Local Assays

■

Books by Dave Smith

POETRY

In the House of the Judge (1983)
Dream Flights (1981)
Homage to Edgar Allan Poe (1981)
Goshawk, Antelope (1979)
Cumberland Station (1977)
The Fisherman's Whore (1974)
Mean Rufus Throw Down (1973)

LIMITED EDITIONS

Gray Soldiers (1984)
Blue Spruce (1981)
In Dark, Sudden with Light (1977)
Drunks (1975)
Bull Island (1970)

FICTION

Southern Delights (1984)
Onliness (1981)

CRITICISM

The Pure Clear Word: Essays on the Poetry of James Wright (1982)

Dave Smith

Local Assays

■

On Contemporary American Poetry

University of Illinois Press
Urbana and Chicago

Manufactured in the United States of America
C 5 4 3 2 1

This book is printed on acid-free paper.

Library of Congress Cataloging in Publication Data

Smith, Dave, 1942–
Local assays.

Includes index.
1. American poetry—20th century—History and criticism—Collected works. I. Title.
PS325.S65 1984 811'.54'09 84-150
ISBN 0-252-01134-1

Acknowledgments are due to the editors of the following publications for permission to reprint these pieces, some of which have been revised from their original appearance:

American Poetry Review: "Robert Penn Warren: He Prayeth Best Who Loveth Best," vol. 8, no. 1 (1979); "Richard Hugo: Getting Right," vol. 10, no. 5 (1981); "Louis Simpson: A Child of the World," vol. 8, no. 1 (1979); "Sylvia Plath: The Electric Horse," vol. 11, no. 1 (1982); "One Man's Music," vol. 9, no. 2 (1980); "The Second Self," vol. 8, no. 6 (1979)
AWP Newsletter: "Notes on Responsibility and the Teaching of Creative Writing," vol. 10, no. 3 (1980)
First Person Singular: ed. Joyce Carol Oates (Ontario Review Press, 1983) for sections from "Assays"
Graham House Review: "Heroes of the Spirit," no. 6 (Spring 1982)
Homage to Robert Penn Warren: ed. Frank Graziano (Logbridge-Rhodes, 1981) for "Notes on a Form to Be Lived: Robert Penn Warren's *Or Else*"
In Praise of What Persists: ed. Stephen Berg for "An Honest Tub" by Dave Smith. Copyright © 1983 by Stephen Berg. Reprinted by permission of Harper & Row, Publishers, Inc.
New York Times Book Review: "The Man from White Center," Feb. 26, 1984 by Dave Smith. Copyright © 1984 by The New York Times Company. Reprinted by permission.
The Generation of 2000: Contemporary American Poets: ed. William Heyen (Ontario Review Press, 1984) for "Beagling"
Poetry: "May Swenson: Perpetual Worlds Taking Place," vol. 135, no. 5 (1980); "The Strength of James Dickey," vol. 136, no. 6 (1981)
Poets Teaching: The Creative Process, ed. Alberta T. Turner. Copyright © 1980 by Longman Inc. "Passion, Possibility, and Poetry" by Dave Smith, reprinted by permission of Longman, Inc., New York.

The Pure Clear Word: Essays on the Poetry of James Wright: ed. Dave Smith (University of Illinois Press, 1982) for "That Halting, Stammering Movement"
Seneca Review: "Thirteen Assays for Poetry," vol. 13, no. 2 (1982)

I would also like to thank the following publishers for permission to quote the poetry which appears in this work:

"False Youth: Autumn: The Clothes of the Age" (entire). Copyright © 1960 by James Dickey. Reprinted from *Drowning with Others* by permission of Wesleyan University Press. "False Youth . . ." first appeared in *The New Yorker.*
"Fog Envelops the Animals" (excerpt). Copyright © 1961 by James Dickey. Reprinted from *Drowning with Others* by permission of Wesleyan University Press.
"At Darien Bridge" (excerpt). Copyright © 1962 by James Dickey. Reprinted from *Helmets* by permission of Wesleyan University Press. "At Darien Bridge" first appeared in *The New Yorker.*
"Approaching Prayer" (excerpt). Copyright © 1964 by James Dickey. Reprinted from *Helmets* by permission of Wesleyan University Press.
"The Fiend" (excerpt). Copyright © 1965 by James Dickey. Reprinted from *Buckdancer's Choice* by permission of Wesleyan University Press.
"False Youth" (excerpt). Copyright © 1981 by James Dickey. Reprinted from *Falling, May Day Sermon, and Other Poems* by permission of Wesleyan University Press.
"The Zodiac" (excerpt) and "Purgation" (excerpt). Copyright © 1983 by James Dickey. Reprinted from *The Central Motion: Poems, 1968–1979* by permission of Wesleyan University Press.
"Women's Tug-of-War at Lough Arrow." Copyright © 1978 by Tess Gallagher. Reprinted from *Under Stars* by permission of Graywolf Press.
"Mrs. Green." Copyright © 1979 by David Huddle. Reprinted from *Paper Boy* by permission of the University of Pittsburgh Press.
"Duwamish No. 2," "White Center," "Montgomery Hollow," "Spinazzola: Quelle Cantina La," "Driving Montana," and "Last Words to James Wright." Copyright © 1984 by the estate of Richard Hugo. Reprinted from *Making Certain It Goes On* by permission of W. W. Norton Co.
"1614 Boren Street," "Montesano Revisited," "Montgomery Hollow," "Plunking the Skagit," "Galleria Umberto I," "Letter to Matthews from Barton Street Flats," and "Port Townsend." Copyright © 1979 by Richard Hugo. Reprinted from *Selected Poems* by permission of W. W. Norton Co.
"Participant" and "Coming Back from the Cliff." Copyright © 1978 by Elizabeth Libbey. Reprinted from *The Crowd Inside* by permission of Carnegie Mellon University Press.
"Port Jefferson" from *People Live Here: Selected Poems 1949–1983* by Louis Simpson. Copyright © 1983 by Louis Simpson. Reprinted with the permission of BOA Editions, Ltd.

"The Daled." Copyright © 1971, 1973, 1974, 1975, 1976 by Louis Simpson. Reprinted from *Searching for the Ox* by permission of William Morrow & Company, Inc.

"Flying Home from Utah," "Show in New York," "October," "Lion," and "A Navajo Blanket." Copyright © 1978 by May Swenson. Reprinted from *New and Selected Things Taking Place* by permission of Little, Brown and Company. "Flying Home from Utah" and "October" first appeared in *The New Yorker*. "Show in New York" first appeared in *Poetry Magazine*. "Lion" first appeared in *Poetry N.Y.* # 4.

"Heart of Autumn." Copyright © 1976, 1977, 1978 by Robert Penn Warren. Reprinted from *Now and Then: Poems 1976–1978* by permission of Random House, Inc.

"Blow, West Wind" and "Interjection #2: Caveat." Copyright © 1964 by Robert Penn Warren. Reprinted from *Selected Poems: New and Old, 1923–1966* by permission of Random House, Inc.

To Catherine Smith Easter

Contents

So we temptiden or assayeden for to abregge in to oo boke, thingus comprehendid . . . in fyue bookis.

Wyclif

It is really a matter, I suppose, of the kind of questions one asks oneself. Some day we may be able to say with assurance, "We came from such and such a protein particle, possessing the powers of organizing in a manner leading under certain circumstances to that complex entity known as the cell, and from the cell by various steps onward, to multiple cell formation." I mean we may be able to say all this with great surety and elaboration of detail, but it is not the answer to the grasshopper's leg, brown and black and saw-toothed here in my hand, nor the answer to the seeds still clinging tenaciously to my coat, nor to this field, nor to the subtle essences of memory, delight, and wistfulness moving among the thin wires of my brain.

Loren Eiseley
The Immense Journey

Preface

In 1978 I began to keep a journal of sorts. Almost nightly for a year and a month, as it turned out, I typed spontaneous commentary about everything I was reading as well as the poetry and fiction I was trying to write. After more than 300 single-spaced pages I lost interest and stopped. I had begun the journal as an attempt to set down a description of my own poems as they appeared draft by draft. I was then very curious about the relationship between verifiable biography and invention in a poem. All poets are asked if what is described in their poems actually happened and much scholarship depends on this sort of inquiry. I thought I might profitably apply that inquiry to my own poems, knowing already that I often resorted to fiction, or invention, while the poem presented itself as an event from my life.

It is natural for readers of poetry to seek what they imagine to be solid ground, the facts, in contemporary poems. We have become ready to assume that whatever is not overtly lyric or a persona's monologue is confessional, or at least radically personal. If the personal poem most interests us, however, it also risks our suspicion as the *merely* anecdotal, the poem which too easily lacks large authenticity, dramatic resonance, a more-than-egocentric vision. I wanted to write poems in which something logical happened but poems whose realistic events would be lenses for seeing the life of the human creature at large. It seemed to me necessary to consider as objectively as I could what I was doing, what I was using from my life, if I hoped to write what I thought was a poem different from those that had begun to feel habitual.

I do not know when the first poet attempted a public explanation of his poem. By now, in essays, formal addresses, interviews, and casual remarks at writers conferences, it comes with the territory. In the summer of 1982, at the Duke Writers Conference, I heard Marvin Bell tell an audience he could not write anything which had not *in fact* happened to him. When the poet speaks about his poem, whatever his forum, his message is: this is what happened. In that message there is another message, often less decoded, which is a statement of why it happened, of poetics. The writing of my journal convinced me that my memory was an unreliable witness to what had happened in my poems. When I told people who had known me all my life what I put down there as actually having occurred, they often proved my memory wrong. I had not intended these explorations of my poems to be published and I did not know what good they might do me. The good came in discovering a need to reexamine everything I thought I knew about poetry and then to say it. I put away my own poems as subject.

Again and again I asked and tried to answer the same daunting questions: What is a poem? How does a poem work? What are its limits and possibilities? Why should a man spend his life making poems? What is the poem I want to write? What is right or wrong with the poems of our age? Innocuously hidden in my own drafts or overt in the poets I ruthlessly dissected, the questions always emerged. I was in a feverish preoccupation with knowing what I could know, fixing it, retesting it. I must have thought I could penetrate to the molecules—or the angels—of the art. When I began to put together this book I went back to that uninhibited, unselective manuscript, thinking much might be useful. Little of it was. I had allowed a version of myself to talk to myself, who responded, and, as T. S. Eliot says: "all literary creation certainly springs either from the habit of talking to oneself or from the habit of talking to others. Most people are unable to do either, and that is why they lead such active lives. But any one who would write must let himself go, in one way or the other, for there are only four ways of thinking: to talk to others, or to one other, or to talk to oneself, or to talk to God." Because I found in my journal certain passages of speculation which I find myself repeating to the first three of those listeners and because I think those passages say what I think about contemporary poetry, I rewrote and joined these fragments into the first section of *Local Assays*. This section is not a journal or an essay. It is an assay.

In the second section I have included only two of a number of chronicle reviews, choosing these as having on the whole more coherence than others and as giving specific examples of poets or poems which illustrate and balance the generalized commentary of the first section. The poets reviewed are those I was obliged to consider by assignment and not necessarily examples of contemporary poetry at its best, worst, or even most instructive.

The third section collects nine essays commissioned by magazines or books. I would be surprised if these essays about senior contemporary poets did not reveal at least some common characteristics in the poets and certainly they constitute a limited evaluation of our poetry. They were not chosen as representative or exemplary but rather because their poems gave me sufficient pleasure to write about them. My intention with each has been to see what the poet put on the page, to seek why and how he did so, and to say what I found of interest, passion, and value. I have not been particularly concerned about their weaknesses.

The final section of *Local Assays* consists of four essays and an interview. "Beagling" was written as an introduction to my poems in William Heyen's anthology, *The Generation of 2000: Contemporary American Poets.* "An Honest Tub" was written for Stephen Berg's *In Praise of What Persists,* essays for which writers were asked to consider what had influenced them. "Heroes of the Spirit," an interview, was conducted by the poet Peter Balakian at the Bennington College Writers Conference. A microphone creates odd distortions in what one thinks and says and I regard this interview as a provisional expression of what I was thinking at the time of those questions. "Notes on Responsibility and the Teaching of Creative Writing" was prepared as an address to a western regional conference of high school teachers of English. "Passion, Possibility, and Poetry" was written for a collection of essays in which poets who teach poetry-writing were asked to examine a specified group of "student" poems and provide a prose equivalent to one's classroom response to those poems. Both essays were done during a time when I felt great uncertainty about both the nature and value of trying to teach poetry-writing. What teaching does to a poet and what a poet can do for students are issues of consequence and interest but they have only a slight bearing on what matters, which is the quality of each poem. I place the essays here because they concern the two indivisible, primary activities of my life, writing poetry and teaching poetry-writing. For better or worse this is the life of the contemporary American poet.

To the extent *Local Assays* is a criticism of contemporary American poetry, it is limited, disjointed, personal, and lacking a singular thesis. I did not intend the focus or exhaustion of scholarship. It is, to some extent, a polemic but I hope it hasn't the bullhorn noise of manifesto. Writing about poetry has been, for me, an extension of writing poems, a necessary act of the mind in which I take pleasure. Pleasure, in all its varieties and revelations, is all there is for the reader of poetry; without it there is no poetry. *Local Assays* is an attempt to know the nature of pleasure and poetry. How far it falls short of truly artful criticism and of any good poem, I am well aware. Yet I hope readers will find a similar pleasure to that of Wallace Stevens who tells us "delight, / Since the imperfect is so hot in us, / Lies in flawed words and stubborn sounds."

Part I

■

■

Total clarity in a poem is an impossibility. The poem is not a photograph or a film. These are the most registrational of the arts, yet each is an illusion which implies a shape of feeling and act, a motion and response. Each begins in representation but ends in symbol. If we examine a photograph by Ansel Adams or Alfred Stieglitz we shall soon enough speculate about what has been selected out by the maker, but we will ask *why*. What begins most clearly ends in speculation and subjectivity.

When someone remarked that Gary Snyder was America's Polaroid poet he made a little poem to illustrate a little poetry. He was not indicting Snyder for a failure of referential clarity but for being unambitious. He meant Snyder was not remarkable for the complexity and depth of experience which is another sort of clarity—a clarity not available to photographers, professional or casual, but which one expects of important poetry. This is the clarity of dimension rather than of surface, the clarity that arises from the music of words, the essence of visionary rather than visual poetry.

Clarity of both sorts is not a virtue of contemporary American poetry. It has not been our virtue for a long time. Probably our lack of clarity was exacerbated by the shift from verse, as a dominant mode, to image and symbol. Even in Whitman the poem as a form of heightened discourse or public communication remains the primary intention. In Emily Dickinson the poem is shifting to intuitive and subjective expression. After the shock waves of High Modernism the poem as a public intersection of maker and recipient is an aberration. The Republic of Verse, and all of its senators, does not die but it is an anachronism. Even

Frost, who was resolute and heroic in attempting to make ordinary speech suffice as the musical dialect of poetry, became for the average reader what all poets became: a creator of fortune cookies. Whether they read the poem or heard it, recipients said, "I didn't get the message." Had poems ever *had* messages? Were they gone? Archibald MacLeish wrote a poem to say that poems must not mean but be—the poem is the message. Poetry had a problem: it lacked authority, status, credibility, utility. Eliot, Stevens, Pound, and Williams wrote manifestos, some of which declared independence from utility (and clarity) while others declared a blue-collar solidarity. Dr. Williams tried to have both in his advocacy of a plain-talking American language which might engage big myths for visionary clarity.

The poets became, for most readers, too hard to understand. They remain well out of the ordinary reader's reach. Most would argue the nature of modern existence, not the poet, is the cause. It is certainly true, as Randall Jarrell says in "The Obscurity of the Poet," that for the modern reader all poetry is obscure when there is no trained, attentive, truly receptive audience. Yet the problem of clarity is not evaded by blaming it on dull readers, poor schools, or the national personality. We are going to have no clarity, either of surface or visionary depth, until poets demand it of themselves. Our problem with clarity arises from our anxiety about the function and value of poetry and it expresses itself in a ceaselessly inclusive referendum over form. It is not that we have no form but that we have an infinite variety of forms and no common sense of purpose. What is a poem? Why is it valuable? To whom? If we could answer these questions we should come to say something intelligent of form, of our choices, and we would move toward clarity, but not otherwise.

I do not mean the clarity we lack and want is easy verse, transparent speech, or even the generally flat language of conversation. Our magazines have plenty of each. I don't mean we want a return to the symmetrical tidiness and public conventions of traditional techniques. Those who proclaim the resurrection of rhyme and meter have displaced religious yearnings. We will not be helped by thinking of form as a good army or a bad army into which we are all inducted. Any form, I suppose, is as capable of clarity as any other, though there can be no clarity without form. There is no poem without form; there is only a chaos of words without form.

Partly, the clarity we lack is just good, responsible writing. Partly, it is better described as accessibility. Good writing takes care to see that words mean what they say. They mean what they are intended to say in a literal, regular, denotative manner. This is what we expect of prose. Too many poets forget Pound's warning that poetry ought to be at least as well written as prose. Responsible writing is accessible because it considers an audience, a communication, and accepts the duty to make referential exchange. The stream of bad books of poetry is thickened more by sloppy, inattentive, aesthetically liberated poets than by anything else. In the service of *freedom,* we have taught ourselves that toleration and not discrimination is the right posture of the mind. But we have thereby become the prisoners of any man's taste, ignorance, or insecurity. Our audience has constricted to ourselves and to those who imagine a poem may mean anything they want. If the audience and the poet are neither one a corrective to the natural tendency of language, which is *unclarity,* then we can hardly expect to create anything but poems unclear and mediocre at even the most elementary levels of comprehension. We have done this and we have justified the unclear poem as a reflection of our true, irrational, nightmare, dream, absurd, and associational lives. Our constant defense is that the poem is what we *feel,* sincerity sanctified. We fail to insist on conjunctions of nouns and verbs which create an action, a context, a unity. We overpraise the jejeune, the silly, the adolescent, the lineation of prosaic urban anxieties. We have pushed poetry beyond fidelity to the referential world and set it adrift in the unrealistic that we can never see or verify. Yet this is not bad. It is, in fact, necessary. But when poetry has proceeded to the point that it has no common language for exchanging what it knows about the unreal and the unseen, then poetry is in trouble. Language must be stretched, its limits pushed in the service of expression and knowledge, but language snaps into incoherence after a point. Tom Robbins, in one of his novels, defines poetry as fucking with the syntax. It's clever and right in the implication of experimenting. Robbins doesn't say poetry kills or abandons syntax. Let syntax here represent poetry's need to speak clearly. Novelists know something about the need for clarity, even if that knowledge is translatable to dollars or their absence. If poetry is to exercise the powers of vision, prophecy, action, and beauty which poets still claim for their art, then poets need to make their poems more accessible through greater discipline, not liberation.

Accessibility means also to suggest a poem of ordinary human experience enacted dramatically. Any poem must have some drama in it or the poem is divorced from life's energy. Energy is rhythm, but it is also the imagination participating with the physical senses. How obvious it is to say we first *feel* a poem, we experience it. Yet many people don't do this. They have been taught to view the poem as a kind of Rorschach test so it becomes an intellectual exercise meant to spew out a decoded message. Or they have been taught a kind of emotional therapy response which consists of endlessly babbled feelings. In either case they are, as Jarrell said, unprepared for poetry. They do not know the poem is not meant to be a time capsule of enigmatic and profoundly mysterious wisdoms, nor is it a psychiatric catalyst for confession. In so far as a poem is a coded organization of words, it is one the poet should be trying to decode. Jarrell might also have said that poets and critics have done little enough in helping to generate clarity and far too much in establishing a national distrust of poetry. If feeling has been first among the poet's loves, opacity, and even egotistic density, has been the usual character of his cohabitation. Americans don't take poetry seriously and they have reason. Yet if the poets might do more to make poetry accessible, the fact is that poetry's intention of expressing the inexpressible frustrates solution and, as Neruda says,

> all night long they struggle,
> nobody knows the weight
> of the harsh clarity that will go on opening
> like a languid fruit.

Perhaps clarity may be approached by allowing poems more statemental simplicity, an easier breathing. We may love the strongly sounded, accentual charger of a poem, but its clots of words—like fat men—tend to lose energy quickly. What is the way to achieve clean, memorable lines and sustained depth of vision? Most of the poems of my generation seem to me like contemporary furniture, more veneer than wood, less built than bolted. Many of us talk too much in our poems, with too much gritting of teeth, too much verbal muscle. This way, too, the real poem slips out the side door. What can be done except to remind oneself to continually seek the better way, to rewrite and rethink? And to remember Thomas Hardy: "Who feels that delight is a delicate growth cramped by crookedness, custom, and fear, / Get him up and be gone as one shaped awry; he disturbs the order here."

Each line and image must serve to advance the whole intention of the poem, the plot, curve of vision, emotion, resonance—the whole. Unity is the dream of every poem, large or small. Does each word carry, embryonically, the intent of the entire poem? Probably not. Even a stout wall has its missing or crumbled brick. But a corrupt line of bricks topples any wall. Each part serves: this is the cleanness we need. But against that we must set the necessary corruption of impurity which is the colloquial, vulgar, rude voice of the referential world. Too much of this, however, and we have glibness. James Wright called glibness the natural enemy of poetry. The glib poem is effect without cause, noise without origin; it is the poem moving toward conversation, which may be artful but is not art. The image poet may also be glib in that the presentation of unmediated objects leaves only a kind of raw data. When we are glib, we are slick. We haven't looked or felt thoroughly enough *in the words*. We haven't made it possible for the reader to move beyond surfaces.

What, in general, can be said about the subjects of poetry? Only, I suppose, that everything has a potential beauty which poetry seeks. But some subjects appear more likely to yield significant results than others. Or is this merely fear of being trivial? Isn't it possible a great poetry might arise from a sequence about fence posts as well as in a sequence involving a blackface mummer and a variety of historical personages? Why does one grow weary of poems about one's father, one's mother, one's sexual disappointments, one's admiration of certain painters? Is it a distinctly modern characteristic that poets seem not to choose large subjects around which poems are then composed, as a novelist might choose to dramatize a war, a family chronicle, or a philosophy? No subject is, in and of itself, the same thing to all readers. No subject is inherently beautiful or meaningful or expressive. Ordinary phenomena are not necessarily interesting or beautiful—but they are where interest and beauty begin, where the poet establishes the appropriate context for revelation. The thing itself is only itself, scarcely art, until art alters it. It is in the measure of this alteration that the artist's skill and limitations may be found, his skill or limitations as a visionary—not as a craftsman. Poe's remarks about the death of a beautiful woman being the most propitious subject for poetry seem a little slippery but it is apparently the case that some subjects, like certain soils, are on the whole more fertile than others. Nevertheless there are no great poets whose greatness resides primarily in their choice of subject. Still I think it can be said that the image poet is handicapped by the severity of his subject as well as by the choice of form. In this, as in the minimalist attitude which is widespread among contemporary poets, the imagist is remarkable not for what he does but for what he is prohibited from doing: he fails to embrace the fullest opportunities of his art.

Art begins in the ordinary, the physical, the material. If the poet is to lift his subject to the value of art he must first recognize the uses and the limitations of both his subject and his tools—his formal skills. Art does nothing on its own. The artist creates and uses art, as a jeweler deploys his stones, toward a context of suggestion. There is no poem entirely without narrative direction, be it epic or couplet; moreover, narrative direction always implies an authorial statement. This statement may be as oblique as Casey Stengel's soliloquies or it may be explicit as a philosophical proposition. Every poem comments on human experience: that is the poem's function. Any organization of words shaped by a man is, by definition, a statement. Statements do not occur in the natural world. Poems do not occur organically as do lemons, worms, or uranium. Human deliberation which leads to a shaping of words, the mere intent to order, is the first step toward any poem's meaning. Meaning, however, is a great deal more than the terse paraphrase of plot and result. For example, the Anglo-Saxon poem "The Wanderer" is about the loneliness of a man who will never see his homeland, his comrades, or any reward for having accomplished valorous deeds. My summary is no more the poem's meaning than it is the poem, for it carries nothing of the feeling that is the poem. Feeling cannot exist apart from the context of generational events and the poem's voice any more than it could exist apart from the creative music of words and phrases in the harness that is the form of the poem.

Every poem makes a statement, as all things in time and space make a statement. The artist shapes time and space and body to discover his statement. Poets seem to agree that they generally don't know what an individual poem will try to say. Some, in fact, resist knowing, as if the appearance of that knowledge too soon or at the wrong time will destroy the art-spell. Frost spoke of a piece of ice melting on a stove as a figure for the poem which the poet watches until he is able to save it just at the edge of dissolution. That edge is the artist in control, but a control sufficiently tentative to permit discovery. The element of surprise, as Frost also tells us, is critical to both writer and reader. It is at the very core of the pleasure we take from a poem—but this is not surprise as trick. It is the surprise of timing, necessity, inevitability that allows one to accept the statement of the poem as emotionally valid. If the poet does not know what statement he will come to, he knows that when he has found a few compelling words he is going to find next a context. Everything is decided according to context, for it is only through context that full, clear expression is approached. Narrative is one sort of context; image and lyric are others. None exists entirely separate from the others but all are matters of emphasis. At its most fundamental, poetry may be imagined as a spectrum. On one end there is the pictograph, the representational image cut into stone. On the other end is the abstract word, entirely nonvisual, such as *honor* or *metempsychosis*. The poem exists most powerfully—as act and as meaning simultaneously—in the middle of the spectrum. At least the poem as ideal exists there.

Art, if it is art, makes a point. It means. The poem must mean or it is no poem. How ludicrously simple that seems. Yet there is no end of aesthetic theory to the contrary and there is a very great deal of bad poetry justified by critics who would find meaning where no meaning is. And there are those who would argue that the absence of meaning is, itself, a statement of meaning—as one poet I know who argues that a poem of hers, half a book long, is chaotic because it imitates chaos. This is solipsistic. The poem which defies referential clarity is unlikely to succeed in meaning anything to anyone, though there are examples of such poems which attain to something like a superclarity. If a vote were taken even now, I suspect Eliot's "Waste Land" would be regarded as massively clear by many and massively murky by an equal number. Having a point to make certainly does not make a poem but where is the true poem which makes no point? Complex and abstract expression is the human act beyond all others. A poem, like an essay, is a sort of hypothesis, a theorem of experience, but it ordinarily abandons the illusion of argument, syllogism, or proof. It exists both for and as the dramatic presentation of what it means. What would Williams's wheelbarrow poem be if it did not begin "so much depends / upon . . ."? It would be a non sequitur.

The first question of value in a poem has to do with the depth, quality, and validity of its feeling. The great poem simply tells us more, and tells it more profoundly, about what it means to be alive. This is so even when we do not accept entirely the statement of the poem. *Paradise Lost* and "Lycidas" are such poems. There are perhaps infinite numbers of ways we know the world but foremost among those ways is feeling—it is still first. We must judge a poem by the truth and size of its feeling and this feeling must be a necessary, inevitable result of the poem's resolution of its own actions. We must judge a poem by submitting it to the testing fire of individual and historical knowledge; we must find it authentic or false. Our assessment of feeling is not, however, a matter of merely agreeing with a poet's sentiment. It is a matter of emotional proportion and rightness generated by dramatic circumstance. We can be touched by melodramatic poetry but moved only by tragic poetry. I mean tragic in the literary sense, in the sense of the work which enables us to embrace great pain and great beauty and great joy because we have seen the inescapable and crushing forces of fate in combat with the largest human spirit. But the poetry is not those forces, that drama, or any resulting statement—not precisely. The poetry is the music which evokes, creates, releases, controls, and clarifies feeling in the dramatic context.

It is, I think, impossible to separate what I would call the context of the poem and what I would call the communal function of the poem from the sound or music. The music is the poem's first order of existence. It shapes the feeling even as it rises out of the feeling, but the poetry is the music and not the feeling. Nothing is harder to speak of in the abstract than this music and it may be that nothing significant can be said of it. One reads the textbooks and the theories of sonics with a sense of hopeless irrelevance. Nothing I might say can have any specific connection to the universe of poetry any more than does, say, Paul Fussel's *Poetic Meter and Poetic Form*. Whatever Fussel or anyone may tell us of poetry's mechanics, no one can give us the next poem's blueprint. Both the reader and the writer remain the subjective unknown out of which the poem will sing or remain mute.

What is common in the sound of poetry in Neruda, Smart, Li Po, Baudelaire, and Emily Dickinson? Very little, I should guess. A comparative examination of sonic strategies employed by each might be profitable but I suspect we would miss the poetry. Much of what we are taught about how sounds operate on the individual ear seems sheer opinion and is occasionally nonsense. If the music and the meaning of a poem work as one act of the mind, these actions nevertheless impel us toward the separate directions of feeling and thinking, which are themselves never strictly divisible. The final value of a poem is to give pleasure, but in what does this pleasure consist? What in any poem pleases us, and how? If our agreement with what the poet says seems suspicious, then how much more so seems that tendency to pluck out felicitous lines or vivid images. Yet it is rare to find the poem whose statement is utterly repellent to us while its music is enchanting. The poetry is in the music, however much or little we can locate the music. But it is also true that insistent rhythmic sound, if that is the only music one speaks of, is not poetry, as Lewis Carroll proves. A friend of mine understands no German, though he has a sense of German sounds. He likes to read Rilke aloud in German—his brand of German—because the soporific rolling of syllables pleases him, just as he is pleased by Dylan Thomas. What he loves is not poetry. Clusters of sounds, however sweet, constitute no poetry when there is no referential meaning.

All poetry asks what is valuable in life. Every aspect of a poem's organization conspires to dramatize a poet's experience of the world and reveal what is both durable and valuable. Readers are, however, too prone to think that what the poet says in a poem is precisely what *he* thinks or feels. While this may be the actual case it is also true that the poet writes through what might be called a second self, a sort of neuter, super-aware, nameless other. It is, at any rate, my experience that I am a different person at the typewriter than the person who answers the telephone or plays tennis. The first-person speaker in my poems is rarely, and then only in part, the person identified with my Social Security number. This means that what happens to the created second self of the poem most often has not happened to me. But those events and that speaker are inventions in the service of what my imagination regards as valuable, although those values arise from whatever I have been able to know of anyone's life. Poetry attempts to objectify and simultaneously dramatize with immediate force. The second self provides distance, objectivity, perspective, form, and tempering for the first self's unmediated rehearsal of experience. In words we repeat the acts of our experience and we do it because we need to know what and how we are in the world. Poetry is perhaps the most concrete and immediate way of knowing, but it must proceed through testing and resolution and speculation, for assertions of value without resistance have no force.

William Carlos Williams and Charles Olson claimed to create new forms of poetry in order to accommodate new thinking about human experience in general and about Paterson, New Jersey and Gloucester, Massachusetts in particular. Can it really be shown in specific ways how the geographical, cultural, or even sociological character of those places had a single influential moment with the formal organizations of words those poets put on the page? That is, what about Gloucester affects Olson's decisions to shape lines and stanzas as he did? It does not surprise me that the critical studies of Olson and Williams, including the several dissertations on the subject with which I have been associated, have little to say about the relationship of biography and formal choices in the area of poetic music. The tendency of such criticism is to argue for a grand form based on a sociopolitical argument about a reflected sociopolitical society. That is, to argue for a poetry composed of verbal architectures and not verbal musics, a poetics analogous in part to the Bauhaus movement. To speak of poetry in Charles Olson and poetry in, say, Anthony Hecht or Elizabeth Bishop is to confuse what is meant by the word *poetry*—or it is to make the term massively inclusive. The result is, I think, a general confusion about form wherein we are obliged to call whatever is lineated *poetry*. At what point does technical innovation collapse into mere eccentricity? At what point does poetry cease to be defined by the devices of musical organization such as lines, stanzas, or any of the pattern-making sound signalers? At what point does poetry exist as verbal architecture? At what point does it exist as feeling?

When we sound a poem in our heads we can experience the effect of form, of lineation, of rhythmic surge and ebb. When a poet chooses a line length, he chooses for the stop and go of a form that alters his perception and the reader's. He controls subject, poem, and reader. End-stopped lines with metrical regularity create a tight control and experience. The experience of continuity which devalues end-stopped lines and disregards the fusion of line halts and eye halts asks for a different experience. One cannot read Galway Kinnell's "The Bear" in exactly the same way one reads a poem by Marvell or Richard Wilbur. One implication is that poetry itself is different for these poets, and not a matter of superficial options. Yet some readers and writers regard form as not merely an option but a reflection of political orientation, as if the writing of sonnets indicates a covert alignment with oppressive conservatism. Free verse, in its many varieties, is often enough described as revolutionary with the full implications of social rebellion. Where then does *form,* even each individual version, come from and what is it exactly? Does form inherently demonstrate a poet's deepest philosophical convictions? Surely rhythm lies at the heart of form—but there is no free rhythm since rhythm is possible only in systematic resistance or containment. Form, it might be said, is that set of disciplines and responsibilities to which the poet agrees with each poem and this would imply the recognition that nothing is free, that everything a poet does has its cost, its obligation, its allegiance.

At the center of form, whatever might be meant by that word, is that most idiosyncratic, most felt, and least describable matter: rhythm. Theodore Roethke says of it that: "We must keep in mind that rhythm is the entire movement, the flow, the recurrence of stress and unstress that is related to the rhythms of the blood, the rhythms of nature. It involves certainly stress, time, pitch, the texture of words, the total meaning of the poem." And he says also that "Rhythm gives us the very psychic energy of the speaker." We should be alert enough to recognize there are at least two kinds, not one, of rhythm in his definition. The first sort not only identifies but also creates the life in the poem, the character of the poem's speaker. It is drawn from the personality of the poem's maker, from the emotional blood-pulse of the heart. Once it is impressed in the poem, it tells the reader's heart how fast to beat, how he should pace himself through the dramatic experience. Darting us ahead, or withholding us from time, now fast and now slow, this rhythm creates immediate experience. It controls psychic pressure and emotional inevitability. This rhythm is analyzable and, as Roethke suggests, may be broken into identifiable components. It is the rhythm, for example, which may be scanned, the subject of prosodic studies.

But there is a larger idea of rhythm which Roethke implies but does not consider. This is the rhythm of change and truth. If the rhythm above is the rhythm common to a single man, the rhythm here is that common to men. It consists of what is changeless, continuous, and may be called the truth. Each man's singular rhythm, in every poem, plays against the common rhythm and it is the resistances as well as the congruencies of the two impulses which provide tension, vision, and discovery. One might picture these rhythms in the lines on a heart-monitoring oscilloscope: the constant line there is death. Any good poem sets the local, singular rhythm against the rhythm of constants; indeed, its act of discovery is to find the constant that is not death, for that is the principle of resistance by which self-definition, self-creation, and all knowledge of self and other achieves measurable value.

This rhythm of constants lies in the imagination of the race. Constant is, perhaps, not the most accurate word for what seems to me to be far from static. Perhaps what I mean are clusters of energies verging on convictions, the images and stories which emerge in great myths as dramatized explanations of what the race considers to be continuous and true. If every poem is an attempt to create, to explore, and to expand consciousness, as I think is the case, then reason suggests every poem is an attempt to contact those constants. But every poem is also a record of the individual's encounter with resistances. The poem's greater rhythm is, then, embodiment of the human's motions in conventional time as well as his continuity out of time. Surely this is the truth of any poem: its ability to hear the heart beating in this world but also beating in synchronization with the heart of the race, or body, of all men. Flannery O'Connor says all this very plainly: "The writer operates at a peculiar crossroads where time and place and eternity somehow meet. His problem is to find that location."

In ways I am not sure I understand, the music of poetry is composed by the constant engagement and disengagement of the individual and the communal psychic energy. Where do those energies come from? To the writer this asks: why do you write? Again O'Connor is helpful. Her answer was that she had a gift. Great poets have that gift and it cannot be taught or in any way purchased. This is, I think, why every discussion of prosody leads inevitably to vision and the location of a poem's value in what it says, and not the other way around. Poetry is poetry and not prose or drama because of its music—but is music far more than patterns of sound even when those patterns are the uncounterfeitable signatures of individual poets. O'Connor says, wonderfully, that the writer "operates" and she means he acts, participates, even cuts through much going on around him. More than anything else he hears and he watches, giving and receiving, a rhythm within rhythms, a truth within truths.

Recently I read Yeats praising Rabindranath Tagore and remembered that I had bought a battered copy of Tagore's poems for a dime. I found it and read Tagore. He is what might be called a *pure* poet. Extremely lyrical and melodious, he is entirely conventional in construction and his subject is most ordinary: love experienced, love lost, love lamented. He seems more in love with the idea of love than with any person, resembling the courtly love of Provençal lyrics. His poems would gag one with their thick sighs did not a reader regard them as the practice of something like an anachronistic skill. The pure poet, in so far as such a creature actually exists, is an escapist. He seeks an ideal, a world uncorrupted, a music which has no intention of discoursing with or walking among the flesh of this world. In Tagore, a twentieth-century poet, one finds no trains, airplanes, wars, scientific discoveries, or news of the world at large. He is all expression, all veneration of a habitual and stiff decorum. He ranges from reticence before love to wallowing in rapture. There is hardly any dramatic tension or occasion; there is no presence of the tough-minded citizen. He gives himself entirely to bald statements of affection with no syntactical, rhythmic, or imagistic surprise. Let Tagore think of grazing the hem of a woman's skirt and he melts—almost literally. He is a sort of ruder Rilke. Not surprisingly, he reminds me of many younger American poets in whom the world seems too weakly embodied, too little explored, too frequently constricted to one voice and one anxiety that simply hasn't the power to sustain interest. Seeking purity, these poets refuse internal resistance.

Yet in Tagore there are the true pleasures of poetry: praise, feeling, direct expression, a cleanness of attention, a sense that the poem may be like the stilled surface of a country pond, virginal and fragrant and, well, pure. The pure poem is successful because it radiates and works exclusively. Tagore can suggest great beauty with his ever-present observation of a young girl's ankle bracelets, but one never quite feels it is a whole, mature vision. One misses entirely that girl's dirty feet, the barnyard smell, even the dailiness of village life. Because of what Tagore does not incorporate in his poem, his pure music is finally dismissable. When we read a Provençal lyric which tells us the story of a man who falls in love with a woman's image, travels years to find her, and dies of love when he sees her, we nod a little. But the story adds that the woman, upon seeing this man, falls in love herself and also dies on the spot. This we cannot accept, however lovely the language. Tagore's eloquent simplicity and his transparent feeling are pure and attract us away from our existence in cynicism, knowledge, and fear—but they do not sustain us. This is also the case with some contemporary American poets. We all want the unsullied expression of quintessential beauty that would be *pure,* yet to have it we must deny the poem any broad connection to this ordinary world. The purer the poem, the more it must exclude the warts and winds of our existence. The consequences of purity are limited expression, limited knowledge, limited audience, and *mere* beauty.

We want, all of us, the civilization of pure poetry, which is the impulse to form. Yet we want also our beasthood, which might be called pure expression. We are human more than beast because we possess consciousness. As Emily Dickinson says, we feel first, but we seek to render permanent and understandable our feeling. We do this in organizations of symbols that assert the formality of thought as preferable to brute act. We do something a white crane and a bulldozer can't do; we do something not possible for a eucalyptus or a newt. The proto-human act is to receive and respond to the world with creative thought. Not all creative thought is equal in quality. The democratic attitude which would argue against qualitative discrimination in poetry is a foolish and naive one. One mark of excellence to be sought in a contemporary poem is the balance of civilization and the beast, of disciplined form and passionate expression.

We cannot reduce what is valuable in any poem to a single aspect or idea and we cannot enlist the poem, as a measure of value, in the service of expressing what is good for the Republic. On the whole, what is valuable is the transmittable and felt human experience a poem contains. Inevitably we must test the validity of a poem against the curve of our lives. If we accept a supernatural vision, an extra-human cosmology, as did Milton and Gabriela Mistral and Mario Luzi, there is another basis for judging the poem's reality and beauty. This is also true of any poem which supports a political idea. Yet for most contemporary poets the poem has no such grounding. Our poet has himself, what he has seen and known and felt, what he has assimilated from history and culture, as touchstone and source. This tends to drive him away from grand ideas and toward the image of himself as minimal, as a voice which can be trusted with only the most local and circumscribed of truths. Yet he must find a way to make the life of his poem congruent with the lives of others. He must find a way to speak for the good of the Republic. What else is so clear in the poems and statements of the Eastern European poets such as Milosz and Herbert?

It is because we must find a way to conjoin the issues of the self with the large issues of the Republic of men that the contemporary poem must above all be emotionally accurate and tested. We should certainly, as well, suspect the poem that fails ordinary journalistic accuracy. The poem that lies must be rejected. The lie is what is wrong with poems of polemical rhetoric, however well-intended the poem's subjective attitude. Denise Levertov's antiwar poems fail as poems to the extent they become propaganda. They do not think or feel complexly enough. Among younger poets, many less skilled than Levertov, we are impelled to ask what the poet thinks and we often enough discover little evidence of thought, the kind of thought which approaches large issues. It is no answer to say, in their defense, that poetry does not think, it feels. Feeling is a way of thinking and in the poem feeling submits to formal organization for purposes of communication. Too many poets lack the necessary intensity of speculation by which poetry moves the reader from sight to knowledge. Much of our poetry is aggressively trivial, as if it feared being thought overserious, righteous, or ambitious. The poem that is trivial asks us that we do not look too closely at ourselves, and it demeans us by that.

The polemical poem, whatever its message, ordinarily makes music subservient to program. Yet the music is the poetry. Only artful sound can lift message to art. No sentiment, however righteous or agreeable or moral, is by itself art. Sound is form, an organization of words, but when matched to an appropriate context the living and free pulse of experience may result. Context is dramatic situation, of course, but I think it is something more. It is the poem's chance for ambitious art, the opportunity for the poet to conduct experiments in ethics and morality, to demonstrate maturity and range of vision. It may be the forum for a truth, a whole truth. For the poet who wants polemic, context is a prefabricated shell meant to support an ideological statement. For others context is something freer, more alive, something which generates a statement and allows its discovery.

The contemporary poet, if we judge by the various published interviews and working papers, begins his poem with an image taken from the imagination. He does not usually know why the imagination seizes on one image rather than another. The image comes to him independent of a context and he is content, perhaps, merely to record it. But soon enough he finds himself asking why this image should matter, what it suggests, what its existence may mean for him. Put simply, he plays with the image and discovers that the imagination has been slowly locating whatever it is in a web of relationships. All things exist in a web of relationships. These may manifest themselves to the poet as compulsive sounds, vivid pictures, or the sense of a narrative; they may exist as all three, in fragments or more sustained units. The poet's process, however, is to choose or establish a context. Successive drafts frequently show the initiating image to be irrelevant and it is dropped as the poet concentrates on the forces, the possibilities invoked by the newly focused context. This is exactly what Richard Hugo describes as the triggering subject. Initially, the poet seems to have little idea of what the poem will say, what its intention is, what form it will seek as appropriate and much of his own pleasure consists in discovering these things. These discoveries, to judge from what poets commonly say, are mysterious in nature and process but are guided by unbidden sounds, words, phrases that simply arrive in the head. Once they exist they seem to generate more of their kind, until a rhythmic direction is established, until everything sonic about the poem is determined. Of course, the poet is able to enter this evolution with his own determinations but the point and force of his entry is both delicate and critical. It is what will determine art. I have, as others have, often enough made deliberate choices to impose a form on a poem and have killed the poem or temporarily hidden the true poem.

The ability to establish the triggering context and the further ability to know when to wait and when to act are perhaps the most valuable of all talents for a poet. They are, I think, the least accessible to discussion. Biographical criticism appears to assume that such contexts are drawn directly from one's lived experience but I think this is not the case. This is why invention is commonly thought to be confession. Just as mysterious to me as the establishment or discovery of context is the relationship between context and evolving music. I cannot say with certainty which precedes the other or which is the primary influence on the poem. Again, my experience is common with other poets. I respond to that overheard music, a sound pattern, and I follow it as far as I am able, always with the initial surety it will lead to the pleasure of a poem's completed act. In the end, however, I shall not be following the music but leading it, fitting it to the context which has emerged. The point at which the transfer from rapt attention to controlling agent comes is impossible to predict or to formulate. Yet I can say the poem is freely made by the music so long as I may add that the poet shapes his music in service of his meaning, a meaning that abides latent and potential in his context. The writer of the polemical poem does not expect or experience the surprise that Frost meant when he said no surprise in the writer, no surprise in the reader.

The surprise is not merely how things fall out but how the sound of words leads to and rests in art.

The American poet wants both a private and a public language for his poem because he is saddled with a need to express the uniquely American experience and humankind's common experience. We believe there is an uninvented American wheel. We chafe at the limitations of form and the witness of history. We want a language of such purity and scope that it might say everything to everyone and all at once. This impulse toward purity is escapist. All poetry is an escape into illusion, a retreat from unselective experience, yet it becomes art to the degree that escape metamorphoses into penetration of that experience. Art moves from raw sensory data to and through organized meaning. The minimalist attitude toward poetry, especially toward language, is a search for pure poetry, but it fails to be more than escapist, more than locally ambitious however it may secrete self-justifying aesthetic theories. What is the appropriate language for our poetry? Is it an echo of English verse? An imitation of the Asian pictograph? A slang-flecked image composed in triadic feet? What will be the language that is identifiably American but not parochially poetic? Perhaps any answer will require the single poem pointed at or leave us with unsatisfactory abstractions. Surely, at least, we want an ordinary language that is referential, connective, and visionary, words that are not *just* there but unshakably, memorably *there.*

Ordinary language is not merely the banal, the conversational, or the eccentric. Poetry is not merely ordinary language lineated. Poetry is not precisely monosyllabic or polysyllabic, concrete or abstract, personal or public. Whoever demands one or the other shills for a half-truth, a half-lie. Poetry is a dialect of the language we speak, possessed of metaphorical density, coded with resonant meaning, engaging us with narrative's pleasures, enhancing and sustaining our pleasure with enlarged awareness. In comparison to ordinary uses of language, this dialect is characterized by efficient discipline: of sharper imagery, focused symbols, connotative power, deployed rhythmic suggestion. It is both affective and effective communication. We ask the reader to participate in our imaginative act but we control, by the score of the language, the limits and range of that participation. We do not attempt to hide what we mean. I can think of nothing which is more central to the actual writing of a poem than that statement: we do not attempt to hide anything. Yet every beginner and not a few experienced writers assume that is the nature of poetry. The fact is that we write as directly and forcefully and carefully as we can—at our best—because we know the complexity of emotions and the conflict of perceptions, which is what any of us amounts to, frustrates clarity in every word, every phrase, every implied or explicit human circumstance.

Language is a rotting corpse of what men have felt, thought, and spoken. We are nothing without the dead and what has belonged to the dead; but they constantly block our clear expression and we are obliged to shoulder them aside, however gently. We attempt to do this every instant when we speak the words that carry an accumulated freight of meaning that is the legacy of the past. We feel, all of us do, that there is nevertheless a clarity our words can reach in which we may express entirely what we feel and mean. But we despair of reaching that clarity, with reason. Some of us settle for the language the dead have left us. Some of us in frustration brutalize the language and try to explode our way beyond the dead. And some are lucky enough to attain to a clarity that is like hope itself. The poems which please us, whether we find them abandoned or finished, seem to have arrived at that clarity but we know the arrival is temporary. We know there is no permanently pure expression. We cannot ever get free entirely from the dead hand of language. We can only hope for a temporary accommodation and the agent of that accommodation is form, specifically a form of music.

The poem, whatever its Platonic shape in our dreams, is the way our minds ingest and use the world. It is what generates beauty. Its commands are *Look! Know! Connect!* No one of these commands is significantly valuable without the actions of the others. In that, the triad resembles the integral motions of a symphony: all the parts working for one purpose and within a unified sequence. What we hope, of course, is that these three imperatives might result in the poem by which the poet shall know himself and the world, and know what cannot be so well and fully known any other way under the sun.

We humans are enigmas, paradoxes. That is not an original thought but it is worth remembering. We live in an isolation within ourselves and with ourselves, a total and terrible isolation, because we cannot and are not, parted from the womb, truly a part of any other. We speak casually of the love that joins us each to each and we speak fervently of religious oneness. In every religious vision I know about, the ultimate rest is a condition of being where all is fused, flowing, emphatically joined. Even this belief is based on the implicit recognition that the fundamental fact of *this* existence is our division one from another, our utter isolation. We bond ourselves sometimes for life and we even speak of how in our love we become a part of another. This is wishful thinking and poor metaphor. Always in the world, we are always and essentially apart, alone. Art that is great and true and complex affords this paradox the full dramatic reality we know. Such art tries to help us force back the borders of the unknown. It helps make verifiable what we can only intuit. Art's knowledge and its province are inevitably interior. That is why the artist follows no law other than the one he makes, though his law will be more strict, more demanding, more impossible to keep or to understand than any exterior law. The forms he creates act according to strictures never acknowledged until the poem is complete. That is, I am aware, an overstatement and it obviously ignores the influences of literary heritage as well as contemporary fashions. But I mean not the many of us who are going into the anonymous dust of years—I mean those poets who will alter the course of poetry, who seem scarcely to know anything of laws until the laws have been felt, obeyed, broken, revised, and recast.

Law is an odious word to any poet and probably has no business here. If the poet is free of anything, he is free of external constraints. Almost, I hear the voices of objection, citations of the terrible and all too frequent cases of those poets bent and broken by the governments of men. I don't forget Miguel Hernandez and Guillaume Apollinaire and Osip Mandelstam and Anna Akhmatova, to name only a few. Nevertheless, I believe each poet has the freedom to choose silence or the poem's speech, whether he speaks it only to himself or etches it in blood on his cell wall. In the poem and with the poem, he is free; there his freedom consists in choosing how he will say a thing as well as what he will say. Men may make their laws to govern a publication, but no law can be imposed on the poem that the poet does not himself accept. The poet is free even if his choice is only to die with courage. He can choose even that in the last instant, and choice is freedom. Because poets are the bearers of freedom and choice, governments fear them and men love them.

We write as history has written. The form of our poems, like the form of our bodies, comes from our ancestors, whether it be an image or an epic. We can and do modify conventions. This is because we imagine ourselves different from our ancestors, hence in need of a new order of expression. Yet in the things that matter to poetry—Faulkner's verities—we are our ancestors; our forms, too, are theirs. Pound is correct to tell us to make it new but we shall never proceed very far from what we have always been in poetry.

John Vernon has written in *Poetry and the Body* that "Naked poetry is the kind of poetry written when the past has ceased to exist, or at least has ceased to be a satisfying measure of the present." Vernon repeats Henry Ford's error in imagining the past is not a continuously and powerfully affective force in every present moment. Moreover the past is the great adjudicator of wisdom, knowledge, and possibility, the very agent of measurement. This is evident everywhere and nowhere more than in the ghostly residue of language with which every poet must contend. It is one thing to suffer Joyce's nightmare frustration with the past and quite another to dismiss the past as irrelevant. The poetry which does that is hopelessly doomed.

But consider *naked* poetry. Does not the term, slightly childish, barbarous, and rebellious, suggest a final resolution of form in formula? Its implication is freedom, as from the inhibition of clothing, but how nakedness is freedom without responsibility is a great murkiness. What is naked in naked poetry? If one answers it is the form, then one must reply that a biblical psalm is as naked as anything in Allen Ginsberg.

Words are representational and chosen. They are not organic. The word *tree* makes no sound inherently connected to or like the sound of wind, leaves, or limbs. The word is a symbolic and conventional sound. We live in time and convention. In fact, time is a convention. We exist representationally, in that world of exchange, and to imagine we could do otherwise would be to resist, if not to ignore, our shared heritage and meaning in history. Necessarily, poets must challenge habit and engage history, but there is a point of diminishing returns. *Finnegans Wake,* to my mind, goes beyond that point. But it might be said that Joyce wants us to confront the referential quality of individual and communal words, not to escape expression but to know its potential freshly. At what point does this alteration of language tip into random sound? So long as sound is even modestly shaped, it has form; it is formed. If we speak of something as anomalous as anti-form, we are still speaking of what must exist representationally: it points at something or it is, itself, nothing. If there is no active selection and arrangement of words, there is no art. The idea of nakedness seems to be the abandonment of artifice or the penetration through form to some preexistent core which is art. This seems to me either a poor choice of metaphor or a sad wrongheadedness.

We write as history has written. This is, to a certain degree, an agreement to live with and by the past, and the past therefore lives. We are not entirely comfortable with this arrangement, to be sure, but there is finally not very much we can do about it. We cannot change the rhythms of the human body. We cannot radically alter language. We cannot look to nature for new forms of poetry for there is no organic poem in the world. To speak of an organic poem is to employ a metaphor, not a fact. Nature is indifferent to poetry. Where does form originate? In the minds and spirits of our ancestors, in history. What we know of the uses and weaknesses and abilities of form we know because history, like a very slow computer, has sorted all that out through trial and error. Form exists because poets have existed, because they have made choices. We, too, will make choices that cause changes—but within strict limitations. That is why the great Modernists, each one a paradox of tradition and revolt, expressed a continuous and bitter frustration with words, with what could actually be said.

Consider Robert Creeley's dictum that form is no more than an extension of content. If it is true, when I have chosen a subject have I also chosen a form? Is it that each content somehow reaches out of the typewriter and takes hold of my fingers, forcing them to punch out the words, the phrases just so? If I obey, is it that I have chosen a form or accepted the inevitable? If I have not chosen, then what comes may well be naked, but will it be form? Why would I exercise a great sequence of choices, selections and discriminations that constitute art, only to appear as no more than what I was when I began, naked? Naked poetry is a contradiction in terms.

If we call what is at issue here *fluid,* in contradistinction to static, what has been changed? Is "Lycidas" less fluid than Roethke? Words on the page do not move, of course, though the illusion of movement is critical to their life. Another term for the new poem is the *open* poem. At its extreme this is the so-called *process* form, a form that is based on the argument that life has no clear beginning, middle, or end, and therefore the poem must have none. Even if one accepts what seems to me a suspicious theory, surely it is only another principle of representation. This form represents what the process poet feels and sees. The process poet wants to expand the available ground for his vision and this is of value up to the point where the poem ceases to exist with referential communication and becomes merely a sort of arcanum dump. We have such poems and theories aplenty in their defense, theories which echo Creeley's line. But there is a simple flaw in Creeley's logic. If phenomena are greatly various, including all that is human, and if phenomena are what content means, then each poem ought to require a different form. An attractive theory, it logically eliminates the poet as chooser, maker, shaper of form. If poetry is music, then the musics are all given with the various contents and the poet need only learn which plug fits which hole. The alternative is, of course, that content does not vary. The evidence of Creeley's poems supports the latter.

All things express. Let that be a given. It is what William Carlos Williams means in his phrase "no ideas but in things." Things express through dramatic context. Much that exists cannot be explained by art, as it cannot be witnessed by science or analysis. Mysteries simply are. Art can draw near to them, witness them, and try to hear the expression of each thing in creation. I mean, I should quickly add, the expression of each thing as it participates in a human story. Imagine each thing talking! Ludicrous. Yet isn't that what Robert Bly does when he writes "the brave alfalfa has sobered"? I simply mean that the poet seeks what is latent in everything he confronts. This is not quite the same thing as hearing a tiny hung over voice in the alfalfa.

If everything expresses, and constantly, the poet's task must be to combine words in ways that release the expression he wants, while clearing away all the simultaneous and irrelevant contender expressions. He trains himself to isolate what most needs to be heard, to provide an amplifying context. This presumes he has made, or experienced, a determination of what the poem's statement might be. This determination is the first discovery in the writing of the poem and it will virtually compel every subsequent decision. In this way, having already come into being through image and music, the poem's content arrives at context. Form follows in the sequence of choices, though sometimes it seems to assert itself independently. This, I think, only means the poet is making choices so rapidly he is not aware of making them, choices he is conditioned by experience and skill to make. He is like an athlete whose body makes split-second adjustments to the competition though the athlete is not aware of choices, decisions, or adjustments until they are completed. Every choice the poet makes is ultimately a choice about form, for form, because there will be no poem otherwise. He knows that six horses under reins will pull no wagon until there is a singletree harness. Without that organized power, the wagon goes not to grandmother's house or anywhere. It sits in silence. Each thing expresses through form.

Some poets do matter more than others though categorizing is irrelevant to the actual writing of poems. It is not irrelevant in the necessary establishment of our sense of what art is. Part of any poet's mastery of his art must involve his attempt to know who matters and why and, if he means to clear room for his own art, he must concern himself with what they have done to be what they are.

I would call these, for lack of a better term, the breakthrough poets, those who alter the possibilities of poetry. They do not drive away from the past, as is so commonly thought, but into it and beyond it, because the world is the past still alive. Conventions wear. Like eyeglasses they get scratched and grow opaque. Poetry loses clear vision. Readers find themselves immune to words in predictable shapes, in habitual expressions, though the poem's subject and even context may change only superficially. The breakthrough poet cleans the lens. He alters expression by altering form just enough to re-view the world and see it freshly, as it always is. The world's richness, even for the least receptive imagination, returns. This renewal of language is an illusion, but so is poetry. We live by illusions. Poetry renews our energy, desire, sense of possibility, our potential to live. To enter the expressive relationships of all being—with knowledge—is to apprehend what we are. The breakthrough poet drives us into the world only to drive us into ourselves, where the world is in us and we are in it. Without imagination we could not possess an awareness of complex, subtle, or contradictory matters. Without language, imagination would be useless. Without form, language would be a chaos of sound. Form is the choice the poet has to make for knowledge and clarity. We tend to think of breakthrough poets as visionaries. They are and must be that, but these are the visionaries of form—or else we would not hear them.

Is there, finally, very much difference between what Eliot tells us and what we are told—about man, I mean—by Frost, Williams, Stevens, or Marianne Moore? I think not. Yet each manages something remarkably unique in his poem, something which lasts and is the poet's individual signature of beauty. This is form. There is about each the character of eccentricity, even pugnaciousness, yet to be eccentric and self-sure is no guarantee of the breakthrough poem. Otherwise Robinson Jeffers, Olson, E. E. Cummings, and many others would rank higher than they do. What is missing? I think it is memorable, sustained, clear vision which composes a large, whole, fully tested image of man through a language which constantly refines itself toward a clarity of statement and resonance. What is missing is a form appropriate to vision. The irony is that no poet could be more addicted to form than, say, Olson. Yet it is too often a form set out mechanically, like a net, set eccentrically where the fish are not.

Yeats says, "There is in the creative joy an acceptance of what life brings, because we have understood the beauty of what it brings, or a hatred of death for what it takes away, which arouses within us, through some sympathy with all other men, an energy so noble, so powerful, that we laugh aloud and mock, in the terror of the sweetness of our exaltation, at death and oblivion." Perhaps Milton could not have said exactly this but I think he would have recognized it as a valuable statement of art's action. If the poem is gloomy, sour, morbid, desperate, or horrifying, it will yet lead us to celebration, for the poem praises that which we must honor and reveals that which we must mightily hate. No less an aesthetician than Wallace Stevens tells us that art is, finally, noble energy.

If we cling with ultimate conviction to a faith in the world's beauty, we cannot blink away the meanness, scum, malignity, and plain scurrilousness that is also the world. In this world poetry shocks the individual to health as a faltering heart is shocked to its best rhythms. It may be that poetry affects only the poets, a small constituency. Yet perhaps that is enough, that local stronghold, to keep alive something of the good that men may imagine. Certainly the testimony of history is that the poem is one of the forces of knowledge, and a knowledge we may attain in no other way. That is why poetry is noble energy. It is the noble energy which compels us to be free, which causes us to understand that the condition of freedom means an active, speculative, responsible allegiance to values whose reality and beauty we must continually test.

What is a poem? What does it do? It is music and statement and feeling and the shape of courageous thought. It says *no* to death and to pain and to the spirit's imprisonment. It denies that it may affirm and witness and celebrate the grace and goodness of life. To the degree that it sacrifices full and complex witness to experience, that it begins to moralize, it is rotten and useless. Art, poetry, does not promulgate a social design nor does it yield up constitutions. It shows us a man in the motions of his life. The poet believes he must seek for life in art but he must first seek for the possibilities of art in life. Art may and usually does improve the quality of life. It may even affect human behavior for the better—but we had better not hold our breath.

Baudelaire says poetry exists only to be poetry. That is like the great wheeling hawks I have loved since my boyhood. The hawk exists as itself above all sophistry or explanation. Its nature is to rise and fall, to be silent and to sing. The hawk belongs to the high air where he circles and everything seems part of a force whose only intention is to keep the hawk what he is and where he is, mysterious, serene, and compulsive. Almost I want to say the poem is that hawk's voice riding out like a final sound of defiance in a final place. Yet a poem is not a hawk nor a place. It is an organization of formed words made by a man or a woman, an undeniable, strongly sounded music of human crying-out, sometimes in joy and often in sorrow, which comes to rest and to live in an apparently natural but always artificial form. In a poem a man may rise and fall with the beauty of a hawk, but he is not a hawk. A man must do and he must be in the world but he cannot, if he would fulfill his destiny as a man, refuse the attempt to know the meaning of himself and the attempt to render it permanent in the memory of his kind. Melville spoke with admiration of the "whole corps of thought-divers that have been diving and coming up since the world began." The hawk, as much as I love him, is a pitiful and limited creature in comparison to the thought-divers, the poets, whose pursuit of clarity and form is nothing less than the will to live for beauty and to make it the meaning, the noble energy by which we shall be enabled to live and to know the fullness of that living.

> ASSAY: from Latin *ex-agere, exigere* to weigh, try, prove, measure, adjust, ascertain, examine, inquire into; the trying (of a person or thing); trial imposed upon or endured by any object, in order to test its virtue, fitness, etc.; trial, tribulation, affliction; experiment, experience; the trial of anything by taste, tasting; the act, latterly perhaps nothing more than complimentary, of tasting the food or drink before giving it to an exalted personage; putting forth of one's strength or energy; an attack, assault; a first tentative attempt or learning; a sample; to determine the degree of purity of one of the precious metals; character, temper, sounding, depth.
>
> *The Oxford English Dictionary*

1

The subject of poetry, whatever the context and with lesser or greater satisfaction, is always man. Poets write about as many topics as there are phenomena in the world. The topic, however, is context: a window which gives forth the nature of a man or woman in crises of passion, a man or woman who has not yet answers to the enigmatic but apprehended shapes of existence. This is why all poems must have a meaning and be a meaning, for any poem is a statement of our relationship to a particular part of or to the whole of the world that is not us. As the word *poet* derives from the Greek word for the shaper, as that which is shaped reflects, the poem is a construction in and of man's image. Pope's admonition to study man never loses validity. Few poets tell us more about man than Milton, yet Milton's *Paradise Lost* could be rightly accused by Samuel Johnson as being too much about angelic instruction and too little about ourselves: "The want of human interest is always felt. *Paradise Lost* is one of the books which the reader admires and lays down, and forgets to take up again. None ever wished it longer than it is." Nevertheless our critics venerate the impenetrable art-poems by John

Ashbery, award prizes to James Merrill's *The Changing Light at Sandover,* and develop a nearly Talmudic commentary about Charles Olson.

2

Every poem is a choice. Every poem is a set of choices. All choices are made for, contained in, and expressed by words. Any word chosen eliminates all other words that might have been but were not chosen. Each phrase shoulders aside every other possible phrase. Each line exercises an influence on each succeeding line. The progressive set of choices from word to phrase to line to sentence to stanza to poem determines patterns of sound and of visual perception. The totality of shape accrued through choices is called form. The choices which lead to form may occur so rapidly and organically as to resist explanation. Poets call these "gifts" but they are not unearned gifts. One informing principle may be discovered as the arbiter of form and that is the poem's attitude toward man, experience, and existence. In dramatic genres this attitude may not be the poet's but that of an assumed or composed speaker; in the lyric we are always overhearing the poet. The poet remains, in whatever generic form, the chooser and he is never constrained by any force except the exigencies and responsibilities of the poem whose obligation is its truth. We can say nothing intelligent of poet or poem until we understand that all life, every act in part and in whole, is choice—even when the choice appears subjective and inexplicable. The most valuable distinctions among poets result from evaluating the seriousness and responsibility with which a poet chooses.

3

Great poetry must be responsible and serious, whatever its genre. The serious poem will be unflinching before the truth of human experience as it has been and as it is, experience recorded by history and understood by consciousness. The responsible poem, however dark its vision, will celebrate images of human health, knowledge, love, and freedom—in potential if not in fact. All poetry is a demand for freedom. This freedom, and whatever the poem may do in its service, begins at home. Therefore we need no better definition of the virtues, pleasures, and actions of the poem than Wordsworth's:

> For our continued influxes of feeling are modified and directed by our thoughts, which are indeed the representatives of all our past feelings; and, as by contemplating the relation of these gen-

> eral representatives to each other, we discover what is really important to men, so, by the repetition and continuance of this act, our feelings will be connected with important subjects, till at length, if we be originally possessed with much sensibility, such habits of mind will be produced, that, by obeying blindly and mechanically the impulse of those habits, we shall describe objects, and utter sentiments, of such a nature, and in such connexion with each other, that the understanding of the Reader must necessarily be in some degree enlightened, and his affections strengthened and purified.

4

All arguments about form are exercises of the intelligence and are speculations born of ignorance and anxiety. No argument should be left unconsidered, regardless of moral, political, aesthetic, or nationalistic position. No argument will be conclusive. None will permit a final, formulaic truth. Form is directly linked to function. In the natural world a giraffe grows a long neck in order to feed upon the particular high leaf that sustains him. But it is not logical, therefore, that form is an organic fact. The giraffe does not achieve his form after a sequence of choices. The poet finds form only after making choices, however accessible or inaccessible those choices may have been to rational thought. Form is intrinsic and may not be altered without creating a different poem. The meaning of Milton's "Lycidas" may be abstractly stated and shown to be common with Auden's "In Memory of W. B. Yeats" and other elegies. Yet what the poem *means,* in this sense, is not the poem. The poem truly means what it is, what its form is. If that form is changed, the meaning changes and "Lycidas" is no longer exactly "Lycidas." When we have asked what we want the poem of our future to do we shall, perhaps, discover some of what it must be. If, for example, we wish the poem to be an enigmatic and near-fabular exploration of natural phenomena, a medallion delivered in terse, slightly reverential but apparently common sensical voice, we may have A. R. Ammons. If we wish it to be the massive intrusion of catastrophic social and cultural malignity on a modest lyric sensibility we may have Denise Levertov. But even the most dispassionate and deliberate attention to form will not write the poem alive. The poet must proceed like the diviner with his water-seeking rod. The poet knows there is no original poem yet to be developed, but that does not stop him from trying.

5

A poem's content is more significant than its outward, imposed form. Yet what content can exist without form? No poem exists without form. It is possible to execute with formidable skill every species of form known and make only inert verse-clones. What is missing there is the heartbeat of knowledge that mere learning, in its arrogance, cannot possess or imagine. We are at the threshold, if not already in the room, of a conservative poetics which threatens a new age of such versifiers and palace tutors. Two examples are John Hollander and William Harmon. Hollander's *Rhyme's Reason* shows us how little relevant is the strict application of rules to making of poems. Handbooks, theories, poetics, maxims are all valuable to apprentice writers for they contain the accumulated wisdom of our heritage. They describe what is valuable and possible beyond temporal and parochial standards, but they give no formula which will result in guaranteed excellence. Conversely, it is possible to write poems about admittedly significant subjects which remain non-poems or poor poems because their forms are inadequate, awkward, insufficient, partial, or even destructive. If no poem can exist without form, no form can make a poem that matters out of insignificant matter. Auden is reputed to have said that two young men came to him to speak of writing poetry. The first is supposed to have said he burned with messages of consequence. The second said he delighted in playing with language. Of the first, Auden said, he will write little. But the second one had a chance. Insofar as Auden said either, he was wrong. It is true that no poet of main consequence can succeed without the obsessive urge to make language bend to his will and desire, but if a poet has nothing to say better he should work crossword puzzles. The world of contemporary poetry spilleth over with those who have nothing to say, who are nevertheless adamant that we shall hear them saying it. What is louder than ennui, exhaustion, darkness, and inertia among us? Many of these voices are in university writing programs, men and women who have fought no war, loved but little, gone but short distance of time and space from their homes, and read not much. In their forgivable immaturity they appear now to be turning to the new glibness of verse. What can *they* say? Yet, Emily Dickinson encompasses the Universe.

6

Men need to speak about what matters. The most succinct, beautiful, memorable, and affective speech is the poem. Words are the poet's enemies, conspirators, and only allies. It is understandable that the poet wants to press language beyond the point of referential communication because he wants to express the apprehended and the unknown. Nevertheless, *Finnegans Wake,* much of Beckett, and almost anything called Surreal is terminally boring. A painter who shoots himself and calls it art may have something in common with Aram Saroyan's publication of blank pages, but in neither case is there art. The poem which does not communicate something to a reasonably attentive and reasonably intelligent reader is no poem. Feeling may well be communicated more easily outside of words—in mime, gestures, signs, and pictures—but not so long, not so fully, not so completely. The minimalist attitude which holds that not much can be said of consequence, or need be said, is wrong and dangerous. It accepts the servitude of man or woman in a technocratic world and collaborates for the littleness of the human spirit. The hermetic and willfully opaque poet risks the further isolation of poetry in a society which already regards language as of marginal value except as its glittery letters march militarily across a computer terminal. This minimalism has nothing to do with the poem's length, as the poems of the New York school reveal. Such poetry seems, like a petulant child, to say pay attention only to me or I'll hold my breath. When the child speaks it is unintelligible, yet praised for cleverness and sincerity. Once I saw a dog at a party piss on a guest's leg and the guest cooed over the dog for its anxiety. Ours is a people that does not want to give or get hard news, even from the interior; it wants flash, dazzle, ease, and surface. Perhaps this is not true. Perhaps in our lust to know and be known we stand docile in the doggy world of the critics who mark us like fence posts. We let a James Atlas tell us what art is.

7

The only story in any poem is life and death. All poems tell this story. The poet's is the voice of life contending with that ultimate survivor, Death. I am speaking of great art, not mere entertainment. Perhaps even the American musical comedy is what Richard Eberhart calls "a spell against death," though it seems to me the slickest, silliest creation of our national imagination. I have heard serious men say the musical comedy is the only original American art form. If so, we shall surely be the jesters among the great artistic nations.

8

The morality of poetry exists though no one wants to be caught holding that particular tiger's tail, especially when to do so suggests card-carrying membership in Jerry Falwell's new Luddites. Poetry's morality lies in the poet's absolute commitment to give experience, known imaginatively and empirically, its most affective, responsible shape in the static illusion of words. It is the will to enlarge experience with vision, to invest speech with the pulse of life. The morality of poetry opposes enervation, misanthropy, and Death. No true poet praises, cultivates, or softens Death—unless in doing so the effect is to heighten the value of life. Yukio Mishima is wrongheaded. When she is sick, so is Sylvia Plath. The morality of poetry is the heroism of vision which helps us to take courage and live, which demands freedom. Ginsberg's "Howl" is a heroic, moral poem however anarchic it appears. Any writer who demeans the will to live—not merely to exist—either by default or intention is nothing more than an interloper among the heroes, a charlatan. To say this, of course, is to recognize a fact, not suggest a choice. It will do no good whatsoever for the poet to take to his work with a New Year's resolution to do good, to seek the heroic and the honorable. We must hope that poets hope for good character, desire to write as they imagine and not necessarily as they are, all of us being considerably less than perfect citizens, but the poet who begins with a cigar-box of ideas, ideals, or programs which he means to flesh out in lines is doomed to stillborn poems. Yet let us have that poet who seeks to understand, to refine the shapes of thought and feeling he can discover in tested words, however he finds them. The poet who does this need not concern himself or herself about morality in the poems that serve life.

9

Any poem achieves its subject with greatest power when it moves by invention. Invention is a function of the imagination. Imagination is the engine of poetry. That this is an antique idea does not lessen its validity or force. Many younger poets misunderstand and regard Fancy as the power. Let them read Coleridge. Fancy avoids knowledge, does not drive through the real to the visionary. Fancy does not seek the shape of our destiny but rather contents itself with superficial entertainments. It refuses life out of selfishness, meanness, cowardice, and blindness—which are the motives toward fashion and fad. This, again, is the minimalist scene. It doesn't struggle with itself for ourselves but connives, deals, weasels. The poet who can write of nothing so obsessive as his frustration with words has an important subject, something at the heart of our age or any age, but it is comparably a stunted subject and will produce stunted poems like those of Creeley. Such poems do not embrace what the anthropologist and poet Loren Eiseley called "matter dreaming." We have too many boring dreamers of little matter whose ambition is no more than a modest journalism. These are the poets of the lineated diary, the humdrum of the incessantly weeping city, the neopastoralists who took Robert Bly literally when he said two hours of solitude under a tree for each line of poetry. Yet is anything clearer than the fact that subject is almost irrelevant to poetry? Poetry arises when imagination invents truth out of whatever subject is at hand. It was always personal experience that poets had at hand. This may have been, may be, what poets do, see, feel, remember; it is also what they are told, what they dream, what they imagine. Not the experience you have but what you do with experience when it has you. Imagination invents the credible context, shape, rhythm of human experience. There are always poets who do not submit to enough personal catechisms, the searing questions about the meaning and nature of experience, which might lift what they know and say to the invented but true level of art. Why is one poet's poem about roast beef merely innocuous when Keats's poem about a tableware vessel is magnificent? It is not subject, maybe not even form, that differentiates them; it is the power of imaginative vision, of connection and revelation, of poetry that one has and one has not. This, maybe, is the power of fiction—or at least the will of fiction to invite into the words the entire shagginess and desultory imperfection that life has. Invention organizes, orders, frames, alters, and synthesizes but only in the context of a right imagination does the poem become durable and fresh. In the weak imagination and in fancy's invention there is only the novel, the temporary. Many among us were not at birth imaginatively gifted and nothing human can be done to provide what nature has withheld. Yet without imagination constantly stretched and worked, as a muscle, poetry will be little more than competent, rote performance. If the majority of our poems are going to be, as they will be, pale scars on the world's body, nevertheless we do wrong to seek less than the heroic will toward Beauty and permanence. The imagination tells us why Yeats says, "Passive suffering is not a theme for poetry."

10

The great poem is the single most revolutionary weapon in our arsenal against Death. In it, we live and are free. It is also the quietest and most subversive. This says nothing, however, of the political or polemical poem. A poem is merely political if it is only a poetical march through righteous ideas. No publication of manifestos and no good engagement in public works, however agreeable, justifies the merely political poem. Much of the poetry written against the Vietnam War, brave and necessary as it was for those poets, is now dated and dull. Much was and is sensational trash. The American poet who takes a political side in El Salvador or Ireland is approximately in the same position as the Bulgarian or the South African poet who writes about American race relations, presumptious, perhaps opportunistic, to the degree the poem points its finger outward. The poem's argument is always with the individual heart struggling to achieve selfhood, its destiny. James Wright said the enemy of poetry is glibness. Strangely enough the opposite of glibness is not sobriety or veracity, not exactly, but more something like responsibility's cost. That cost is local and immediate in the self and in the poem. If we abandon pursuit of the most ambitious poetry we can imagine, we abandon ourselves. Poetry is nonfunctional, nondemocratic, and nontemporal. Poetry answers the spirit's need for Beauty, which lies beyond all brutal, physical needs. In boxing they say cut off the body and the head follows. To cut off the head will do equally well. In poetry both head and body serve but the heart is critical and necessary in the spirit's battle.

11

The music of poetry *is* poetry. Poetry, however, has many musics and there is no ear fine enough to hear them all with equal pleasure or sympathy. Each music, if it is a true unity, contributes to and participates in the orchestration of the song of freedom. All forms of poetic music are partially open and partially closed. All forms tend to assert the individual's unique selfhood while simultaneously asserting the common nature of humanity. The peculiar American argument about the validity of open and closed form is only a reflection of the American social experiment which exists on a paradox: the democratic principle proposes the rightness of the majority while it proposes also the individual's right to uncompromised independence. We like to say each man's opinion is as good as another's but this too easily becomes, in the public mind, an opinion of equal rightness: each opinion is correct but never to the exclusion of another opinion. Because this paradox influences what and how we think of poetry, we need to remind ourselves to value unity, clarity, totality, and purpose, which are the benchmarks of music. In the music of poetry lies Beauty. Beauty is all that poetry is, all that it does. Yet this Beauty must be a constant testing and restatement of what is valuable. Therefore the greatest poetry will be that which evolves toward a seemingly systematic vision of human society, a big vision as Jung calls it. For this poet the poems of a lifetime are like the scrupulous digs and delicate brush strokes of the archaeologist who patiently reveals a whole shape, an order of being with boundaries, contingencies, relationships, and vivid dimensions. Poetry which does not move in this direction is less Beauty than the record of a moldering civilization. We must try to hear all the musics as the archaeologist feels his puzzle. If we are poets we are also, inescapably, critics, judges, adjudicators. If we are critically democratic to the exclusion of passionate discrimination we fail ourselves, our responsibility, and worse we fail the future entrusted to us.

12

Poetry does not exist outside the human voice. Matter may dream, as Eiseley says, but only the human voice lifts that dream to articulation. Only through the voice of words may it be fixed and known across time. The song of the nightingale and the bellow of the moose may cause rapture but they are not poems. They are only sounds. Dandy Don Meredith may call O. J. Simpson's broken-field dash for a touchdown an example of poetry in motion, but he is wrong. No painting, symphony, movie, or prose is, precisely and actually, a poem. No poem of significance has been written by computer or committee. The true poem has a single human voice speaking under the pressure of character, passion, circumstance, and necessity, yet it is also the echoing voice of all men and women.

13

If poetry were no more than what men and women think, we should regard what they have thought as little more than the curious costumes of our past. What we think about the world and ourselves has changed and poetry has also changed—but not so radically as literary criticism might suggest. Poetry is not primarily the expression of thought but is the embodiment of feeling as thought. I do not think what people *feel* has significantly changed. As Yeats worries about becoming an old man who cannot get the girl he shows he has more in common with "The Wanderer," Matthew Arnold, Li Po, and Galway Kinnell than any differences implied by course descriptions. The poet who begins with idea is a poor philosopher and, unless he is very lucky, is a doomed poet. But the poem which begins with the Ur-cry of the heart will convince us we are at least on the road to Truth. It has the chance of sustained pleasure for the reader. The beauty the poem seeks becomes the pleasure the reader seeks. The name of the man or woman found at the poem's end is of no final consequence; the generative gravity of the poem itself defines the poem as the speech of a man given to men about men. We know the real poem when we touch it just as we know the electric touch of the lover's body.

14

The relationship of all statements about poems to the poem itself, to its felt reality, is approximately the relationship of sexual instruction handbooks to sexual intercourse. The thing is ever various, ever potential, never less than mysterious, never exhaustible. Men speak of intercourse as "making love" but this is nonsense. One can discover love. One can fall in love. One can nourish and care for love. One cannot *make* love, not so long as *to make* connotes deliberation, calculation, or formula construction. Yet intercourse is certainly a function of love at its best. So, too, is the poem. Just as sexual intercourse is fundamentally inexpressible experience while it is perhaps the most essentially and biologically known fact of our being, a poem and its power are both known and scarcely to be known by discourse. Of both, we might say that nothing said after the fact changes the fact; nothing said in advance of the fact changes the fact. Perhaps this is why Baudelaire tells us, "The object of poetry is not truth, the object of poetry is poetry itself." He does not tell us we will not find truth in poetry or that we should not seek it there. He merely says there is no necessary end for poetry but the creation and continuity of itself. The poet engages in poetry in order to experience reality. Poetry, like love, begins with what the imagination makes, ends in the reality of the senses, and affirms possibility for matter dreaming. The contemporary poet's task is, as Pound said, to make it new—but also to know there is nothing new under the sun. Except, perhaps, the stories of Ecclesiastes, the poet's unique life, and his way of saying before which all acts of love and music stand locally, radiantly, for his assay.

Part II

■

One Man's Music
The Second Self

One Man's Music

■

Contemporary American poetry is frequently accused of "becoming slight and fantastic, abstract, unreal, eccentric. . . . It must reclaim substance and sense, and physical and psychological reality." What critic, reviewer, or ordinary reader would not agree? Yet, what is slight? What is unreal or real? What is poetry? Are not these terms subjective and applicable by anyone to anything which is set up as a poem? Risking imprecision, I suggest tentatively that whatever is poetic is real. In poems this reality inheres in an intensity of passion and a shapeliness of music. One music shapes toward prose, another shapes toward poetry.

That imprecise critic I cite above, Robinson Jeffers writing in 1938, was bedeviled by trying to define poetic music, knowing that only in music could poetry be shown to be itself and not prose. Prose, that is, represents imperfection's tendency; poetry shows the tendency to purify, to seek purity of expression. That is why prose is inclusive and poetry is exclusive. If we follow this over-neat categorization we may argue that there are two kinds of poets among us, just as Jeffers implies: the physical and the psychological, the impure and the pure, the objective and the

Reviews of David Huddle, *Paper Boy* (University of Pittsburgh Press); Margaret Gibson, *Signs* (Louisiana State University Press); Jane Shore, *Eye Level* (University of Massachusetts Press); Ricardo Alonso, *Cimarron* (Wesleyan University Press); Brian Swann, *Living Time* (Quarterly Review of Literature Poetry Series); M. Slotznick, *Industrial Stuff* (Quarterly Review of Literature Poetry Series); E. G. Burrows, *Properties: A Play for Voices* (Quarterly Review of Literature Poetry Series); Reginald Gibbons, *Roofs, Voices, Roads* (Quarterly Review of Literature Poetry Series); David Galler, *Third Poems: 1965–1978* (Quarterly Review of Literature Poetry Series); William Mills, *Stained Glass* (Louisiana State University Press); Richard Shelton, *The Bus to Veracruz* (University of Pittsburgh Press); William Heyen, *Long Island Light* (Vanguard).

subjective, ad infinitum. As he also implies, the good poets are both in one, though some are more one than the other in concentration. Current critical practices divide our poets thus: there is the poet bored with the exterior world, distrusting of language, cool in posture, urbanely natured. He is dedicated mostly to a world that is the jaded intellect, one marked by interior and self-reflexive poems which prize refinement, sensitivity, education, arcane information, a subdued yet insistent attraction to Spanish politics, French painters, etc.

There is also the poet who views the sequentialities of fiction as the poem's proper ground. Here events become exfoliations which seek revelation. This poet emphasizes objective detail, place (usually suburban or rural), and much prefers language to silence. His music is roughened and aggressive, rather than tidy and demurring. Regardless of the backing and filling qualifiers we supply, categories tell us little of how the poems from either poet are, in fact, poems, how reality is summoned forth, or what excellence is achieved. A poem is a poem to the degree it manages the emotional illumination and infectiousness of music. But what music? And what is poetic music?

Those who write of poetry's music usually define it by external or internal manifestations; that is, by talk of technique, device, and facility—or by talk of intensity, scope, immediacy, and effectiveness. Their theories of *why* range from phoneme function to Derrida. Doubtless, one or more of them is right. It isn't possible in this review essay to attend to the many explanations of that various thing we call poetry's music. One thing it isn't: the Beatles. Nor is it anything subject to standard musical notation. Onomatopoeia, that changeling tribe, won't give it to us. And really, have you ever read one handbook of prosody that didn't seem so much mist once you'd turned the last page?

For me, although music is the conventional term, *music* in poetry cannot fully disclose what is simply the saying and staying power of the ruthlessly human voice courting its most precise, clear, and vivid articulation *in the awareness* it must become more interesting and more durable than any other form of speech. We find what we look for, perhaps, and we find this music in the poet's attitude toward his written experience. I look for a surprise in the sentences, which is a kind of dancing of sound, an expectation aroused by lines and stanzas, a phrasing that is charged with tension yet careful—because the experience is conceived to matter within the language, not because of it, not in spite of it. It is only when the body's speech-music is missing or sputtering that we need talk of the horse-and-buggy conception of form and content. Still, we all have our vague notions of an ideal music, what we most want to hear, which is why my music is only another man's noise. I think this is why we can identify poetry only by pointing at a poem and can identify reality only by pointing through the best poems. The function of poetry's music is to make us hear reality.

II

There is no question in my mind that David Huddle's first collection, *Paper Boy,* aims at defining reality. His book, a kind of *Spoon River Anthology,* authentically explores a rural Virginia town and comes complete with eccentric characters, set-jawed relationships, civil decay, small jobs, first loves and true fights, and Death. It is very like fiction, like Southern fiction: dedicated to the psychological imprisonment of people whose lives are demeaned, abused, and yet impacted with the tonnage of explosive possibility. These stories are human, about real people, and grit-true as facts. Huddle makes us believe that in spite of everything wrong back there they throve. So far, so good. I don't think the poem exists unless it has a story to tell, even if it is the severely repressed winker in a haiku. But a story is not, ipso facto, a poem and Huddle's narratives are only stories. They don't have enough poetry, aren't enough poetry. The poem about strikers getting shot for their action cannot be allowed to end "things like that / can happen anywhere." Poetry's truth is greater than fact, larger than the story which is fact's embrace. Huddle's lack of music, his nonchalance within words, trivializes rather than illuminates reality.

The compositions of *Paper Boy* are poems primarily because they have similes and are lined. We are drawn through them not by poetry's compelling sound but by fiction's suspense. The language is too inert to engender either transcendence or transformation of factual and local detail. Everything here comes to seem thereby predictable and stereotypical, truly formulaic: in honky-tonk world we cannot have *real* emotional responses to *real* people. Real, did I say? Well, complex, resonant, the difference between people in a film and people in a Polaroid snapshot. Too often Huddle's poems settle for the narrator's joke, especially the stud-colloquial, pseudo-intimate leering and rib-nudging that is one boot short of vision. Huddle has the necessary tools: an eye for realistic detail, a sense of dramatic organization, a feel for moments of crisis that go to the heart of what it means to be alive. He can be interesting and he is readable. In fact David Huddle is rarely a bad writer, but as poet he has no ear and is mediocre. His poems are, I would say, semitough prose anecdotes. For example:

MRS. GREEN

At the screen door
a pretty woman just
married and in shorts
on a Saturday in May,
she was sweet to me
when I came to collect,
offered me something cold
to drink,
                which I refused
for the sake of dreaming
the whole summer I was
twelve about what it
would be like some
morning to walk
softly into
that lady's
kitchen.

Margaret Gibson's first collection, *Signs,* superficially marks her as a nature poet. She writes much of the northeastern seacoast, plants, gardening, fruits, and birds. But her precise and lyrical observations of "edges / and outlines" show her to be looking beyond things to the emanations of a sacramental energy in all things. "Will we ever be raised / incorruptible" she asks of the earth's body, echoing the Christian dream of perfectibility, because she feels imprisoned by mutability and decline while she is driven to celebrate physical reality. Gibson's poems are less events than the meditative siftings of an unusually sensuous mind. Her speaker sits at a window or lies in bed or stands before the sea; she describes textures of apples, onions, sea-winds, snow, light, her body. From such static origins, because description becomes penetration rather than registration, she can speak as "a peasant pushing / a wooden cart / piled high with / brilliant gourds." This terse two-stress line helps her achieve a blunt clarity. Gibson calls herself "transparent / a magnifying glass" because she intends to clear away what is unnecessary to or obstructive of the radiant surfaces she imagines to contain the secrets of being. Merely to see, however, will not be enough, for Gibson is not an imagist but a celebrator; she intends to derive from the natural world a philosophy of feeling. Love, given and received, is her primary subject.

Yet Margaret Gibson is as much rationalist as rapturist. She shows more than a few poems that are remarkable for a pronounced strain of discursive comment, some of which is engendered convincingly and some of which is ad hoc. Not too surprisingly, she is a bookish thinker and she invites Colette, Dostoevski, Flaubert, Sartre, and others into her poems, the effect of which is to temper rapture for the natural world while making the discursiveness seem more to be feeling than it is comment. A skilled and formally various poet, Margaret Gibson has yet, perhaps, to find quite the style to harmonize her sense of art's control and her need for full revelation. She can be too static and austere and she is also indulgent with shopworn mythmaking that fuses pop song lingo, natural symbols, and Homeric travel ("I empty my mind and listen for green / cadences, taste salt / wind on sunburned roads"). But *Signs* is, on the whole, a strong book by a poet whose "Canticle for the New Year" says:

> I praise the thunder
> which shakes seed from
> its pod
> swift clouds, the
> galloping horse
> fierce love.

Jane Shore's *Eye Level,* another first collection, is concerned with a world much like Margaret Gibson's, a world of love undervalued and abused. Her ground, too, is domestic and northeastern. Unlike Gibson's poetry, however, everything here seems as temporary as the present tense. Though this is a world continuously, closely observed, it yields only the rarest sense of conclusion. About life, Shore seems to feel a constant guilt born of an inability to change or deflect the forces of destruction. The guilt is too easy and is the mark of a young poet. The awareness, with intensity, of those forces of destruction is characteristic of a matured poet. When we speak of the unevenness of first collections we often speak of faltering skills but it is more ordinarily this disalignment of response which makes a poem and a book less than wholly satisfactory.

In Shore's best poems there is an admirable toughness which wants both to possess life and to energize it. Too frequently she settles for mere observation rather than the looking-through that is poetry's strength. This is endemic with America's workshop-trained younger poets. Though Shore, like Gibson, tries out numerous formal approaches she prefers a blunt and statemental poem which usually lacks the charged phrasing that makes her composition more than lineated and clear prose. Her lines can be leaden, such as "I watch for clouds." This is the portentous conclusion to "Ararat." Where a conclusion ought to satisfy our aroused expectations, such a line asks that we anticipate something we are nowhere given. Shore is more affecting in longer-lined poems which focus less on the speaker's conscious awareness and more on clear dramatic contexts. "Witness" is about a child roped by his feet and pulled from a "lumberyard cesspool." It ends:

> He swung a long moment over us, shiny,
> bigger than we thought, his face bruised blue
> by that metallic light. Cold gravity; release.
> He whined like nothing in my arms.

The poem is emblematic of Shore's vision and talent. A chilling, immediate, yet virtually typical poem of urban violation, it is marked by its melancholy and the speaker's helplessness. In this stanza three lines are precise and strong, one is derivative. Indeed the stanza suggests Shore's poetic apprenticeship: Dickey's "The Lifeguard" is its dramatic predecessor and James Wright's "St. Judas" provides the last line. (Wright's presence is also here in the echo of his poem "The Anniversary.") If Shore's book shows a cool and canny ability from time to time, its greatest weakness is that it is premature: she has not dispensed with the learning ghosts. Her imitations, necessary to any poet's development, remain both obvious and unassimilated. Besides Dickey and Wright, Creeley's terse nominational poems are abundantly evident. But worse, I think, are the poems which deploy that chill, chatty, hypersincere, entirely ordinary idiom of America's schooled poets: we can't tell which writer wrote these poems or why, only that things are bad in a monotonous way. Unlike Huddle, Jane Shore is capable of music but not consistently enough yet to break through or beyond her manners into what she calls "The spark / deepening in the brain."

Where Jane Shore suffers from uncertainty about which discipline will be hers, Ricardo Alonso's first book, *Cimarron,* shows a poet who needs some concentration to wring the most power from a considerable talent. Alonso is a Cuban who is "from" the darkness of the American barrio experience. His subject is the exile and social imprisonment of "his people." One almost says that technique is irrelevant to a poetry so affecting in its hard loneliness. Yet it is precisely technique which allows Alonso to make us feel the pain of his poems. He is nearly a natural poet who proceeds by repetition of image and phrase, by refrains and folk rhythms common to blues songs. Yet he fails to resist the most banal language: "I / must be going / crazy / because today / it really matters" (the *it* is a gamble). Alonso has not yet learned that in poetry words matter most—that the great poems of revolutionary fervor and righteous outcry are memorable because of the music of poetry, not because they are morally or socially agreeable. Yet he writes, in spite of laziness, an elegaic poetry that mixes bitter sting with rapture as easily as he mixes Spanish with English. In poems about fathers, mothers, lovers, and lost homelands he portrays the "cimarron" or runaway slave in whom there is a defiant courage to live, and that is worth a good deal, technical weakness or not. Alonso's finest poems are the longer ones which allow for cumulative effects of anger, tenderness, sorrow, and pride to alter both the dreams and the lives of his people. In these he succeeds by drawing us close to the whole lives of the family. His short poems seem mere breathing space when compared to, say, "Rain" or "Rumba." *Cimarron* is a political indictment of the American promise, but Alonso is wise enough to see this is the indictment of human idealism and wise enough, therefore, to make a book of love for all those still able to dream "life is green / and thick as the air." If Ricardo Alonso will refuse parochiality and retain his will toward a poetry that speaks to the cimarron in all of us, we shall have much to look forward to in his future.

III

Theodore and Renée Weiss, as most readers of poetry know, have been long and singular friends of the art. As editors of the *Quarterly Review of Literature* they were diligent in discovering and printing poets whose work is now part of our heritage. Currently they continue their service to poets as the publishers of the Quarterly Review of Literature Poetry Series. Each volume in the series contains five "books" of poems, or two more than the long defunct Scribners Poets of Today series which is the model for Weiss's new venture. Volume I includes Brian Swann, M. Slotznick, Reginald Gibbons, E. G. Burrows, and David Galler. Unless I have a particular point I wish to illustrate, as with David Huddle's *Paper Boy,* I generally prefer to ignore books that seem to me entirely poor. The format of the QRL series would require me to be markedly rude if I said nothing of some of these books so I want to say that this volume is an attractive, welcome bargain in spite of some of the following remarks.

One reason the volume is worth having is Reginald Gibbons's first collection, *Roofs, Voices, Roads.* Gibbons is sheer delight to me, a writer whose every experience is made to resonate in nearly sculpted language. His world is complex and rich, ranging from seamy Southern hotels to Ezra Pound. The poems have dignity and refined music but they know they speak to people and they take seriously their responsibility for communication. They are as intense and charming as a good sleepy-eyed fiddler who slides without warning into chamber music. What may be best about Gibbons is his ability to do the right, unexpected thing. Who else, I can say now, would end a poem about melancholy dusk by turning to a man out walking his dog this way:

His chest is in flames.
What a relief to see the fire of loneliness
there too, breaking

from another man's heart.

And who else would turn the "angel of desire" into a mugger as Gibbons does in "Body and Soul"? Like an instinctive musician or athlete, Gibbons seems to have moves we cannot explain but do not question. "Pine Island" is a poem I think most readers will wish they had written. I don't know of another poet, except perhaps Ransom, who catches the tension of lovers who would but can't break away from each other—as Gibbons does in "Pine Island." There is little use in saying what his poems are about; they are about our lives—but our lives seen with a clarity that is rare enough to preserve the "stories / and stories rising from / rubble" or to celebrate the poets who "croak out a few spells" to keep the imagination alive. Gibbons sometimes reminds me of Philip Levine's slightly angry, deeply sympathetic portraits of places and people there is no way to sustain or keep except in memory. Gibbons, however, is less a narrative poet than Levine, more lyrical, and certainly more bookish: his poems often translate, imitate, and celebrate such poets as Guillen, Vallejo, Alberti, Gongora, and Paz. Not surprisingly the most common poem in Gibbons is the elegy, brief, prophetic, less well-lit rooms than shadowy passageways and terse gestures. It is, in fact, a poetry of roofs and voices and roads. Gibbons is a young poet who has his flaws and the good readers will find them, but I am confident he offers us "the broken thread of a melody that can / awaken from desire or despair / the entire remembered chorus."

I am less enthusiastic about the other four "books" in this volume. Brian Swann's *Living Time* is set entirely on location in Italy and no one could say it is remarkable for bad writing. But I cannot find for the life of me a single urgent, compelling poem. Swann's writing is mediocre at worst and competent at best. It is never memorable or brilliant or even eccentric. Yet it is sometimes curious. When, for example, Swann writes "The sun is climbing the door / like a wind" nothing in the simile or the poem discloses what is meant. What could it mean to say about a café that "Each chair and table has the crust of its shape upon it?" Or to write that "A hen begins to cackle in iambics" and later in "spondees"? This is mechanical poetry-work of the sort that well-meaning professors write, often after they have retreaded themselves into creative writing classes.

When Swann writes about the Italian scene it is all clear and communicative enough yet I feel like a tourist who wandered away from the bus: you see everything all right but it doesn't seem different from anywhere else. In the midst of it all there's "Summertime," a six-and-a-half-page reminiscence of boyhood in England, mostly in prose and in coy sex, whose purpose I cannot discover. There is a current fad which mandates the inclusion of prose swatches in books of poetry, sometimes defended as prose poetry, but I can think of few examples where the effect is more than padding. I am tempted to say that Swann's book is faddish but that would imply a model. Rather, it seems, Swann writes in all the bland modes one discovers in magazine after magazine so that you are never certain what *his* poem is. Whatever it is, it lacks musical character of any real distinction.

Swann's book provides the opportunity for me to add that Weiss has asked each of these poets to append a prose "Afterward" in what must be anticipation of obtuse readers. Some of the observations are aesthetically interesting but it seems likely they will do little more than pique our curiosity. One must wonder, for example, why Swann's is fairly testy and snide in its cracks about Mark Strand, Richard Schramm, Galway Kinnell, and others. Still someone may be helped to care about Swann's poetry when he reads, "I suppose the real challenge is to let something speak through you without shaping it with your own previously achieved expression." Aha. Aha!

M. Slotznick's *Industrial Stuff* reminds me of Buckminster Fuller's poetry, a constriction of words and theories. It might also be poetry by, say, Howard Cosell, convinced of its clear thinking, its cures for social and industrial dilemmas, but dazzled into speaking a nonsense that is smart-alecky. Slotznick would make a good workshop student if he were willing to think and feel clearly. He is not. In his "Afterward" he writes, "Our industrial hegemony . . . forms the vast, fabulous weft of the American mantle; its reverberations within our political and spiritual space are booming, immeasurable." Does a mantle reverberate? Slotznick shows no sign that he cares, any more than he cares in poems which read, gosh, this way: "A sparrow mordants, thunderous, yes, / lax guardians of the useless, our petals crackle little ciphers / from the branches, and the branches are cracking." Near as I can figure, this is that weft aforementioned. Without the contrived obliquity and the geopolitical smirk that regards everything for one-liners, we might take pleasure from Slotznick's poetry. It has energy; it goes its own way; it wants, like John Updike, to bring together art and the daily world of smog, politicians, and machinery. Unfortunately there is no poetry here. It's industrial stuff.

E. G. Burrow's *Properties: A Play for Voices* is a radio play. That's a venerable form in which National Public Radio has succeeded in re-interesting writers. But we will have to stretch definitions to call it poetry. Here, the "story" of Pierce Butler and his wife, actress Fanny Kemble, circa 1849, unfolds in court amidst Butler's suit for divorce. The marriage has rotted because of her opposition to his ownership of slaves and his opposition to her publication of journals concerning their domestic life. The play's themes are slavery, marital cruelty, suppression of free speech, feminism, chauvinism, lust, and a whole bunch more. Ms. Kemble speaks long noble monologues in what Burrows calls "the spoken verse of today" while Butler gets terse, uninflected courtese. No slaves speak because Burrows is unsure how "the black peoples . . . spoke in the 1830s." This is surely the imagination copping out. Readers, as they must in every case, will have to decide if this is a dice-loaded melodrama (as I think) or a worthy rage against human filth. As for the poetry, it is sometimes vivid, sometimes Homeric, sometimes banal. It is possible that I just haven't heard this "spoken verse of today" but I think if I knew a woman who spoke it I would be terrified into reading novels.

Finally, there is David Galler's *Third Poems: 1965–1978,* and Galler's "Afterward" provides an excellent one-sentence description of this poet: "I should have to describe myself today as a radical conservative in versification." A guardian of the classical and immaculate Way, Galler has an "intellectual hatred" which Yeats feared. He is extremely hostile to what he calls "spontaneous" writing by "punks" because it doesn't lead to "sense." Such boundary patrolling gives poetry a bad name and a bellyache. Yet there are increasing signs that the wheels are grinding once again in this direction and not a few poets now in their fifties are alarmed about a return to the Fifties and a literary McCarthyism. Galler's bile is an unfortunate distraction from his often skilled and moving poetry. Much of what he writes about now, however, is the lurking barbarians who don't agree with him. When he stops worrying about such matters he shows himself to be a poet of nuance, discretion, mystery, and not a little passion. "The Escape of Icarus" and "The Root" are impressive while "The Stonecutter's Resignation" and "The Archer" rise nearly to the quality of Anthony Hecht's work. Lest this book misspeak Galler's ability, readers should seek out his earlier *Walls and Distances* and *Leopards in the Temple.* Galler should remember *Honi soit qui mal y pense.*

IV

In my introductory paragraph I tentatively pointed at poetry as the fusion of a special music and an intensity of passion, but have reserved until now comment on that *passion.* Poets can make a middling, even an excellent music by most standards and yet write a poem easy to dismiss. Often enough this seems accounted for by absent, deflected, uncultivated power, the power of dreamed and mythic energy whose potential is to connect us with the full truth of being alive. In the mature poet this power informs both "psychological" and "physical" reality; indeed it fuses them through the poet's unique music into what we perceive as the authentic body of reality: the poem *is* and the poem *does,* and is successful to the degree it achieves an appropriate balance of act and statement. Each poem determines what that appropriate balance is, not superogatory rules. The poem is successful to the degree the poet sees, understands, and transmutes what is temporal to what is chancy and permanent. Passion, then, is an attitude and poetic music is both a function of and a revelation of that attitude. William Mills, Richard Shelton, and William Heyen are all poets of powerful and matured passion whose musics are radically divergent and yet entirely appropriate to their purposes—and to poetry's, which is to possess and express the part and whole of reality.

Stained Glass is William Mills's second collection of poems but he remains, I believe, mostly an unknown poet. Partly unknown because he chooses to publish little in magazines, his poems do not invite a large audience. They are not particularly fashionable. They are restrained of personality, diffident, and even seem unwilling to ask a reader's attention. They are sometimes gnomically philosophical. Always short, terse, salt-edged, his poems can appear oddly slight, like an oblique radiance of sun under a leaf. In the book's community of poems, however, each piece sustains and strengthens the other until you feel the slow inexorable motion of life that is infinitely sad and yet vivid with potential.

Mills is a poet who writes about the hard-scrabble life of Arkansas and Louisiana but he resists honky-tonk windiness and posturing, somehow combining the matter of a James Agee with the luminously realistic portraits of a Doris Ullman photograph. His "life" is not only sad but is almost entirely lived in an interior condition of fear, a fear occasioned by the knowledge of historical existence which has ground away dreams, hope, and love. As Mills writes in "Louisiana Night":

> A man has to watch himself very
>   carefully
> When late at night
>   he lies alone and listens,
> And the cicadas
>   suddenly
> Stop.

In spite of his reticence and distance in the poems, Mills writes so strictly that you feel the curious intimacy of a voice that *knows* our secrets, our questions, our "series of guesses, / Rebuttals, silences." Almost all of the poems, even those softened by wry wit, attend to the psychological carnage of love and testify that against fear and grief love is life's only weapon. But love has many forms here, sexual passion, tenderness, grace, the forbearance of intelligence, even poetic style.

The emblematic poem for Mills's book describes a stained glass window assembled, amateurishly and for consolation, by the survivor of "an old marriage." As the evidence of personal history and translucent vision, the image evokes our larger histories, faiths struggled for and lost—faiths that, like art, continue to shape what we are and what we know. "Stained Glass" concludes:

It was no window at Chartres,
We both knew that.
Still, on certain days
It brought some pleasure.

A fact of stained glass and light:
Stained glass dies at night.

If dirge is too large a word for what that last line does, loneliness is its matter. Mills speaks as a man who would like to avoid the piece-by-piece revelation of how close to the abyss we all live, yet one who cannot help himself. He would like to discover a constellation of consoling beliefs but he can only tell us that each moment, however terribly beautiful, is finally ours alone, unsharable.

In his poems and their music, William Mills is perhaps nearest to the courtly medieval lyric where anguish is bravely countered by love's willing resistance to defeat and contingency. "A Philosophical Evening in Louisiana," "Louisiana Night," "Stained Glass," the exuberant "Weddington Woods" and "Coming" ought by themselves to earn Mills a new readership. His final elegy, "Our Fathers at Corinth," is an exceptional poem that evokes comparison to Lowell's "For the Union Dead" and Tate's "Ode to the Confederate Dead." *Stained Glass* has wine, women, and song, but it also has passion's dream of love and wisdom, which makes it a poetry of real interest.

I have liked by fits and starts the poems of Richard Shelton, feeling some of them, like "The Tattooed Desert," would make the north wind stop and listen, but feeling others were arbitrary, a patchwork of quasi-surrealism which I could accept only by suspending my own entire consciousness. It appears now that I have not read Richard Shelton closely enough. He is far better than I had thought and his fourth collection, *The Bus to Veracruz,* has driven me back to previous books, as I hope it will affect other readers.

In attitude, Shelton is not unlike Mills. Life is a tragic business which teaches us "never to trust / one another, never to trust anyone / who is dying of thirst." Of course, if one means to live, especially when we are speaking of poets, one can scarcely do otherwise than to trust, to expose oneself to continuous betrayal, unless life and poetry consist not of a willing vulnerability before existence—in which case I have little business writing this review and Shelton is not the poet I think he is. In fact, Shelton knows the poet must speak that truth of isolation while he stands bodily for its opposite. "The Prophet" tells us that the poet is doomed to be *"Citizen of neither country"* but to be the one left behind who "looks toward the east / knowing the sun would rise there / if it could." Though his passion is as complex and lyrical as anyone's Shelton's stance is idiosyncratic. He casts the speaker of his poems not in the solitude beyond love but in the social and communal exile of Ricardo Alonso's cimarron. In this way Shelton makes a curious identity with outcasts who remind us of Richard Hugo's seekers. Shelton, though, writes much of prisoners and prisons both inside and outside penal walls. The risk of such an identity is always the liberal cant which sentimentalizes, and lies, as it seeks to ennoble. Shelton, to my way of thinking, is partially guilty of distortion in "The Last Time," a poem about a prisoner stabbed forty-seven times by his fellow inmates. The poem is based on a factual event. Some who know the story of this prisoner's victim might argue that any sympathy for Shelton's hero is misplaced, but that might turn into the chicken-and-egg argument about who victimized who first. What is at stake here is the poem. Shelton turns it on himself, taking on a social guilt which very nearly convinces me we are all responsible parties in every particular. But I'm finally not convinced by *this* poem, though the large ideas of human responsibility, which might lessen our tragic cruelties and render walls irrelevant, are traditional and, I think, affective as ever. We may argue with Shelton's conclusions but we cannot argue with the authenticity of the feeling or the world he presents. Yet the poem, if we are not convinced, must remain less than satisfactory.

Shelton is a restless and impatient poet, which suggests his virtue and his vice. He continues to write what I take to be gratuitous lines: "It is yourself, the dream you are / never allowed to remember," he says of a woman lying beside him, one who has no other participation in the poem. And, can we actually be forbidden to remember? Shelton says she wants to be the dream she can't remember and presumably this means to suggest a lot of unspecifiable longing. In fact it is filler language. Shelton too often pushes his poem to say big things rather than allowing it time and context for big things to evolve from what the poem does say. It is a particular difficulty for the relatively brief lyric which Shelton writes.

Thus he causes the moon to become sentient, to speak not as a projected human voice, but as itself and the moon "forgives us all." For those of us who can't accept that moon-speech, he says "They are blind." The result of this impatience, then, is to draw a line in the dirt, placing us on one side or the other. Yet, in this way, language does not reveal but censor. We don't cooperate with our music toward discovery and resolution but use it for the drive toward balkanizing message.

Nevertheless, Richard Shelton's restlessness is a large virtue in that a part of him refuses to allow poetry to be less than the agent of prophecy and vision. He is never tame, quiescent, dispassionate, or dull. In the new poems of *The Bus to Veracruz* I believe he is more attentive to the clarity and symphonic potentials of language than in his previous work. The result is a poetry of more than ordinary accomplishment, of a musically shaped passion which may not be fashionable, especially to eastern ears, but is unblinkably there. His poems are so much achieved bodies that I choose not to violate them with quotation but, instead, to suggest readers turn to the excellencies of "Guilt," "Landscape with a Woman," "Mexico," "The Prophet," "Reaching for the Gun," "Harry Orchard," and "Softly Softly." No American poet now writing has established himself more completely as the voice of the desert than Richard Shelton has. Is this as oddly reductive as it sounds? I say it in admiration. It is an accomplishment to speak with the character of any place, as the least poet would admit, and the harsh music of our deserts has quite as much beauty, quite as much story as anywhere else. *The Bus to Veracruz,* in telling that poetry, leaves little doubt that Shelton is a necessary poet.

Writing reviews reminds me of the blind man asked to describe what an elephant is like. I imagine, as the blind man must, that no one could possibly conceive these remarks do justice to the books or be prevented from going to see for himself what the poems are. It occurs to me that I have not fairly suggested how Mills, Shelton, and Heyen employ like musics. Briefly, Mills prefers the poem of the terse and distanced lyric, Shelton prefers the immediate image and alogical progression. William Heyen, to dig this hole a little deeper, employs both approaches within a poem of longer and often sequential context. Technically, Heyen is perhaps the most traditional of the three poets. In some ways, *Long Island Light,* his fourth book, might be seen as a manual for how to do the variations of Modern American Poetry. Heyen is not the tinkerer with perspectives that Shelton is nor does he look as far backward into received form as does Mills. There is always a firm structure in the Heyen poem but he is so subtly flexible with it that he manages to be both an intensely private and a confidently public poet. Of him it is true to say, as of any good poet, that no label or category will adequately identify him.

I am tempted to describe William Heyen as an ecstatic poet and a nature poet. He stands by self-admission in the line of the Emersonian visionary (though increasingly, I think, of the Whitman branch) and his poems evoke contemporary models of the line: Roethke, Dickey, James Wright, Robert Bly, and more prominently of late Galway Kinnell. As poet he is extremely close to the land, to the sea, to the beasts and fish and fowl, and he hurts because "the land smells of metal." He feels almightily the powerful and wild energy that for the American ecstatic poet has been pretty nearly the single sacramental connection. And he feels, too, the darkness of the American heart so that talismanic presences like Faulkner, Twain, and Whitman coexist in his vision alongside westward-ho painter George Catlin and the glitter-chronicling Fitzgerald. Like Roethke and Bly, Heyen begins with minimals, small subjects, but like Kinnell he is possessed by "desires / for the deep water" and its cast-up reliquaries of "the jeweled claws of crabs, / strands of seaweed shining like saints' hair." His primary ground of vision is the Long Island shore and its relatively stable and preurban life, but the range of Heyen's poetry is national and as wide as Audubon's horizons, who is another presence in this collection.

The American ecstatic poet seems to have, for all his praise of abundant variety and soul-glory, two prepossessing themes. Apart from nature and its expressive exuberance, he feels spiritually vacated, impotent, and regards the phenomena he loves as a sacred text of dissolution. Yet in the natural world, even as it includes the imagination, all is the body and dance of spiritual vitality. For Emerson, perhaps, this was literally true; for Heyen it seems more a metaphorical truth. He writes "Your dead Lord lives at the wheel's hub" and exchanges the deep water image which is never far from his consciousness for an image of centrality—but the desire to move far and deep toward the secrets which the objective, natural world must hold remains. There is, as usual in this line of American poets, a strongly moral dimension to Heyen's poems and even, at times, the moralistic tones of Bly. As public conscience in perhaps the last credible way, the ecstatic poet is expected to prophesy and Heyen does—though with rare exceptions he resists the soapbox of polemic. When he preaches it is ordinarily in the service of ecological rectitude and an enthusiasm for brotherhood that is as faintly tacky as the latter-day injunction for worshippers to shake hands over the pews. But Heyen more often creates the beauty of a land that was and is a vision, a land always imperiled by the imperfect hearts of vision's makers, and he makes it the task of his poem to enter that vision and reclaim what is gone while he praises what endures. His task, that is to say, is to speak the poem of the nation, a big job indeed.

The wildness and ferocity of the human spirit's struggle to find its place and name its nature, Faulkner's passion, is alive in *Long Island Light,* a book that evolves from Heyen's earlier *Noise in the Trees.* His method of arranging, rearranging, revising, and recomposing books parallels Whitman's. He has now added twenty-eight poems and ten prose sections which, as they are more extensions than additions, suggest Heyen is best read as a writer of a long poem in progress; hence, a poet whose individual poems have an especially tentative feel within the slowly emerging and larger orchestrations. If his poems are in the ecstatic tradition, his prose implies certain connections with the Williams-Olson heritage of homegrown comment. Bardic, mythic, faintly saintly, the prose does not, I think, supplant or even distract us from the poems but I am not entirely convinced it is necessary.

If Robinson Jeffers read *Long Island Light* he might find it a little soft at its edges but I think he would consider Heyen a mature poet and one whose music shaped the physical and psychological reality of the American spirit that is always a combination of driving ambition for purity and a yearning for escape. Jeffers would, perhaps, agree that Heyen can write us back into connection with "the pond's old father, its brain / and dark, permanent presence" ("The Snapper"). Whatever kinds of poets or readers of poetry we are, we must believe with William Heyen in a poem that places before us, as "The Elm's Home" does, the bittersweet tenderness of American wanderings toward home:

> when I touched the loam fill over the elm's stump,
> its clusters of tiny noctilucent mushrooms,
> I saw through them
> into the ground, into the elm's dead
> luminous roots, the branches of heaven
> under the earth, this island home,
> my lightning lord,
> my home.

Heyen is a large talent in a man of exquisite skills and great delicacy. The kind of poem he is intent on writing, the lyrical epic of an extremely pluralistic country, requires all of that and more. My own guess is that he will become one of the more significant poets of his generation but to do so he will have to discharge more completely and quickly the ecstatic voices he has carried with him so far. He will need something more of the ruthlessness which Jeffers had. He has the music, the words, the ambition, and the rare chance for a true, convincing ecstacy. It would be vile to ask for more from any poet.

The Second Self

■

Many among us want to be poets. Many others want to write poems. It is easier to understand the former than the latter: those who want to be poets imagine a career of glamour, fame, and integrity. They consider that the poet will speak profound matters and be widely honored, including the cash and flesh and good life which is, say, the rock star's existence. Others are satisfied to write poems, to hope for poems, without concerning themselves too much about the career. In America now we write by the hundreds of thousands and always we write, properly, about ourselves. For some, the merely autobiographical exposes what most of us are by birthright: unimaginative, ungenerative, mediocre. Often enough the poem which begins in revealing the little wounded thing we are ends in a large attempt at cauterization. I have grown weary of all the echoes of Rilke's charge that we must change our lives, not because Rilke is less than right but because he has a slippery, easy, patronizing echo among poets whose glibness is astonishing and ubiquitous. I would venture to say that the bulk of our poetry now consists in an extraordinarily self-righteous assertion of what we must *do* and this attitude seems based on the conviction that self-discovery and self-growth is synonymous with poetry. No one can doubt

Reviews of Elizabeth Libbey, *The Crowd Inside* (Carnegie-Mellon University Press); Robert Winner, *Green in the Body* (Slow Lorris Press); Tess Gallagher, *Under Stars* (Graywolf Press); Wanda Coleman, *Mad Dog Black Lady* (Black Sparrow Press); Felix Pollak, *Subject to Change* (Juniper Press); Leon Stokesbury, *The Drifting Away of All We Once Held Essential* (Trilobite Press); Stanley Moss, *Skull of Adam* (Horizon Press); William Matthews, *Rising and Falling* (Atlantic-Little, Brown); Donald Hall, *Kicking the Leaves* (Harper & Row); Allen Grossman, *The Woman on the Bridge over the Chicago River* (New Directions); Philip Levine, *Ashes* (Atheneum); *7 Years from Somewhere* (Atheneum).

that is one of poetry's functions but god knows it is fuzzily articulated and ludicrously sentimental more often than not. In poems we have the chance for growth but it is a rare, frail chance. Those who regard the poem as a hand-mike and a public service announcement write both fashionably and formulaically, which results in the weakly thought, the unmusically droned, and the superficially artful poem. Oddly enough, those who posture in this way are sectarian evangelists, careerists as intense as the myopic fortune-seekers. Both types produce a sadly tedious, predictable poetry which is, curiously, without a self.

One such poem, to me static and boring, is that whose form is built around the direct address of pseudo-mysterious statements to an anonymous *you,* and about that same you. The motif is entrenched sufficiently for Jon Anderson to consider it in his poem "Witness" (*Antaeus* 30/31) where he asks why so many have given their hearts, feet, and diction to this stranger. Contrasting this *you* to a fifteenth-century Dürer engraving, Anderson says, "He is himself / As you are not," and, moreover, "if you are not yourself, neither / Are you any other." To be no self and to have no self, before all, prohibits any imaginative extension of understanding. Mr. Anderson suggests that poems "fill in, not contour, but color" and implicates the gray bodilessness of so many poems. I would dispute only the suggestion that a colorful abstraction is full compensation for a non-self.

The fear of inconsequence, of having no self, a non-self, or a false self, may explain why some poets abandon all assertion of a character voice not for an ordinary narrator-monologist but for a super-anonymous voice which is neither communal nor individual. Such poems risk becoming contrivances exactly in the degree they are not locatably human. I do not mean the revelation of biographical congruence with poetic details. I mean the poem exists, or does not, because of the pressure of human crises which we may recognize and feel as having consequences in our own lives. Mr. Anderson touches deep nerves in our society and reveals what I think is a widespread deception among many poets: that the creation of a de-selfed and hyperplain language is the same thing as simplicity of and accessibility to subject. The voice on the PA system, however, is not necessarily art, not even if the voice whispers. Mr. Anderson uses Dürer to suggest that poetry requires a creator who projects human possibility, strength, vision, and tempered character in the vice-grip of experience. Dürer engages what might be called a second self, a voice rooted in the autobiographical *me* but enlarged by the imagination to include us all, our selves. Good poetry must have, I think, a colorful, contoured self whose speaker is this second self, a voice which serves the human need to witness what we are in all our complexities, and does so in language we cannot forget. Such poetry inherently resists the formulaic expression just as it resists the programmatic social instructions about what we *must* do. Such poetry does not create vitality in its form of saying but urges us to rediscover vitality in language because it is already there in ourselves.

Elizabeth Libbey's first book, *The Crowd Inside,* has sometimes this vitality and also the strength of real talent. It is equally, disturbingly remarkable for that "anonymous shape / in stories you've read," a shape that undercuts her power. Consider this:

PARTICIPANT

You wait for something to happen.
Your breath is so many ice petals
dropped to the floor.
Watch out, even now
a tune deepens the erosive air,
even now the sinewy dancer
wakes and unfolds from his chair.
Your breath dances
with his, your mouth is his.
Only then does he whisper
what you want most
not to hear: you must not inhale
him so, there is no more room
for breath, let it
stand in your throat like so much
loose change. You wait, and
how brutally the dance continues.
How brutally
nothing is asked of you.

Who speaks here? To whom? With what excellence, freshness, or precision of language? Has the poem color, shape, memorable expression, human character? Is it "so much" fuzzy whining in "so many" tenuously related similes? Is it sentimental—or a cool evocation of real grief? Is this the venerable Cinderella story revitalized in its updated lyric or only a stylized ennui? Does it cheat us with what happens "brutally"? Does the anonymity reexpose deep nerves or smother us with smarmy clichés? Most important, does the poem demonstrate particular observation that initiates feeling? I don't mean to ask sarcastic questions. Many are writing this poem and may well feel it possesses qualities I find absent and necessary. It seems to me a typical example of what our poets are doing, and doing wrong.

Diction and stance seem naturally to follow from a tactical choice of that "anonymous shape" and lead, apparently, to a formula. This cultivation of the non-self, which denies rather than extends the biographical base, must make the poem interesting through a compensatory music or particularly arresting context, scene, act, or discovery. If it does so the poem may result in the magic of a Merwin. If it does not we have the ordinary dimmed by pose and mediocre poetry. Of course our own late Senator Hruska argued once that mediocrity should be represented in the national Supreme Court. The fact is that we are not going to eliminate mediocrity anywhere but in poetry we ought at least to recognize what it is and seek, as Thomas Hardy says, the better way. Nevertheless, mediocrity has its followers and Ms. Libbey's book is frequently one of them.

The Crowd Inside, however, does offer its moments. Libbey will sometimes go into the chancy interior where the self is necessarily alone and she can be convincing. In "Ceremonious" she quotes Emily Dickinson's "letting go" and in her best writing there is a similarly controlled wildness. "Ceremonious" tells us "Let's walk with her off the curb." And we do. We move into that life of danger felt in traffic which, by risk, confirms consciousness of self and community. Here is a poem which suggests Ms. Libbey at her best:

COMING BACK FROM THE CLIFF

His voice disappears inside her.
She is hollow.
Below her, the soapy gray eyes
of canyon rocks. His eyes among the eyes.
Suppose the clear lake is not the bottom; suppose
another cliff to follow down, and
never the lake. Walking back without him,
she sees him in the leaves, balanced
on the points of blue needles.
Still clinging in her throat.

Libbey is deft in evoking the residual (and Dickinsonian) feeling of domestic life. The history of feminine entrapment is painful in "Making His Bed One Morning" where the poet feels herself become her grandmother who "flapped her way / out of the blackness in me." In poems about ancestors, lovers, and those who remind us (not lecturing us) of our frail humanness, as in "Bloodline: Grandmother Elander" or "Love

Poem," her speech becomes what ours would be if we were poets enough. In "Come into the Night Grove," a tour de force whose speaker convincingly exchanges being with a forest of cedars, and in "Concerning the Dead Women: The Munitions Plant Explosion: June, 1918," she moves through intense feeling with fine, lyrical control. Both are the poems of an inclusive imagination, a second self whose power to let go is generative of commensurate feeling in the reader. Ms. Libbey writes, "What we let go of with every pore, is / what keeps us alive." Though we may argue with *The Crowd Inside* we must hope for poets who take us to that place of consequence.

Robert Winner's *Green in the Body* shows some of the infelicities of first books but the poetry is serious in its attempts to create "the unexpected self." Mr. Winner's poem "The Banjo" describes the ennervated life that poetry opposes by its very existence:

> All of them nailed to their careers
> like handles on boxes!
> There is some other game for me,
> another reality could walk in any time
> and become the boss,
> shouting Dance! Dance! Dance!

Elsewhere he writes that the "sky without an identity bursts upward"—a teasingly opaque notion. I think he means that anonymity is no life, while identity given leads to identity received. Most of his poems celebrate that conventional source of identity, the rural landscape; yet there is often a surprise, a complexity of language and thought, as in "Eden" which begins "The truth has never needed us." This poem concerns an abandoned railway station. *Green in the Body* is a grave and good, though not somber, collection remarkable for its spirit and clarity, its horses, hunchbacks, penguins, and frisbee. Winner is elegaic about a lost pastoral life, caustic about the urban world. "Miss Alderman," "The Banjo," and "Learning to Mourn" are accomplished poems in a style Winner describes as "reckless, fatal singing." He makes us feel often enough that his is the way to live in the world.

Few younger poets write with the passion and the discipline that Tess Gallagher brings to the pain of missing, isolated, thwarted selves. The twenty-eight new poems of *Under Stars* confirm the excellence and felt experience of her earlier *Instructions to the Double*. If there is a change, and I do not know why there should be, it is that *Under Stars* is less private, more social, more accessible. Gallagher creates lyrical events organized by syntax and paragraph rather than by line or image. For her, the voice of the second self is everything and it depends on phrasing that is consequential and resonant with ordinary speech made eloquent. Her speaker, instantly recognizable, seems partly hurt child and partly world-wise crone. One hears both in two stanzas from "Four Dancers at an Irish Wedding":

we are all stolen and grieving
in the tender arms.
I have seen the magpie in the morning
on the back of a cow
singing: One
is for sorrow. One
is for sorrow.

Drop the strange hand, be
lifted, child, held
there on your father's swaying shoulder
for we are one and one and
one with ourselves
on the polished floor.

Ms. Gallagher's movement is intentional and complex, beginning with the personal statement of violation within those synecdochic arms and funneled to the singular absurdity of magpie and cow that turns a child's numbed rhyme. The poem alternates affirmation and denial as one voice speaks through another. Cinderella and her prince are, inevitably, doomed but there is still the joy of parental tenderness, of dance, and song still deflects anguish. By leading us precisely to that image-doubling floor through nearly syllogistic cadences and a properly matched event and tone, the poet moves us beyond confession to pathos believable because it emerges obliquely and is tempered beyond indulgence. Poems should be interesting and they should provide a definite pleasure, a kind of specific gravity of experience. Ms. Gallagher's poems do both, perhaps because they are inherently about the moments of love, simultaneously growing and withering, around which our lives spin. Her faces, gestures, voices are like letters we would write to ourselves, if we were not ourselves. She says in "Under Stars" that "I am the found one, intimate, returned / by all I touch on the way." Just so are we re-turned by this haunting lyric:

WOMEN'S TUG OF WAR AT LOUGH ARROW

In a borrowed field they dig in their feet
and clasp the rope. Balanced
against neighboring women, they hold

the ground by the little gained
and leaning like boatmen rowing into
the damp earth, they pull
to themselves the invisible waters, waters
overcalmed by desertion
or the narrow look trained to a brow.

The steady rain has made girls of them,
their hair in ringlets. Now they haul
the live weight to the cries
of husbands and children, until the rope
runs slack, runs free
and all are bound again by the arms
of those who held them, not until, but so
they gave.

If the second self suffers from the formula in which nobody is at home, it is also betrayed by omnipresent *me. Mad Dog Black Lady,* Wanda Coleman's first book, shows this weakness. Speaking for and from the subterranean world of exiles, her pose as revolutionary reveals a well-known haberdasher: the conviction of superior suffering, the hackneyed refusal of grammatical order, the innocent little "i" with the foul mouth, sexual shock, demands for dispensation as a street writer. How indulgent and faddish are the tricks of mediocrity rediscovered! Yet Ms. Coleman is more than mediocre in spite of herself.

Mad Dog Black Lady is rude, vulgar, and formulaic, yet it has the set-jaw of art on its own terms. It has what poetry must have to give pleasure: human passion subdued to memorably shaped speech. Ms. Coleman's poems are angry, loving, hurtful, and cunning; they are spoken by a black whore who rails at the world's abuses, as if her railing were not laced with Latinate syntax, Anglo-Saxon phrasing, and vivid imagery. There seems nothing undone, foreign, or unexamined in this shadow-life raised up to daylight. But this book is a *tale,* similar to Gogol's or Grimm's, of the struggle for love and dignity. Under the mad dog-murderess-thief-whore ("black ahab") waits a black lady; under the lady is a dreaming child ("the kid in the yellow organdy dress"). It is this tension of human innocence within violation that powers Coleman's visionary self beyond the screw-you formula. I hope she will consider the value of her own words ("it ain't the act—it's the style") for while it is hard to make a deep and durable art of squalor, suffering, and buck-shifting accusations, good poets find ways beyond caricature. We must be both ourselves and one people, as she knows:

> all i do is remember, think of us / our people as we were
> or could have been—apart, the awful silence
> together, the awesome storm
>
> "Luz"

I do not believe chapbooks ought to displace full volumes in omnibus reviews, space being a scarce item. Space an item? Still, I want to note Felix Pollak's *Subject to Change* and Leon Stokesbury's *The Drifting Away of All We Once Held Essential.* Mr. Pollak's pamphlet demonstrates a thread of objective and sharp image poems and a counterthread of poems which speak discursively, and painfully, of a world of images lost, lost because the speaker has gone blind, "transparent skin has grown" so that his "eyes reach out / but cannot touch." This is unforgivably bad language but it is rare in a memorable little book about the beauty we cannot keep the world from devouring. The beauty, for example, of a woman loved, but unseen, her voice entering a room "followed by her form and only last / her face, a flower, a small cloud / of smoke." All poetry can do is *see* and Pollak's does so clearly on the whole. This is a talent shared by Mr. Stokesbury, who is more given to the terse, ironic, funny, urbane poem of love which he calls "semi-sentimental." Both poets are good at but not hemmed in by traditional verse formulae which they make vigorous, especially Stokesbury, by a blunt contemporary diction. Both poets are Romantic in temperament and elegaic in mood. Mr. Stokesbury's sense of loss is perhaps less personal than Mr. Pollak's and perhaps funnier. As Stokesbury says in his title poem, there is a tide in the affairs of men and "it will drag your ass right out / to sea and dump you, if you aren't careful." I would add, even if you are careful. The octet of his sonnet "Morning Song" concerns a lover in sickness and shows Stokesbury has skill as well as a sense that the right tool, as sayeth carpenters, makes a job a smart easier:

> The tired eyes open. You see now that I see,
> Swirling and tangled, inverted, how
> In this firmament the blood streams and races.
> Your smile and damp hair rush up to meet me,
> Or is it I to them? This skin's blaze and glow—
> The beads of dew on these moist secret places.

For Stanley Moss the right tool is neither the self absent nor immediate but the reverberating self. Should an angel come to claim in a blinding light what a thing is man, I am sure Mr. Moss would answer something like "Come here, Bub, I'll show you what a thing!" But his poems sometimes make us believe he would be right. Mr. Moss is a poet of the eastern city, a lover of urban life, a poet of Whitmanic exuberance, skyrocketing joys and Talmudic sorrows. His second book, *Skull of Adam,* begins "This face without race or religion, / I have in common with humanity," and he is *that* democratic. Like Mae West, when he is good, he is encompassingly good. When bad, he blusters. And he doesn't seem to care that an old movie Indian has already told Dustin Hoffman that "Any day is a good day to be born / any day is a good day to die." Precise language matters less to Mr. Moss than Truth's big hands. His poems mean to be brother to all and soul of all. This leads to an enlarged sense of reality and a cheerful view of everything in sight. It makes us cheer his spirit. It also leads to some sentimental verse about his dog and about political martyrs, as well as to "Snot," "Vomit," and "Shit," that memorable hound which bays "Let the mysterious ghost / of a turd pass between us." Even as communion parody it would set the teeth on edge. Mr. Moss also forgets that one side of Everyman is no man. To celebrate ghetto dwellers, migrants, and "working class clouds" for existing *as such* trivializes the imagination, the individual, and makes political cant of poetry. A man, for god's sake, is more than excremental gas, class identity, or street address. How long must we go on cashing Whitman's bad checks? And yet, and yet, Mr. Moss is interesting and infectious when he makes poems about a collection of hats, spray-painting the city, or fishing with his father. Clearly he reveres the least things of life, as in "Clams":

> Ancient of days, bless the innocent
> who can do nothing but cling,
> open or close their stone mouths.

Mr. Moss's *Skull of Adam,* whatever else it may be, has the uncommon wildness of a large spirit, a self that is more precious than anonymous flocks of peepers.

Rising and Falling is William Matthews's third collection. Perhaps too hastily, I thought his earlier poems had the odd effect of losing substance upon being read a second time. His first two books were clever, gnomic, and glib. But he has a book now which has singular depth, weight, and clarity. Everything in it is touched with intensity and taken care of with integrity. In "Living among the Dead" Mr. Matthews examines his responsibility to ancestry, history, and artistry—those parental figures:

> To love a child is to turn
> away from the patient dead.
> It is to sleep carefully
> in case he cries.

How that *carefully* resonates with loving alertness. It is exactly the responsibility Matthews shows not simply for children but for all that exists, what he calls "the scripture of matter," and not least for art's forms: music, painting, poetry.

The poems of *Rising and Falling* do not glitter or dazzle, but shed a steady light. Often speakers in these poems are swimming or sleeping, or addressing those buoyant conditions (obviously they speak *about,* not from, sleep), conditions calculated to manage poems of meditational stasis that are yet interesting motions. Mr. Matthews creates dream states without pyrotechnic obscurity; he wants to look quietly and speaks to us always like an intimate or avuncular friend. He intends to illuminate emotional time and space as well as their communal roots in memory. Meditation properly leads to a control of rising, falling breath; it means to slow down for suspended examination all that may be known or apprehended. Poetry, however, has to translate the apprehended into the tangible and Matthews makes a poem the art of the "meditating mind." Art rises, poetry falls; thought looks, life is. He speaks of this in a stanza from "In Memory of W. H. Auden":

> They were not painting about suffering,
> the Old Masters. Not the human heart but
> Brueghel turns the plowman away
> for compositional reasons
> and smooths the waters for a ship he made
> expensive and delicate.
> The sun is implied by how
> the sure hand makes the light fall
> as long as we watch the painting.
> The sure hand is cruel.

Cruel, yes, because it creates accurately "the scripture of matter" and its shadow or absence. The durable image of character and crisis provides all there is of emotional range and ultimate consolations. When imagination composes memory into the recurrences of art, history turns biography, biography turns meditation and "fields / become one field," for the second self on whom nothing is lost. Mr. Matthews's poetry is distinguished by a music made against all odds, the music of survival which he calls "undertow and stutter" in his poem "Alcide 'Slow Drag' Pavageau," the music of ambition, work, and faith:

> the halt and lame can strut.
> You can hear it yourself. Buy
> a few records and think how big

a bass is to a small boy,
his fingers bleeding to grow deft.
Bandages are for amateurs

and they blur the tone, that habit
a bassist and his bass conspire,
the way a couple learns a stride

though the man's taller by a foot.

What I have called the voice of the second self must, as Matthews says, "conspire" for the largeness of human experience. We are suspended in this self which cannot, therefore, be truly formulaic or conformist any more than a community of individuals is. This voice has, finally, little to do with pronouns, much to do with particularity and angle of vision, and everything to do with spirit that sustains the felt quality of experience. Autobiography is no more than the place where imagination stands, looks, changes, reveals, or it is lineated journalism. We are the little we have always been, we humans, and the much we continue to hope to be; that paradox means no poem can be conclusive, no art ultimately sufficient. The struggle to transform what is *me* into what is truly a better *us* requires the dramatic gravity of imagination's enactment beyond formula. Donald Hall's veteran career demonstrates this struggle. In 1958, Mr. Hall wrote:

Now Whitneyville is like other places,
Ranch-houses stretching flat beyond the square,
Same stories and movies, same composite faces
Speaking the language of the public air.

How tidy, cool, neatly composite, and public is that stanza! However, just as Whitneyville is anywhere-USA, the poem is uninhabited by a man. This was the formula self of the Fifties, which after a while we had got plenty of. It strained to say a lot, never mind feeling. By 1971, willing to risk failure to escape formula, Mr. Hall published the dreadful poems of *The Yellow Room*. From nobody at home to silly old *me* in pieces that must have cracked up the muse:

You send me a smile
like a postcard from Nova Scotia:
"Always be happy, Tubsy.
Remember,
turn off the daisies."

Mr. Hall's *Kicking the Leaves* is a return to Whitneyville and a look at what was always there in the imagination. Hall begins with "Eating the Pig," about a dozen surburbanites gathered to roast and eat pig. But they have to read a book to find out how one roasts things, so anonymous have they become in their civilized selves. Hall's purpose, aside from social comment, is to recreate and reidentify the human self as both animal and celebrant. His pig becomes brother and Lord:

> "Fire, brother and father,
> twelve of us, in our different skins, older and younger,
> opened your skin together
> and tore your body apart, and took it
> into our bodies."

No longer composite, now communal, Hall's faces are "different" because particularity is essential. "Eating the Pig" is a sacrament of communion and the prologue of thirteen poems braiding one cord back to Whitneyville, the home-ground of all beginnings. Even so, the poem suggests that Mr. Hall's eyes may yet be bigger than his stomach, for it contains the eating of all human history (including Hannibal's elephant and Hannibal himself) as well as a questionable conversation with the roasted and decapitated pig. "O Cheese," the second poem, is, for me, inexplicable.

But the poems of *Kicking the Leaves* read best, and very well indeed, as tissues in one muscle of poetry. "Maple Syrup" discovers and opens, in Whitneyville, a jar of "syrup / my grandfather made twenty-five / years ago" and it is "the sweetness preserved / of a dead man" and not a societal abstraction. Hall has reached, it appears, a sense of life moving downward and inward to earth, of imminent cohabitation with the dead. He knows, and makes it a strength in his poetry, that, as Pascal says, "We shall die alone." It is the strength of the courage to live.

Whitneyville, for Mr. Hall, is no longer at arm's length, or formula's. It has become the village of life's single story in "Names of Horses," "Ox-Cart Man," and "Traffic." Every plain acre and thing of the earth exudes a selfhood as eccentric and commonly strong as the "barrel / hooped by hand at the forge's fire." Paradoxically, but naturally, these poems take power from allowing the "speech" of phenomena and act to conspire with details of memory that are necessarily personal as well as communal. No poem here is more carefully, affectionately, and affectingly wrought than the seven-sectioned "Kicking the Leaves" in which Hall and his family, "as we walk home together / from the game, in Ann Arbor," scuff their feet in dying leaves. The scene has the feel of the most tribal moments in Whitman but one thinks more immediately of Frost and his invitation to clear leaves from the well. Like Frost's, Hall's poems mean to speak names and to become actions set against anonymity, inconsequence, and fear. He is past complaining of superficial matters. Now he speaks from inside "the only long pleasure, of taking a place / in the story of leaves." He knows now who survives, and what and how, and imagines the self as the voice of desire hidden in contingency:

5.

This year the poems came back, when the leaves fell.
Kicking the leaves, I heard the leaves tell stories,
remembering, and therefore looking ahead, and building
the house of the dying. I looked up into the maples
and found them, the vowels of bright desire.
I thought they had gone forever
while the bird sang *I love you, I love you*
and shook its black head
from side to side, and its red eye with no lid,
through years of winter, cold
as the taste of chicken wire, the music of cinder block.

There can be, for those who love poetry, nothing more exciting than the discovery of new poems by a favorite writer, unless it is the discovery of a poet previously unknown. The delight I have taken in the poems of Allen Grossman's *The Woman on the Bridge over the Chicago River* can't be more than suggested in a review's inadequate remarks. The author of three collections unknown to me (and so far impossible to find), Grossman exults in virtues of poetry often minimized or absent in his contemporaries. He is challenged by traditional forms, undergirded by classical allusions, avoids bald statement for coolly balanced implications, and views a poem as a proper vehicle for argument. Above all, he writes poetic music, heroic songs, lyrics of grave and intricately orchestrated sounds that seem to suggest many writers while remaining always Grossman's own. One can hear in him James Wright and John Crowe Ransom as well as Whitman and Hardy, can hear them as if they were instruments in a splendid orchestra. His sonnet "By the Sea" is a masterpiece that enhances the blank verse tercets of "The Holdout" as well as the more characteristic free verse (I use this non sequitur term loosely) in "Pat's Poem" and "The Department," both powerful elegies which are as personal as can be imagined.

Perhaps Mr. Grossman's poetry is best described by its strategic net of paradoxes. In "Victory" he speaks of "the / Peril of high seeing—bed and abyss" and suggests the polarities of experience each poem somehow examines. Elsewhere it is the contention of left hand and right, of fact and theory, "storms of unwriting" and the face of a "howling infant." Or it is "Eternity and Time," ascent and descent, memory and absence, motion and stasis, all engaged in what he calls "a war in the wind." His subjects include runners, writers, fisherwomen, children, and natural landscapes. He impresses with an acute and *feeling* intelligence attempting to penetrate chaos in order to preserve evidence that "The earth remains and cures." The paradox, from "Villanelle of Keeping," is that "Battered by absence the tablet earth endures" while "Everything will perish, everything that lures—." That this is ancient wisdom (one hears it almost exactly in the Anglo-Saxon poem "The Wanderer") does not make it less accurate or less in need of reassertion. Mr. Grossman is bold, funny, loving, and sad, the full range of feeling we hope for in poets but infrequently find. Some readers, however, will find him tedious for he requires patience and tolerance. On the whole, his is a world of the mind and nature, tenuously balanced and contending, as perhaps this sample from "Victory" will show:

> And so if I bind on Apollo's phylacteries
> I do it now to tell the plain truth.
> Come, I will stop this talking. This is what
> This voice inside you I am saying means.
> Let us draw the black ship down to the divine sea—
> Set the purple sail to the great death winds
> Of the South, and empty
> Out of the burden of our singing, you and I.
> This is the whole ocean. Also the end.
> After the wind stops,
>   the sound of the wind.

When I read Philip Levine's two simultaneously published collections, *Ashes* and *7 Years from Somewhere* I think that, well, maybe one simply likes what one likes—and this is it for me. My opinion is that I would as soon give up reading as give up Mr. Levine's poems. Still, what accounts for such delight? Especially when I have not altogether dismissed some prickly objections. Some have said that Levine has written the same poem for years, that he lacks variety and vision. This is the American habit of demanding a new Buick every season. The real question should be the quality of the poem. Nevertheless, it is true that his poems speak in one doleful cadence. True, that his vision is such a relentless denunciation of injustice that he has occasionally engaged in reductive oversimplifications. For example, the political underbelly of *The*

Names of the Lost comes uncomfortably close to cadres of the good, the bad, and the ugly. His prose piece, "To My Brother on the Death of a Young Poet," (*Antaeus* 30/31) seems irresponsibly blindered thinking and is, I think, reprehensible. Mr. Levine has a polemic streak which makes some of his work strident, manipulative, and at least ungenerous. It has been observed, perhaps fairly, that there is a level of violence in his poems which few poets equal, whether the violence be reflective of contemporary experience or gratuitous. Those who observe this violence ordinarily object to it. In spite of what his weaknesses may be, in spite of my own objections, I cannot help believing Levine's poetry is nearly a national conscience and many of the new poems in *7 Years from Somewhere* are as good as or better than anything he has written.

Ashes contains thirteen poems from the long out of print *Red Dust* (Kayak 1971) and nineteen new poems. The former have been characterized as surreal by way of the Spanish, an influence Mr. Levine admits. The analysis is based on images and phrasings, rather than on entire poems, which are more dreamlike and associative than rational and linear. For example, "Blood runs to the heart and finds it locked"; or "rifles are brooding / in the closet"; or "the grave blooms upward / in sunlight and walks the roads." I suspect there is less surrealism here than a vitally alive and active landscape whose every particle possesses the ability and need to express itself—and a nearly symbiotic integrity. Another way of saying this is that Mr. Levine seems to have an extraordinary capacity to sense and give witness to a man's relationship with all that exists. He is no painter of mindscapes nor a primitivist nor a canting ecologist, though dream life, fundamental states of being, and a world abused matter greatly to him. He is distinctly American, a consumer and a mensch. When he writes, "The clouds go on eating oil," he indicts industrial greed as well as projects an emotional abuse beyond individual proportions. But it is the activity of his metaphor, its visual accumulation and poisoned ingestion, which causes a visceral rather than a mental response. He does not, even in *Red Dust,* rely very much on flashed and extra-worldly conjunctions but on the charged interaction of all things which he so acutely feels.

Importantly, Mr. Levine's poems always begin and remain grounded in a single, highly receptive consciousness which is a man's alone. The language, the figures of speech, the narrative progressions of this consciousness are never so private, so obscure, so truncated as to forbid less sophisticated readers. Though he takes on the largest subjects of death, love, courage, manhood, loyalty, etc., he brings the mysteries of experience down into the ordinarily inarticulate events and objects of daily life. His speaker and subject is the abused and disabused spirit of the common yet singular self. He risks the maudlin, the sentimental, the banal, and worse because he cannot live in the world fully enough; because the world is so much with us all we must sing or die of its inexpressible presence.

Mr. Levine has been writing this way throughout his nine books, even granting the shift from regular verse after *Not This Pig* and some slight reorientations of stance after *Red Dust.* With *They Feed They Lion, 1933, The Names of the Lost,* and now *Ashes* and *7 Years from Somewhere,* he has shown increased technical control, a growing mastery of image and phrase, a deepened power to dramatize the suffering and potential of each moment. But there is no radical change in "A man alone, ignorant / strong, holding the burning moments / for all they're worth." The style of a man's poem need not change in pace with Detroit's assembly lines. It might be said that Mr. Levine has a formula and I would answer that we all should be so fortunate, for what he has is a style patiently developed to fit his need to speak the hurt and the joy that in all of us remains unshaped and embryonic. The point is:

> What would it mean to lose this life
> and go wandering the hallways
> of that house in search of another self?

If we can speak strongly and accurately enough our own love of life and hatred of diminishment, we may speak for all our selves. In such poems as "Toward Home," "Andorra," "Planting," "Let Me Begin Again," and others, Levine has moved well past caricature and glibness, past concern for anything but the honest reality he can forge in words. I think it not surprising that his poetry appears more accessible to large, non-poetry-reading American audiences than that of most of his fellow poets. And yet these poets themselves afford him enthusiastic admiration. He not only speaks for us but as if he is us. A poet of main force, like the sun, he speaks the individual communion of "every / man and woman" contained in the imagination. He is wise, proud, eloquent, and excellent because, like Dürer, he is *himself* and more. Here is the voice of poetry in "Lost and Found":

> He is beside me as he always
> was, a light spirit that brings
> me luck and listens when I speak.
> The day is here, and it will last
> forever or until the sun fails
> and the birds are once again
> hidden and moaning, but for now

the lost are found. The sun
has cleared the trees, the wind
risen, and we, father and child
hand in hand, the living and
the dead, are entering the world.

Part III

■

Robert Penn Warren

Richard Hugo

James Wright

May Swenson

Louis Simpson

Sylvia Plath

James Dickey

Robert Penn Warren: He Prayeth Best Who Loveth Best

Robert Penn Warren is seventy-three. He has published his eleventh volume of poetry, this thirty-second book, and he has never written better. His first book, a biography of John Brown, appeared when he was twenty-four, in the year Faulkner published *The Sound and the Fury* and Hemingway *A Farewell to Arms.* With others he is known as the architect of the New Criticism; his textbook, *Understanding Poetry,* is one of the first stones in the foundation of contemporary American poetry. There is no genre in which his fierce and craggy and formidable talent has not manifested itself. There are no awards in American letters which he has not won.

Why is it, then, that every recent review of Warren's poetry (he has published three collections in this decade) tells us how unrecognized *as poet* he is? Why are we all constrained to note he is recognized as novelist? I suspect the reasons have little to do with poetry and much to do with the business of America. The fact is that no living poet more deserves or receives the respect and admiration given to Mr. Warren. The publication of his books is, simply, an event.

Robert Frost is said to have remarked there can be only one person in the tower at a given time. There is, of course, a poverty of spirit in that. But if there is any truth in the remark, if the space is sufficient only for one, right now the occupant is Warren. James Dickey wrote of Warren that opening one of his books is "like putting out the light of the sun." It is also like entering the unbearable light of the sun—Warren affects one both ways—for in his poems darkness and light are ever present, dialectical, and scorching.

Warren is, if anyone among us is, a poet's poet. We each feel we have discovered him, hence the natter about his anonymity. He is not and never has been glamorously valued. He has been, involuntarily, the object of literary mischief and maliciousness. Yet rarely has he been a strikable target, being so reckless he outpaces adversary and admirer alike. For Warren, a life in the art has meant a continuous and private wrestling not with the shades of literary politics but with the angels of existence.

We can only conjecture the magnitude of Warren's shadow over generations of our poets and this may be an irrelevant consideration in any case; yet we may suggest that he is ancestral to such writers as Dickey and James Wright, Fred Chappell and Stanley Plumly, Bin Ramke and David St. John—three generations. Auden told us that one of the measurements of poetic greatness lies in the poet's literary progeny. The critic Harold Bloom has been scouting this territory.

And it is Harold Bloom who has recently attempted to canonize Warren in an article in the *New Leader* (Jan. 31, 1977). Bloom, king-making, tells us Warren alone now stands with Eliot, Hart Crane, Frost, and Stevens. But it is difficult to characterize Warren this way or any way, to speak to the incredible blossoming that has come in his late years. Warren has spoken often of Randall Jarrell's admonition that the true poet stays out in the rain and waits to be struck by the lightning. (Jarrell, another poet much influenced by Warren, appears to have had his own influence on his old freshman composition teacher.) In poems that range from early iambic monotony to images of virulent, if disorderly, power to a late and soaring architecture of the individual heart, Warren has submitted himself to that lightning. His character, his art, is the conduit of the violent and essential energy of the universe.

Bloom, rightly, has said that Warren wants to be a hawk of life. As poet, he is hawklike, imperial and imperious, gliding over and holding in thrall everything that is. He rarely relaxes or clowns or indulges in the slighter uses of poetry. He has explored a continuous anatomy of ideas, a spectrum of recurrent images, with the doggedness of a prospector. Calvin Bedient said in a recent *Parnassus* that Warren was without a "vision," but nothing could be less true if we are not limited by the term to a seamless polemic. Warren has a vision: the unraveling tag ends of the world's body. We have no poet truer to a comprehensive, sustained evocation of the nature of existence; no one who grapples more with the nuances, the variations, the shadings of a core of thought. Warren's nearly obsessive pursuit begins in these lines from *Brother to Dragons* (1953):

But we must argue the necessity of virtue:

In so far as man has the simplest vanity of self,
There is no escape from the movement toward fulfillment.
And since all kind but fulfills its own kind,
Fulfillment is only in the degree of recognition
Of the common lot of our kind. And that is the death of vanity,
And that is the beginning of virtue.

The recognition of complicity is the beginning of innocence.
The recognition of necessity is the beginning of freedom.
The recognition of the direction of fulfillment is the death of the
self,
And the death of the self is the beginning of selfhood.
All else is surrogate of hope and destitution of spirit.

In *Audubon: A Vision* (1969), that poem of few contemporary peers, Warren made everything he knew as clear as he could: the poems must define "the human filth, the human hope" and would be inextricable in filth and hope; all poems must regard the human in his true humanity. The language became what it had been in fits and starts, a voice-instrument calibrated to final experience. Warren found what Ransom had called for, a poetry of the right head, heart, and foot. He created a poetry which expressed and formed sacramental force as it flowed through events of Love and Knowledge. Man, Warren says, must understand love is knowledge if he is to understand his fate and, moreover, to accept his fate. Audubon, the killer of birds and beauty, the creator of beauty and a possible joy, is Warren's deep analogue. For Warren, the end of poetry must always be to "make it possible to look with joy upon the irremediable things." To do this is to see the world as the hawk does, unforgivingly, that bird whose name means both *taker* and *accepter;* it requires opposable and dialectic vision, a union with the world and a dramatization of that union which tests its philosophical and ethical character. for only in full and mature union can one be human, abstractor, formulator, participant, cause and effect. As Warren says, "literature is knowledge by enactment, imaginative enactment." Put another way, "Man lives by images. They / Lean at us from the world's wall, and Time's." The definition of reality: that has been Warren's vision and his mission. It begins with explorative meditations on the self, Time, History, Love, Knowledge, Family, Community, Religion, and Art; it ends with the self and that glorious, though anguishing, initial love of the immanent world.

If Warren's vision began with *Brother to Dragons,* his breakthrough came in *Promises* (1957), of which he has said, "Seeing a little gold-headed girl on that bloody spot of history [an Italian island-fortress which was both site and subject of the poems] was an event!" The image of beauty counterposed against the symbol of history's continuous and random grinding out of beauty suggests a medallion of Warren's art. It is at once the doubleness of reality, darkness and light; and though the mind must try to know multifoliate meaning, must rage for reconciliation, reconciliation fails; art witnesses and holds in tension the antinomies. All of Warren's poems are events rendered in a holding fabric of image, narrative, and meditative gloss; all attempt to do one thing: "what you are concerned with is a sense of contact with reality. And it's maybe a pinpoint touch or a whole palm of a hand laid, or something; but the important thing is the shock of this contact: a lot of current can come through a small wire" (*Fugitives Return*).

Touch, the laying on of the hand. What Warren has called a single, vital image. Contact. Always the figure of connection, the poem of reconnection, the failure of that ability to receive the energy, disruption, and the possibility of rejoining. For Warren, such poems function: the "poem does involve a potential action, it modifies our being in some way." That is, the poem is not a simple picture, but a picture with extended or exploded events ordered to demonstrate a right relationship, with moral and ethical resonances.

II

Now and Then: Poems 1976–1978, more objective than previous books, is a deeply moral vision, a continuation of Warren's long consideration of the "moral history of man." The book contains, looming like a granite cliff, one of the great poems in our language: "Red-Tail Hawk and Funeral Pyre of Youth." It stands with *Audubon* as emblematic of his full effort. Warren told Peter Stitt in a recent interview (*Sewanee Review,* 1977) that the poem was sparked by Harold Bloom's remarks on his recurrent hawk imagery and its relation to an Emersonian vision of transcendence. Warren has long rejected Emerson's easy dismissal of evil, depravity, and moral irresponsibility. But the antecedent of "Red-Tail Hawk and Funeral Pyre of Youth" is less Harold Bloom and less Emerson than it is Coleridge and "The Rime of the Ancient Mariner." Indeed, Warren's poem is a mini-"Mariner" in plot, vision, and construction. In his essay on Coleridge's poem, "A Poem of Pure Imagination," Warren writes: "The fable, in broadest and simplest terms, is a story of crime and punishment and reconciliation. . . . The Mariner shoots the bird; suffers various pains, the greatest of which is loneliness and spiritual anguish; upon recognizing the beauty of the foul sea snakes, experiences a gush of love for them and is able to pray; is returned miraculously to his home port, where he discovers the joy of human communion in God, and utters the moral 'He prayeth best who loveth best.' " Warren also says "we are confronting the mystery of the corruption of the will, the mystery which is the beginning of the 'moral history of man.' " The issue in both poems is: why does a man commit gratuitous violence? Why does he not see the interconnection of everything—a blindness that means his violence is self-wounding? Warren argues that man commits Original Sin, sin original with each man—not inherited, because he is driven by corrupted will and lacks knowledge (love) to prevent it. He must do harm, must suffer, must heal himself, and then the world's violated body. Coleridge's Mariner passes from innocence to experience, a passage culminating in a wedding and the ability to pray, the life-purchased testimony to the existence of joy in an unjoyous world.

Warren's "Red-Tail Hawk and Funeral Pyre of Youth," divided into ten sections, dramatizes the motiveless boyhood shooting of a hawk. It travels back and forth in time and memory around the event and comes to its own prayer and marriage. The poem reveals what it will celebrate in section 1: "That all is only / All, and part of all." It begins by describing a boy who climbs a hill, rifle in hand, toward "the center of / that convex perfection" and immediately sets up the basic image contrast of the boy's blindness and the hawk's vision. "Gold eyes, unforgiving, for they, like God, see all." The event of the poem comes in section 2:

> There was no decision in the act,
> There was no choice in the act—the act impossible but
> Possible. I screamed, not knowing
> From what emotion, as at that insane range
> I pressed the cool, snubbed
> Trigger. Saw
> The circle
> Break.

To refuse choice or its exercise is to be morally corrupt; the hawk only kills to eat. Nature, the circle, perfection, innocence: these are violated. But the act is also a birth, or might be. Thus, the boy, "the bloody / Body already to my bare flesh embraced, cuddled / Like babe to heart," has the chance of a life, a knowing. He takes the body home and stuffs it, saying "Oh, yes / I knew my business." The Audubon analogue: killer and creator. The poet *rationally* knows. His business is to freeze life, to make dynamic models of life in art. Yet there is something he doesn't know and Warren is compelled to write, in hindsight:

> It was molded as though for that moment to take to the
> air—though,
> In God's truth, the chunk of poor wingless red meat,
> The model from which all was molded, lay now
> Forever earthbound, fit only
> For dog tooth, not sky.

The murder of hawk and the murder of albatross are parables of man's fall from continuity with the natural world.

Warren tells us now that he kept the stuffed bird atop bookshelves to "guard / Blake and *Lycidas,* Augustine, Hardy and Hamlet / Baudelaire and Rimbaud" and tells us that its "yellow eyes, / unsleeping, stared as I slept." Among tragic poets of joy, nature, unforgiving, keeps its own watch. But the poet, still blind, turns away and his personal history, in retrospect, seems filled with the "meaningless motion of life" as well as with a sense of imminent vengeance. He asks, "Could Nature forgive, like God?" But he postpones answering, and in section 7 rediscovers the stuffed bird among "the relevant items" of his life, items he burns in a gesture of clearing toward final sight. Like the Mariner, he kills the bird a second time, "so made a pyre / For the hawk":

> 8
>
> Flame flared. Feathers first, and I flinched, then stood
> As the steel wire warped red to defend
> The shape designed godly for air. But
> It fell with the mass, and I
> Did not wait.
>
> What left
> To do but walk in the dark, and no stars?

The moral awakening has still not come to full term. In dream, then, the bird continues to reappear as it had in that first instant of its immanence. The hunter is doomed to repeat the old violation, to live in history, but the repetition of the act provides opportunity to know the meaning of action, choice, and responsibility. He says:

> —and you come
> And always the rifle swings up, though with

The weightlessness now of dream,
The old .30-.30 that knows
How to bind us in air-blood and earth-blood together
In our commensurate fate,
Whose name is a name beyond joy.

In the final section, Warren prays for this recurrence "To bring me the truth in blood-marriage of earth and air— / And all be as it was / In that paradox of unjoyful joyousness." That is, the Coleridgean One Flesh, the matrix of Being, will be restored because understood, because man learns to accept himself, his fate, the necessary condition for the gaining of joy, having now reexperienced the event and the moral history of all that event portends.

But two key questions—the question of Nature's forgiveness and what one might do besides walk in the dark—remain unanswered. In fact, Nature cannot forgive; the hawk stares, unforgiving, only itself. If the hawk had human will it could forgive, but then it would fall in violation and abrogate what it is. The hawk is the symbolic embodiment of sacramental energy. What one must do in the dark is to both know the hawk and be hawklike. The poem, thus, evolves from event to revelation to vision; moral history enacted, the imagination as alembic; the poem reveals itself as prayer for definition and responsibility, which is to say, an awareness of the meaning in as well as the cost of action. The poem is the story of human consciousness. It is dramatically and aesthetically and ethically true to experiential as well as emotional life. It is a grand, unfolded, unified, and felt experience.

III

Warren's *Now and Then* is divided into two sections, "Nostalgic" with ten poems and "Speculative" with twenty-six, these subtitles paralleling the temporal *now* and *then* in reverse. Typically, Warren takes a position, tests it emotionally and philosophically, then does the same test from an obverse position.

If "Red-Tail Hawk and Funeral Pyre of Youth" is the set piece of both "Nostalgic" and the collection, the initial poem, "American Portrait: Old Style," also looms grandly. It returns to home ground and innocence, its event a visit with a boyhood friend who had won glory as an athlete and who had been an early companion in the imaginative fictions the two men shared as children. The visit occasions meditation on Warren's oldest subjects: Time, Self, Love, Mutability, and particularly the Imagination:

What imagination is—it is only
The lie we must learn to live by, if ever
We mean to live at all.

Through imagination, Warren says, we *may* learn the world's name—that essence of reality (usually figured in the touch of a hand, the stare into a face, various images of flow and dark/light). He warns us again that "of all things the worst, the not knowing / One thing from the other"—is to stand not in innocence but in willed ignorance, in corruption not struggled against. For without the struggle there is no way to know "what makes a man do what he does—." Only in attempting to recreate himself can a man know reality. In "Amazing Grace in the Back Country" Warren flees from revivalists and winds up "By the spring with one hand in the cold black water," which is exactly the figure he employed in "The Ballad of Billy Potts" where the boy-murderer comes to revelation, and again in *Brother to Dragons* where he spoke of the "perfect adjustment" of the catfish which "is in the Mississippi and / The Mississippi is in the Catfish and / Under the ice both are at one with God." This is the state of intuited connection to and immersion in sacramental energy and epiphany, often sexual, always accompanied by the sensation of being dissolved and silent in the world's flow. In "Star-Fall" Warren writes:

For what communication
Is needed if each alone
Is sunk and absorbed into
The mass and matrix of Being that defines
Identity of all?

That communication beyond speech, atavistic and premoral, is the oldest dream in Warren's poetry. But speech, art, is necessary precisely because we remain unconnected to the matrix. Art has been Warren's way back. Having spent more than fifty years to vivify and make whole this reality of interconnection, he has earned the right to rest and say: "I love the world even in my anger, / And love is a hard thing to outgrow." We expect the confirming, consolidating poems of "Nostalgic" at the end of a man's career, in his seventh decade, even should they sometimes recover old ground, even with glibness of glory.

But when we move into the poems of "Speculation" we discover once again that Warren has gone ahead of us. He surprises us with a darkly insistent mood in poems rooted in dying seasons, sunsets, autumn, gray light. As "Departure" says, "Time is up." Others before me have written that Warren was likely done, but no book shimmers so with the recognition of impendent death which is a "truth we must all face." The collection radiates a *Tempest* tone while it hovers toward the few answers which might reveal at last "The possibility of joy in the world's tangled and hieroglyphic beauty." Has Warren, then, turned sour? No. But he has invoked the conceptions, the ideas, the imageries of his career only to question them again. In "Code Book Lost" he suggests he has failed the tenuous meaning he had worked to find; the world isn't revealing anything. It is as if Warren has forced himself to start over entirely. He has, in fact, begun to speculate not simply on what death will be like, hence what value in any values, positions, hypotheses, but on what life is as *husk*. "From what dream to what dream do we / Awake" he asks. And in "Unless":

> All will be in vain unless—unless what? Unless
> You realize that what you think is Truth is only
>
> A husk for something else. Which might,
> Shall we say, be called energy, as good a word as any.

All bodies of the world's body are husks, vehicles, containers, for that current which may pass through even small wires. Energy is life. Warren is recalling the totemic and hieratic images that for fifty years have served toward defining the condition of joy: hawk, owl, beasts, lovers, landscapes of crag and sublime contrast. But he remembers another immediate truth: "So many things they say are true, but you / Can't always be sure you feel them." Have these images become, even for Warren, a push-button reality? Are they only the tired furniture arranged in poems? For Warren, inevitably, the only things true are the felt survivors of literal experience, reflected and reengaged.

And death, always Warren's main character, is nearer than ever. The figure of a hand's touch assumes a new context. Now it is the physician who stares into the patient's face "and you wish / He'd take his goddamn hand off your shoulder." In this poem, "Waiting," everything that has mattered seems now stripped away. The woman a man has loved all his life says "she cannot / Remember when last she loved you, and had lived the lie only / For the children's sake." Is this what one comes to, is this reality? Is this the ease which comes to a man's seventh decade? You must wait to know. Warren, like everyone, must "pick the last alibi off, like a scab, and / Admire the inwardness." As he says in *Democracy & Poetry* (1975), it is ever the poet's task to face the deep and dark inwardness of man's nature—to endeavor to be so much of the matrix that there will be no need to flinch before the hawk of reality.

Warren, indeed, demands more vigorously than ever to know the nature of a man's purpose in "The Mission." Here he creates an *Ur*-dream of horses, long dead, in static and graceful pose, who seem to promise some answer but give only themselves, their beauty. How could they, like the poet himself, be in the world and then not? Waking, he thinks of a hibernating bear who will come alive like the world, and thinks of the snow-blinded world that keeps the bear, the icy stream of reality that continually flows:

> It has a mission, but,
> In that blackness, has forgotten what. I, too,
>
> Have forgotten the nature of my own mission.

What terror now not to know what had been certain reality, to have to conjecture "perhaps" and to relive the old contingencies, the old hope of continuity—and what courage to make this choice! In "When the Tooth Cracks—Zing!" all Warren can do is to try to make new definition by the remaining evidence, pain:

> But even
> The pain is something—is, you might say,
> For lack of a better word,
> Reality.

With "Sister Water" Warren evokes his venerable "Original Sin: A Short Story," and an old man rattles the night-door as had the premoral monster who first announced Warren's claim that "nothing is ever lost," not even the will-corrupted and nightmare self. But in this new poem we cannot be sure time exists, much less continuity: "But is there a *now* or *then?*" Surely time is not of the matrix but of the human—or is it? Without definition, what human gesture is any good? Warren says, "You cannot pray. But / You can wash your face in cold water." How ironic and caustic. The story of these poems tells us that we must do precisely what we cannot do, if we hope to know reality.

"Speculation" is a tragic and necessary movement which insists again that Warren will not live the unexamined life but will, must ask, as he asked in *Audubon,* "what / Is man but his passion?" He had answered this ambiguously lineated question in *Or Else* where he said, "Passion / Is all. Even / The sleaziest." The poems of "Speculation" reinforce Warren's idea that man is defined by passion, and once again he submits the idea to the stress test of experience. None of the poems seems to me more blisteringly beautiful than the Ouroboros-like "Identity and Argument for Prayer" and the book-ending "Heart of Autumn." The former functions as a summation:

And whatever
Vision or anguish
Swelled in the heart to be uttered was
By wind crammed in the throat back, and all
I recall is the shadowy thought that
Man's mind, his heart, live only by piecemeal, like mice
On cheese crumbs—the cheese itself, of course,
Being locked in the tin
In God's pantry.

Well, you might, of course, go to bed, and stare
Up at the coagulate darkness and know
How beyond the frail rooftop darkness piles skyward—
Thinking now that at least you are *you,*
Saying *now,* saying *now,* for
Now *now* is all, and you *you.*

At least, for a minute.

This may be taken as an argument for prayer.

As always, there is no *then* in the moment of connection. When the event of definition, however incomplete, leaps into timelessness it is both argument in favor of prayer and prayer itself; man's mission is to celebrate and to participate, which is prayer. But Warren still asks, in "Heat Wave Breaks," "For what should we pray to our God in the rumble and flare? / That the world stab anew in the lightning-stricken air?" The answer is what Elizabeth Bishop calls that "peculiar / affirmative"—yes! For even if the promise of reality will be only the scalding of flesh and the not-knowing, passion is all. Passion is feeling; man is feeling; poetry is feeling. In his self-interrogation Warren rejects his earlier *Tempest* tone and, like Lear, calls on the crack of winds.

For the heart loves no matter what, it fills with love of the world, with delight in being, no less in autumn, the turning-time. In his fine short lyric, "Tell Me a Story," the conclusion to *Audubon,* Warren became Audubon himself, went back to his boyhood and the dark flow before experience—where he had heard "The great geese hoot northward."

I could not see them, there being no moon
And the stars sparse. I heard them.

I did not know what was happening in my heart.

He prayed. The event of the poem became prayer: "Tell me a story of deep delight." That story is man's moral history that yields the full curve of specific individual experience, which is not abstract but archetypal. Warren asked to start with the world and to know how to live in its reality, to know the world's name and his own, to know love which would prove "all is only / All, and part of all." It is not, therefore, surprising that even in this ferociously eschatological reexamination of everything, Warren would return to those geese, to his feeling for that image of what was moving in the blind darkness. He had felt his passion was mirrored in the unchosen and lyrical yearning of the geese. No one describes what Robert Penn Warren has been *as poet* better than he does when he says, "The palm of my hand was as / Wide as the world and the / Blaze of distance." With Warren, the love of the world is not cant, but reality itself. Let him speak again for himself in the last poem of *Now and Then: Poems 1976–1978,* and let it be far from the last time:

HEART OF AUTUMN

Wind finds the northwest gap, fall comes.
Today, under gray cloud-scud and over gray
Wind-flicker of forest, in perfect formation, wild geese
Head for a land of warm water, the *boom,* the lead pellet.

Some crumple in air, fall. Some stagger, recover control,
Then take the last glide for a far glint of water. None
Knows what has happened. Now, today, watching
How tirelessly V upon V arrows the season's logic,

Do I know my own story? At least, they know
When the hour comes for the great wing-beat. Sky-strider,
Star-strider—they rise, and the imperial utterance,
Which cries out for distance, quivers in the wheeling sky.

That much they know, and in their nature know
The path of pathlessness, with all the joy
Of destiny fulfilling its own name.
I have known time and distance, but not why I am here.

Path of logic, path of folly, all
The same—and I stand, my face lifted now skyward,
Hearing the high beat, my arms outstretched in the tingling
Process of transformation, and soon tough legs,

With folded feet, trail in the sounding vacuum of passage,
And my heart is impacted with a fierce impulse
To unwordable utterance—
Toward sunset, at a great height.

Notes on a Form to Be Lived: Robert Penn Warren's Or Else

■

In his *Essays of Four Decades* Allen Tate remarks frequently about the shoddy state of poetry in the twentieth century, an occupation much favored by critical minds haunted by the demon of *form*. Tate asks, "Where shall a poet get a form that will permit him to make direct, comprehensive statements about modern civilization?" Tate, acutely and restlessly intelligent, could not shake himself free of the conviction that form is to be found externally. If poetic form meant a composition of elements acquired outside of the personality, then both a sanctification of history and a quasi-scientific objectivity were possible. This was the dream of the Modernist. But the poet, even the poet named Allen Tate, finds no form except in himself, in the personality as reservoir and catalyst. The poet's dream of form is a dream outside of time, name, or critical categorization.

For the poet, not the critic living inside the poet, form is virtually everything brought alive into the poem. That this is far from definitions of form given in conventional criticism and classroom ought to be obvious. To speak of form now is to evoke the antiseptic smell of clinics and the faintly hovering potential for pain. It is to observe how a writer declares himself ostensibly through ruminations on unalterables, if we understand those declarations reveal economic, political, and cultural opinions. When a man discusses form and poetry—whichever form he inclines to favor—we can read his personality. Marshall McLuhan says the medium is the message. Creeley says form is no more than an extension of content. Both statements are true and both are incomplete. Both echo the persistent occupation with form as authority in contemporary poetry.

The poet's problem with form is not so much that he has not got one, but that he has got a great variety of forms which seem to offer authority for a credible poetry but which all too often offer only the illusion of order. He has got a confusion. Perhaps this is because "comprehensive statements" are themselves suspect and "modern civilization" is such an anomaly that few agree what it is or where it exists. The result has sometimes been that poets shift forms the way Americans trade cars. Our poets are pressured from within by a suspicion of authority, or personality, and from without by a consumer criticism. No one demonstrates this better than Robert Lowell. He mastered early on a high Modernist form, moved to a much hailed "open" form, retreated to a rigorous and belabored period of sonnets, then concluded in an elegantly conversational poetry. Whatever else may be said of Lowell's body of work, it is clear that he regarded form as the dream of a dream; he continued to seek a way to express the world with the authority of felt experience. Robert Penn Warren, a greater and more accomplished poet than Lowell, shows the same process in a poetry that now spans almost six decades. Lowell called his work a sort of autobiography. In a section of poems from *Selected Poems 1923–1966* subtitled "Notes on a Life to Be Lived," Warren wrote, "if I look at the stars, I / Will have to live over again all I have lived / In the years I looked at stars and / Cried out, 'O reality!' " One way to define the most characteristic quality of the contemporary American poet is to say that he lives through form. Form is the pressure of life to be lived.

What, then, is form? The heart shrinks at the question. Samuel Johnson once remarked in answer to Boswell's question about what poetry might be, that, Sir, it is easiest enough to recognize and nearly impossible to define. I am not tempted to tread where Johnson feared to enter. Yet this may be said: to feel sufficient to the poet, form must be prophetic, dynamic, and emblematic. It must, when it has come into existence, seem to cast a visionary light onto the darker configurations of reality. This reality must be composed of internal and contradictory motions, as a man is. But this reality must also appear stilled, beyond time, caught out of the vicissitudes of change and impermanence. This need, I think, explains the great attraction of our time to the image. The thing itself is the door to all knowing and it is no easy task to bring that thing to clear embodiment in words. Yet the greater task, the task that mere image fails, is to give motion and contradiction, the illusion of life's action. Such an action allows us to discover meaning and to express it. For this, form is needed. Form shapes not merely the world the poet sees, the referential cosmos of men and mud and caprice and vacillation and decision, but also the personality, the character of the poet seeing. The rhythm of the poet is both a point of reference and an intersection. Form is the personality of a man becoming—to the degree it is large in love and deep in knowledge—the personality of men. Poems may exist in forms but poetry exists only in form, in the fused moment of language where we seem to behold the beauty and curve of life freed from the bondage of time, place, and effort.

No poet currently living has so resolutely wrestled with or turned to advantage the problem of form as has Robert Penn Warren. He has settled upon form as dialectic, as conversation between dramatic monologue and lyric speculation. The personality of men formally created by Warren exists in the citizen of intense passion, philosophical introspection, moral violation, and ethical study. This man acts and is acted upon by nearly blind forces, yet his mission is to know those forces, to recreate them in dramas of the self. Unlike the poet who demands we make it new and theoretically casts loose from the past, Warren seeks reality in the ever-newness of the past and his attitude toward form is essentially historic. He renovates form.

Warren's formal accomplishment in poetry is dazzlingly various. His *Selected Poems 1923–1975* contains poems of every identifiable generic type and, like Thomas Hardy, he has created originals. His book-length poems, *Brother to Dragons* and *Audubon,* are as close as American poetry has come, with any degree of success, to the epic. He has written verse plays. Between 1974 and 1981 he has published four collections which have won him a late but widespread recognition as the preeminent American poet. *Or Else* (1974), *Now and Then: Poems 1976–1978* (1978), *Being Here: Poetry 1977–1980* (1980), and *Rumor Verified: Poems 1979–1980* have been received as collections of lyric poems touching on the enigmatic subjects of Time, History, Identity, and Mortality. There has not been, however, much attention to Warren's experiment with form, that subject being overshadowed by Warren's preoccupation with vision.

Because Warren's poetry comes from a mind that is deeply speculative, one which never refuses but cultivates the immanent meaning of all it has ever encountered, Warren is a pronounced thinker among poets. But he has not been so obviously a thinker about poetry, in the poems, as Stevens or Williams. Among those who seem to write as if the poem were beyond all else the poet's subject, Warren has remained committed to the tale, the story, the narrative—with an interlineated commentary which has ranged from stage direction to head-shaking befuddlement to homiletic moralizing. He has, that is, seemed to play Joseph Conrad's Marlow. Marlow thinks and speaks about almost everything known to man. Except, it might be argued, the form in which he participates. But if we argue that the essential definition of form is feeling then it is clear that both Marlow and Warren deal in nothing else so passionately as form. Feeling is the form by which we know and understand whatever the world gives us.

Critical response to Warren's recent collections has correctly identified the lyrical nature of his poetry, and the feeling in it. But there has been little linkage of this feeling to his evolution of form. Annalyn Swan, reviewing *Being Here: Poetry 1977–1980* for *Newsweek,* has written that Warren now "achieves the sort of profound simplicity that marks the best autumnal poetry." It is a remark one might have expected to hear about Frost, suggesting as it does the venerable qualities of sweetness, purity, wisdom, noble song, natural harmony, final vision, etc. Swan is accurate as far as she goes, but since she does not go far enough she is deceptive. For while Warren has become that most lucid of thinkers, the dramatic observer of feeling, what he thinks about feeling is never simple and never conclusive. In fact Warren's thinking and feeling exist in such a tenuous balance as *lyric,* a formal existence no historian or philosopher can quite be comfortable with, that he has constructed a larger, subsuming form whose shape—in the outline—is the tale and whose character is the dialectic of philosophical allegory. His purpose is to confront and engage the nature of human existence. He has tried to find, develop, and refine a form in which he could make Allen Tate's direct, comprehensive statements. But not, I think, statements about "modern civilization" as in any way divorced from the past. Warren's statements are directed at knowing the eternal condition and circumstance of men. This presumes the conviction that the modern is *new* but also that it reflects historical continuity, that the only understanding possible is that which absorbs and knows the living past. Excluding *Audubon,* to my mind Warren's most successful poem is the book he has called *Or Else: Poem/Poems 1968–1974.* Because in this book the form is the poetry, he has done what Browning required of art, a requirement as sufficient now as in the nineteenth century:

> Beyond mere imagery on the wall,—
> So, note by note, bring music from your mind,
> Deeper than ever e'en Beethoven dived,—
> So write a book shall mean beyond the facts,
> Suffice the eye and save the soul beside.
> (XII, 864–67)

Warren has long considered the responsibility of a collection of poems to be the discovery of coherent meaning. *Or Else* blurs, as the title indicates, the distinction between a collection of poems and a poem. He believes that meaning is dynamic, not static: it shifts constantly, altered by circumstance and by perspective, and needs continual refocusing. Warren's poems are constructed as temporary, necessarily pragmatic lenses employed not just to observe reality but to dramatically experience events while the mind is allowed to sift and comment. Such a poetry places crucial dependence on the image, but his image does not constitute the poetry. If the image is actual experience, whether resurrected from memory or entirely imagined, Warren must still create a form which will tease out the luminous, usually refracted meaning of the image. His construction of the tale causes the image to become the mind's stepping-stone through time and space.

Warren, however, makes a distinction between what we might call the lower image and the higher image. The lower image is the literal thing pointed at by words in the line-by-line movement of the poem. The higher image is the figurative and form-enacted vision that the tale represents. It is helpful to hear Warren speak about his distinction before considering the form of *Or Else*. Nowhere has he been more specific than in his comment to Sidney Hirsch, published in *Fugitives Return,* after Hirsch has suggested that some of the Fugitives believed that a poem's greatness was to be defined by its "lofty subject matter" while others thought the true poem inhered in "the treatment, the stylization, prosody." Warren said this to Hirsch:

> it seems to me greatness is not a criterion—a profitable criterion—of poetry; that what you are really concerned with is a sense of a contact with reality. And it's maybe a pinpoint touch or a whole palm of a hand laid, or something; but the important thing is the shock of this contact: a lot of current can come through a small wire. And there you are up against, well, big subjects and little subjects. It's just so it's a real subject, and, of course, you've got this word to deal with; you've got to have something that will actually create human heat in that contact. Well, language can in certain ways, because language drags the bottom of somebody into being, in one way or another, directly or indirectly. But if I had to say what I would try for in a poem—would hunt for in a poem—it would be some kind of vital image, a vital and evaluating image, or vitality. That's a different thing from the vitality you observe or experience. It's an image of it, but it has the vital quality, rather than a passing reflection, but it has its own kind of assurance, own kind of life, by the way it's built.

In this impromptu response Warren dismisses the abstract issue of *greatness* and moves directly to a figurative definition of poetry itself. His argument moves from effect to cause. A poem is "built" and it is mechanical like a wire on its most elementary level. The essential building material is the lower image. We can understand this just as we understand the physical reality of electrical wiring. But poetry, Warren tells us, is electrical current, a flow, and while we are all familiar with the flow of electricity such energy remains for the most part beyond observation. It remains mysterious and enigmatic, but not the less active and present in our lives.

What then of that energy which leaps through the laying on of the hand, that image laden with faith-healing religious connotations? Where does it come from? What does it fit? This cannot be diagrammed or made manifest by wires and switches in our stores. Because he is a lyric poet, Warren does not compromise that mystery; he merely asserts it. He allows this other energy to snap and crackle like a raw-ended wire. Yet it is not vital enough, for it is only a limited view, a limited medium. The poet in *Or Else* creates a form which includes such lower imagery but which extends, weaves, and conjoins it toward establishing a higher image. In this *Poem/Poems 1968–1974* he has caused thirty-two poems to operate as something like panels which exist in a loose sequential movement that is a *tale*. It is a tale which moves freely in and out of time, space, and history, but a tale whose meaning is created by and released through lyric, or feeling. We might say that Warren's mission in individual poems as well as in the sequential poem is to create a circuit. The circuit, then, is the vital, or higher, image by which reality, in its fullest and most contradictory dimensions, may be apprehended. Through laying hand to this circuit-reality the self may be seen and felt to become, by acts of experience driven to emblematic stillness, continuous with the world from which it has been divided. Warren remarks about this function of the poem in *Democracy & Poetry:* "The 'made thing' becomes, then, a vital emblem of the struggle toward the achieving of the self, and that mark of the struggle, the human signature, is what gives the aesthetic organization its numinousness." It is also helpful to recall something Warren had said twenty-five years earlier in "Knowledge and the Image of Man": "The Form is a vision of experience, but of experience fulfilled and redeemed in knowledge, the 'ugly' with the beautiful, the slayer with the slain, what was known as shape now known as Time, what was known as Time now known as shape, a new knowledge."

A tale, strictly defined, is only a sequential movement in time and space by characters more archetypes than individuals. The tale employs a plot whose complications intend to reveal simple moral actions; the tale means to dramatize these actions rising toward the status of unalterable truths. The plot is, however, not complex. Frequently, the tale is the product of oral and folk traditions and its linear narrative movement, evolved rather than designed, functions to inculcate and demonstrate the values, wisdoms, and images that a culture wishes to preserve and transmit. Tales involve common actions, even when they are dream actions, which show the local citizen making his or her way against the enigmatic forces of the world. There is often a folk spookiness, an intense animism, and an allegorically aggressive landscape. If a primary value of the tale is to show one can make one's way in the dissembling world, the allegorical nature of the tale points through referential action, place, and character toward nontemporal signification and a meaningful reality that is permanent. Often those engaged in the tale have no awareness of this signification and the tale-teller only dimly reveals what is figured.

Readers of Robert Penn Warren's poetry know that the image of the child at the foot of the experienced elder who is transmitting the events of history is common. They know, too, that this elder interprets whatever he describes, though this interpretation is limited, suspect, and personal. The image is that of Virgilian guide and innocent apprentice, if we wish to give it literary categorization. In an early poem setting forth this image, "Court Martial," Warren describes his Confederate grandfather and himself:

> Under the cedar tree,
> He would sit, all summer, with me:
> An old man and small grandson
> Withdrawn from the heat of the sun.

Earlier still, in "Letters from a Coward to a Hero," Warren contrasted the old man's recitations and self-speculations with the child's desire for absolutes and he wrote "But piety is simple, / And should be ample." The conventional tale assumes what Warren's child assumes, an ample, simple piety, a code of existence. Yet Warren's earthy realism, a product of modernism, combines with his folk heritage to upend the tale's operation. In effect, the story which age tells of the common lot does not come to easy resolution but rather to antinomies and increasing paradoxes. This, truncated and muted, is the form and world of *Or Else*. Here Warren's tale is told by memory about those who are dead and dying. It recites the acts by which they lived, describes the sometimes hostile and sometimes indifferent—never supernaturally supportive—places where they thrived or did not thrive, with as Warren writes "particular emphasis on the development of / the human scheme of values." It is a tale of time, the past, mortality, love, illusion, knowledge, and all of these as they whirl like a snowstorm in the consciousness of a single man, a consciousness in which all time is present and one. This man, unlike Faulkner's Benjy, knows what is past and what is present but the distinction seems meaningless.

In effect, the narrator of *Or Else* stands in the dusk of knowing, as he stands in literal dusk with the initial and concluding poems, and stares into the sky that is "Saffron: pure, pure and forever" and the sky is the image of time passing but slowed enough for him to seize the fragments of experience and objects which it carries. These fragments the poet attempts to assemble in a form of revelation. Warren says, "Man lives by images. They / Lean at us from the world's wall, and Time's." To force these images into a coherent and discursive plot sequence would be to falsify the felt experience of life—which is primarily lyrical. But to deny the sense of an unfolding and unified story, even one whose end is enigmatic, shifting, or unknown, would be an equal distortion. Warren's task is, therefore, to suggest through both an alliance and a juxtaposition of lyrical poems the forward motion of the human story, the function of the tale, while he lifts the sequence to the understood radiance of what he has called a vital image, or emblem. The tale built from associative images, constructed as a sequence of lyrical fragments which mean to cohere in the higher image—the human signature, is the tale of a man whose end is to know, to achieve knowledge. Only through form will this be possible and then only if the form is as dynamic, complex, contradictory, and numinous as the acts and personality of a single man.

Poets do not ordinarily speak prescriptively of form, even Allen Tate. For Warren, whose descriptions of form have always been democratic and individual, form must be inclusive but discriminating, a balance of elements, rhythms, and movements. It must see and shape, juxtapose and juggle—what else is life but pulse, motion, rest, change, current? The poem must create meaning by assimilation that results not in transcending truculent details but in fully engaging such details to generate the effect of "human heat." Warren has always invited into the poem what he has called the world of imperfection and prose. He disavows both the theory and fact of pure poetry. His authority for this practice is Coleridge:

> In short, whatever specific import we attach to the word, Poetry, there will be found involved in it, as a necessary consequence, that a poem of any length neither can be, nor ought to be, all poetry. Yet if an harmonious whole is to be produced, the remaining parts must be preserved in keeping with the poetry; and this can no otherwise be effected than by such a studied selection and artificial arrangement, as will partake of one, though not a peculiar property of poetry. And this again can be

> no other than the property of exciting a more continuous and equal attention than the language of prose aims at, whether colloquial or written.
>
> *Biographia Literaria*

Like Warren, Coleridge has not prescribed an ideal and external form; he has merely asserted the need for the worldliness of prose, the electrical ground, in poetry. And he has insisted on a unity of parts, a created harmony whose end is to give the superior pleasure of meaning. Had Coleridge said that poetry and prose should compose a dialectical argument he would have described the principle of form in *Or Else.*

Of course within the emblem architecture of *Or Else* there is a plenitude of conventional poetic forms. Within the metaphor of electronic circuitry, these might be regarded as different kinds of wire, each having its specific ability to affect the kind and degree of current Warren wants to send. Among them are meditations, dreams, fairy tales, songs, narratives, elegies, dramatic monologues, still-life compositions, and prose commentaries. Many of the poems blend forms. Too, within the poems there is a masterful shifting of dictions, tones, voices which sets what might be called the hard fact against the soft and the gentle rhythm against the harsh rhythm. Yet all is ultimately created by and takes its form from the single voice that is, as it were, the teller of the tale. This poetic speech is the peculiar style that is distinctly Robert Penn Warren's.

Critical response to Warren's poetry has been almost entirely exploration of themes, motifs, philosophies, that which could be abstracted and contrasted with bodies of discursive thought. Warren's poetry, of course, lends itself to such examinations. Yet it is ironic that one of the architects of a major critical methodology designed to look at *how* a poem operates and what it is should have received so little and so superficial an assessment of the form his poems have taken. His style is generally observed to be one of dense verbal textures, turgid and distressed syntax, one studded and layered with grand abstractions. Such characterizations are often accurate but usually offered without exploration of cause or function. Perhaps this is because Warren's style, preternaturally violent in its clarity of expression and adamantly opposed to lyrical resolution, has taken the path less traveled by the majority of contemporary poets. Warren's style is designed to glide, step, swirl, plod, and dance through cadences which come abruptly short in order to give the impression of narrative motion halted. The operation of a Warren poem depends on syntactical suspension, image association, aggressive Anglo-Saxon stresses, dictions that bark. Here, from "Chain Saw at Dawn in Vermont in Time of Drouth," is an example:

> Dawn and, distant, the steel-snarl and lyric
> Of the chain saw in deep woods:
> I wake. Was it
> Trunk-scream, bough-rip and swish, then earth-thud?
> No—only the saw's song, the saw
> Sings: *now!* Sings:
> *Now, now, now,* in the
> Lash and blood-lust of an eternal present, the present
> Murders the past, the nerve shrieks, the saw.

Beginning with two dramatic statements couched in one sentence which he suspends over three lines, Warren's clustering of hard sounds is explosive and abrupt as he associates the image of dawn stillness with disorienting noise. It is at once the figure of birth and the figure of a rending universe that is absolute time, absolute present. There is no tranquil recollection here, but immersion in repetition and combination that is a violent, halting, shrieking, surging song of life. The song of the chain saw is a lower image which Warren employs as a sort of leitmotif to hover over and weave through the collection that is *Or Else.* The landscape of Warren's tale, hostile and dangerously chaotic, is not merely described by the word combinations, the ripping phrases, the bestial behavior, but is sonically imitated. The rhythm of this passage mirrors the pulse-and-stop rhythm of the tale just as the mind in which the elements of the tale are held mirrors something like the mind of the world that is happening now.

The form of *Or Else,* even in the verbal style of individual poems, is therefore analogous to the multilayered personality of the man who writes. It is only through evolved form that the images in his rhythmically swirling consciousness can be brought to a temporary knowledge, an epiphanic glimpse of what a man is—since while he is immersed in time he can scarcely hope for sufficient quiet and distance to know anything. Warren believes that a man is inherently flawed, sick, self-deluded, but he has the power to *know.* He shall know by feeling and by poetry. What he shall attempt to know is the nature and power of passion, himself, and his potential for magnificence. As he writes in "Folly on Royal Street before the Raw Face of God,"

> For what is man without magnificence?
> Delusion, delusion!
>
> But let
> Bells ring in all the churches.
> Let likker, like philosophy, roar

In the skull. Passion
Is all. Even
The sleaziest.

Man the magnificent and man the sleaze, but man against the looming sky and landscape, is the vital emblem at the heart of *Or Else*. Warren shows him in many forms: elders dancing in the rain, the ghosts of parents, derelicts, and the mad in New York, a penitentiary warden, an Indian setting fire to rattlesnakes, adulterers, Theodore Dreiser and Flaubert, a shopkeeper turned lynch-master, an assassin, a little boy with a lost shoe, drunks, lovers, etc. This is the emblem of man at the edge, the dusk of time. Warren's poems attempt to flood that silhouetted figure with an illuminating current so powerful that he will be seen in his most significant acts and will be understood as representative, in the sense that any character in a tale is larger than life through the nimbus of signified meaning. Too much "current" would make this man all dazzle; too little would leave him an allegorical mouthpiece. None of the wires which each single poem is—generic form, point of view, rhythmic variation, etc.—is sufficient by itself to hold and reveal the mysterious complexity which any man is. Yet Warren appears to believe the orchestrated circuitry of the tale might do precisely that. The hero of the tale might attain knowledge, might become the living emblem of man with knowledge, without sacrificing lyrical intensity that is ordinarily foreshortened in fiction.

In an especially canny but not unpredictable strategy, if one keeps in mind Warren's long-standing habit of binding poems into thematic sequences, Warren has constructed the individual poems of *Or Else* as reflectors, baffles, mirrors, and back-lights. In addition he has introduced what he calls "Interjections" whose function is to counter the theme, tone, and meaning of the twenty-four titled poems. They are the interjections of a second voice into the unfolding tale of the primary consciousness. These poems—and they are not always poems to any real extent—tend to be terse rather than lyrical and tend to speak for the concept of man's continuity and glory rather than for his isolation and world-sickness. There is, however, an equally interesting feature to the formal construction of *Or Else*. Warren has brought forward from his *Selected Poems 1923–1966* seven poems he had originally printed in a sequence called "Notes on a Life to Be Lived" and he has dispersed these into the fabric of the poem called *Or Else*.

The seven poems imported from his earlier book allow Warren to create the dialectic with the newer poems of *Or Else*. More than any others in this book, these poems are sweet, lyrical, sonorous, and amorous. They are the voice of another poet. They are quite literally older in composition and publication, but are also older in their conformity to an older tradition of poetry. Warren places them in deliberate contradistinction to a newer voice, a contemporary mode whose accent is harsh, relentless, and interrogative. The poems from "Notes on a Life to Be Lived" are evocations of glistening moments when vision is sudden, epiphanic, and clear. They are romantic and rapturous. The twenty-one new poems are mostly dramatic, plotted, with a flattened and tortured sound. They are thematically more pessimistic and are less songs than poems influenced by prose. My comments are, however, impressionistic observations of tendencies, not absolutes. Nevertheless it is through the juxtaposition and oblique continuities of remarkably varied poems that the form of *Or Else* manages a vision of an individual existence which is dynamic, complex, and emblematic. Two poems will illustrate my meaning. The first, printed opposite the second, is taken from the seven old poems:

BLOW, WEST WIND

I know, I know—though the evidence
Is lost, and the last who might speak are dead.
Blow, west wind, blow, and the evidence, O,

Is lost, and wind shakes the cedar, and O,
I know how the kestrel hung over Wyoming,
Breast reddened in sunset, and O, the cedar

Shakes, and I know how cold
Was the sweat on my father's mouth, dead.
Blow, west wind, blow, shake the cedar, I know

How once I, a boy, crouching at creekside,
Watched, in the sunlight, a handful of water
Drip, drip, from my hand. The drops—they were bright!

But you believe nothing, with the evidence lost.

This poem seems almost entirely a skein of sound. From beginning to end he marshals that mournful O, rhyming it internally, at line's end, weaving it through stanzas until it becomes the wind itself. In that wind Warren locates all the lost: the speaker, the dead father, the haunting kestrel, and the death-shaken cedar. The poem is a construction of repetitions, even to the phrase that envelops the poem, yet so wonderfully liquid is the sound that we nearly fail to see that the poem's progression is by image association, not lyrical discourse. We are told no one can speak, then all those images speak eloquently, if enigmatically. Because we are carried in the poem's electric current we come, like the boy, to an amazement at the water's brightness when it falls away from us. Again, we nearly fail to see that this water is a communion with the father's sweat-laden mouth—and it is an image of continuous contamination. Had the poem ended with its penultimate stanza it would have been a beautifully credible implication of continuity between past and present. But Warren's dialectic requires doubts. The poem's abrupt shift of voice in the last line reveals those doubts.

The concluding line forces us back to ask what evidence is lost, evidence of what, and what it is we might have believed that we do not now believe. It appears the evidence is of certain *knowing*. It appears we may not believe in the joy experienced by the child or the speaker's reaching of the father through the act of communion. Yet is not the poem an emblem of continuous joy, even as it is undercut by the guileless and debunking adult voice? This giving-withdrawing balance is carried forward by Warren's next poem, though the form now exactly reverses the process.

INTERJECTION #2: CAVEAT

Necessarily, we must think of the
world as continuous, for if it were
not so I would have told you, for I have
bled for this knowledge, and every man
is a sort of Jesus, but in any
case, if it were not so, you wouldn't know
you are in the world, or even that the
world exists at all—

but only, oh, on-
ly, in discontinuity, do we
know that we exist, or that, in the deepest sense, the existence of anything
signifies more than the fact that it is
continuous with the world.

A new high-
way is under construction. Crushed rock has
been spread for miles and rolled down. On Sunday,
when no one is there, go and stand on the
roadbed. It stretches before your eyes into distance. But fix your eyes firmly on
one fragment of crushed rock. Now it only

glows a little, inconspicuously
one might say. But soon, you will notice a
slight glittering. Then a marked vibration
sets in. You brush your hand across your eyes,
but, suddenly, the earth underfoot is
twitching. Then, remarkably, the bright sun
jerks like a spastic, and all things seem to
be spinning away from the univer-
sal center that the single fragment of
crushed rock has ineluctably become.

At this point, while there is still time and will,
I advise you to detach your gaze from
that fragment of rock. Not all witnesses
of the phenomenon survive unchanged
the moment when, at last, the object screams

in an ecstacy of

being.

Whereas everything about "Blow, West Wind" had seemed the mark of sweet poetry, almost nothing about "Caveat" does. The first poem is an example of purity and the second of impurity. Yet the former leaves us deflated and the latter leaves us buoyant. Instead of the communion of water we have come to an epiphany of rock. Indeed, Warren has composed "Caveat" not as a lyric but as a quasi-syllogistic pronouncement. We must, his thesis tells us, regard the world and man as continuous. His evidence now is the testimony of faith and, he informs us, it is reliable because he has suffered to gain it. We know that a man in the world must suffer; if he does not suffer he is not in the world—or he does not know he is, which is the same thing. To suffer is to be betrayed. It is also to be responsible, hence capable of magnificence. Yet this, Warren admits, is not the whole truth. Paradoxically we have to experience separation to discover what we are and what the other is. Only in discontinuity discovered is it possible to conceive of union, which is knowledge.

An argument demands truth. Warren shifts to something like a hypothesis and fact: a highway is under construction. It is the Christian Sunday. Warren advises us to go and stand on the gravel roadbed, not to stare at the distance but to stare at the gravel fragments. Doing so, he asserts, we will experience a disorienting vision of luminous beauty. This will be dangerous because it will change us. In this Wordsworthian spot of time we, too, may scream in "an ecstacy of / being." The further danger Warren leaves unsaid. The road is going to be blacktopped soon and the evidence lost. If we do not soon come to this vision we shall come only to a road and distance, a wandering.

"Caveat" and "Blow, West Wind" exist in a dialectical configuration but they arrive at the same place, as *Or Else* arrives at its vision of continuity through rhetorical juxtapositions. In poem after poem *Or Else* chronicles the lost, the dead, the abandoned, and yet we recall that in one of his earliest poems, "Revelation," Warren wrote, "In separateness only does love learn definition." And in "Original Sin: A Short Story" he had said, "Oh, nothing is lost, ever lost!" In order to accommodate continuously that which is only apparently lost, he has now created a form of such multiple and interconnected perspectives that it has had to take on the shape, however ghostly, of the completed story: the tale. The end of the tale, that sifting and organizing of memory's images toward emblematic vision, will be the primal scream of joy. At the conclusion of "I Am Dreaming of a White Christmas: The Natural History of a Vision," which is the exemplar of *Or Else,* Warren steps boldly out of his role as tale-teller and speaks to his reader:

> All items listed above belong in the world
> In which all things are continuous,
> And are parts of the original dream which
> I am now trying to discover the logic of. This
> Is the process whereby pain of the past in its pastness
> May be converted into the future tense
>
> of joy.

In this long and associative poem Warren dreams he has returned to the house of his parents, both long dead, and he stands first at the procreative bed. He turns then to rooms lying in desiccation and describes, while he looks at old furniture, his mother and father. He sees the remains of a Christmas tree, some package wrappings, and is surprised by how real all is: "The holly / Is, clearly, fresh." In section 9, stilled to the point of breathlessness by the dream that has carried him into the living past, Warren abruptly shifts the scene, the time, and juxtaposes himself and a brutally mad woman to the eerie calm of the world of the dead:

> Where I was,
>
> Am not. Now am
> Where the blunt crowd thrusts, nudges, jerks, jostles,
> And the eye is inimical. Then,
> Of a sudden know:

Times Square, the season
Late summer and the hour sunset, with fumes
In throat and smog-glitter at sky-height, where
A jet, silver and ectoplasmic, spooks through
The sustaining light, which
Is yellow as acid. Sweat,
Cold in arm-pit, slides down flesh.

The flesh is mine.

What year it is, I can't, for the life of me,
Guess, but know that,
Far off, south-eastward, in Bellevue,
In a bare room with windows barred, a woman,
Supine on an iron cot, legs spread, each ankle
Shackled to the cot-frame,
Screams.

She keeps on screaming because it is sunset.

Her hair has been hacked short.

Even this inhabitant of Baudelaire's unreal city seems, according to Warren's poem, to belong to that dream whereby the past may be redeemed into a future of joy. Now Warren spatially suspends himself in no-time with a prisoner of illusions. The woman is sick. Everything, even the air, is sick. She screams, apparently, because she faces the darkness following sunset. Or is her scream an "ecstacy of / being"? We cannot know.

Section 10 of the poem extends this portrait of the unreal city to include those going home from work with "some hope" and old men exiting pornographic theaters. Then Warren shows us a mounted policeman who is "some kind of dago" and describes him as being "as beautiful as a law of chemistry." He is given beauty because he is a man, however, not because a law of chemistry is beautiful. Warren had flirted with Naturalism in his early poetry but there are no people possessed of beauty in that ideology and there is precious little hope. Naturalism did not explain away evil and it did not explain why "between the event and the word, golden / The sunflight falls." Naturalism did not demand or value responsibility and love and knowledge by which the human dream might be converted to the sustaining emblem of joy. But men did, especially in light of the fact that "every man / is a sort of Jesus" carrying in himself the tale of continuous hope and life. Warren's dream is the natural history of a vision at the center of which stand all those who face the dark recesses of the self where inchoate images whirl and wait for coherence. The tale of *Or Else,* that is to say, is the tale of man thinking and feeling himself toward the revelation of his destiny, which is the continuity of self with and the responsibility of the self for all others. As his own personality enlarges to include the evidence and contradictions of the "original dream" it becomes the form, the very dynamic personality of men.

There is, certainly, much more to be said about the operation and character of form in Warren's *Or Else.* I must hope, however, to be suggestive rather than exhaustive. In "Time as Hypnosis" Warren describes on snow "the single / Bright-frozen, red bead of a blood-drop" and makes it a profound symbol of one of the tales of time. There are many such tales subsumed in the man's life which is the emblem of *Or Else.* It is a book of notes not on a life lived, finally, but on a life yet to be lived. The unity of these notes as poems results not by adherence to verse conventions but through the active contours of the vital image which develops: a man in pursuit of human values and human schemes of being. When we feel ourselves in the presence of a life wired and illuminated so it reveals surface reality and the current that passes beyond what is merely finite observation, we are likely to feel what Warren calls "human heat." This is art's task. It is what Conrad meant when he said he wanted to show of life's fragments "its vibrations, its color, its form: and through movement, its form, and its color, reveal the substance of its truth—disclose its inspiring secret: the stress and passion within the core of each convincing moment."

Poetry exists only when such a form has come into being. With *Or Else* Warren has found a form capable of Conrad's hope. *Or Else* is the tale of a man in his passion, a man caught out of the surge of time, a man who simultaneously thinks and feels. In what other position could he understand and begin to express anything beyond himself? *Or Else* moves from one dusk to another and there is little in the human progress that it fails to touch; there is little that does not insist "You must reevaluate the whole question." We need to remember that a tale depends on the magical, mysterious, cloudy past to reveal its secrets. The tale imagines a basic continuity with the historical and the imagined past, continuity of sustaining values, manners, realities, and even truths. Warren's tale suggests we must find some way to reconnect with our continuity—or else. We must find some operative principle of joy—or else. This principle of joy, the essential resolution and form of the joy, is what we have to assert against the darkness of mind and heart that is upon the earth. Warren says it clearly in "Interjection #8: Or, Sometimes, Night":

The unsleeping principle of delight that
Declares the arc of the apple's rondure; of, equally,
A girl's thigh that, as she lies, lifts
And draws full forward in its subtly reversed curve from
Buttock bulge to the now softly closing under-knee nook; and of
The flushed dawn cumulus: the principle
That brackets, too, the breaker's crest in one
Timeless instant, glittering, between
Last upward erg and, suddenly,
Totter and boom; and that,
In a startling burst of steel-brilliant sun, makes
The lone snow-flake dance—
                                        this principle is what,
Intermittently at least and at unlikely moments,
Comes into my mind,
Whether by day or, sometimes, night.

This is the principle of beauty and passion that *is* form, the principle Warren applies when he asks at the conclusion of his finest poem, *Audubon,* for what any child wants. He says:

Tell me a story.

In this century, and moment, of mania,
Tell me a story.

Make it a story of great distances, and starlight.

The name of the story will be Time,
But you must not pronounce its name.

Tell me a story of deep delight.

Richard Hugo: Getting Right

■

I had been rereading Richard Hugo's poems during the 1979 World Series in which the all but trounced Pittsburgh Pirates made a stunning and memorable comeback to win going away. I remarked to a friend watching that last televised game that Hugo was the George Raft of poetry. I meant to imply that Hugo was a player of tough-guy roles. My friend, without blinking, said that Hugo was instead closer to the manager of the Pirates, or would be if he chewed. We were, I think, both right because Hugo as poet is the creator of scenes whose players are always constructed figures that speak with Hugo's unmistakable voice. Pressing this comparison of Hugo to a Pirate, however, I think less of that doughty manager than of the great Willie Stargell, whose face is a marvellously active and yet enigmatic mask upon which knowledge and emotion dance briefly and are gone. I can easily imagine a Baltimore pitcher trying to guess what in the world that man is thinking while everyone in the stands feels with absolute clarity what Stargell has in his mind: home run!

Stargell and his family of champion Pirates are iconoclasts of tradition. One feels they possess just enough barbarity to be exiles and mavericks, while they are just civilized enough to function in society even as they remind us that society's numbing rituals kill the spirit. Some of us would call them reluctantly adult with their devotion to a game, their nineteenth-century caps, their enthusiasm for Stargell-Stars. Some of us would point out how Pirates appear, on occasion, to play lethargically, as if winning were less important than keeping the game going. To be a professional athlete with style, skill, and desire is to participate in a traditional activity heavily ritualized and civilized. It is also, sui generis, to be regarded by society as a man who has yet to enter fully into the mature world of work. Such a man must be obsessive in his self-creation even as he becomes the exile he never wanted to be. Many athletes live not in the towns where they play, but where they grew up. They have been ousted from their hometowns, however, in spirit if not in the fact, by virtue of what they are and do. They can't really go home since home doesn't exist. Plato might very well have ousted the Pirates as well as the poets. All this is equally true of Richard Hugo and, like Willie Stargell, what he has constantly in mind is survival and getting home. I think there is hardly a better explanation of why his poems have touched so many of us so deeply.

Reading Richard Hugo's *Selected Poems* one discovers a poet of unusual continuity in vision and execution. There are the benchmarks of change and of some evolution, but he does not show the radical alterations of style or thought which mark his contemporaries such as, say, Adrienne Rich, Robert Bly, James Wright, or Donald Hall. Indeed, the poems he includes here reinforce the sense that Hugo was born to say one kind of poem and knew what it was from the start. This is slightly deceptive. Just as Hugo has always tempted readers to see him as an immediate confessional poet of self-degradation, his *Selected Poems* eliminates work that shows his struggle to create an art characterized by tense passion and tragic joy, an art of the durably made thing. He has, for example, cut nearly one hundred poems from his long out-of-print first three collections, *A Run of Jacks* (1961), *The Death of the Kapowsin Tavern* (1965), and *Good Luck in Cracked Italian* (1969). He has cut another eighty-seven poems from *The Lady in Kicking Horse Reservoir* (1973), *What Thou Lovest Well, Remains American* (1975), and *31 Letters and 13 Dreams* (1977), all of which are in print. I regret that so much of the early work, some of it admittedly weak, was sacrificed for reprinting later work, but that half of his accomplishment which remains is not distinctly different, it is only more clearly accessible.

All poets labor to make increasingly transparent and accurate what they have to say. We do not necessarily agree what this thrust toward clarity means, hence divergent responses to Merwin. Still, poets usually begin in overwriting and opacity. The best slowly win through to a special luminosity that has little to do with being either discursive or imagistic and do so at the point they have manipulated tradition to be adequate and sufficient to their purposes. More than many of his contemporaries, Hugo began and has remained in the middle ground of discourse and image, satisfied to work at being clear at the level of communication while increasing the vivid and resonant images he owns in the power of implication. Reduced to the most absurd distillation, Hugo writes in a private code of the single confrontation of a man with an inevitable fate: he must survive by finding a way home and he will always fail in his attempts. The most characteristically Hugo and, perhaps, the best poem in his first book illustrates what I mean. "1614 Boren," a street address, begins:

> Room on room, we poke debris for fun,
> chips of dolls, the union picnic flag,
> a valentine with a plump girl in a swing
> who never could grow body hair or old.

In what is typical strategy for him, Hugo has returned to the scene of a crime, the abandonment of vital life. In the next stanza, having seen a slick picture of a pastoral scene still hanging on the wall of this emptied house, he asks "What does the picture mean, hung where it is / in the best room?" He describes the conventional portrait of trees, house, vines, canals that hide "the world of harm behind the dormant hill." With no transition he jumps to the absent roomers, identifying them only as rooms 5 and 7, telling us how sordid their lives were, and noting they called this *place* and *house*. Home would be "a joke on the horizon— / bad proportions and the color of disease." Weaving by contrast this ruined address with the picture it yet keeps like a lost secret, Hugo concludes:

> But the picture, where? The Netherlands
> perhaps. There are Netherland canals.
> But are they bleached by sky, or scorched
> pale grey by an invader's guns?
> It can't exist. It's just a sketcher's whim.
> The world has poison and the world has sperm
> and water looks like water, not like milk
> or a cotton highway. There's a chance
> a man who sweated years in a stale room,
> probably one upstairs, left the picture here
> on purpose, and when he moved believed
> that was the place he was really moving from.

That picture of the Netherlands is a calendar cliché and we all know it, but Hugo means for us to see also that it is the netherland of dream as equally phony as the girl who never grows body hair, or grows ugly. But Hugo, if he has brought us back to the debris that, realistically, all homes become, has no intention of abandoning dream. He believes that dream is the right way to vision, and images of spiritual vision (and blindness) proliferate from beginning to end of the *Selected Poems*. Therefore whoever left the illusion of what home might be has also taken it with him. The netherworld can't exist and yet it does.

"1614 Boren" reveals a great deal more of what is essential to Richard Hugo. We see first, perhaps, that it is a landscape poem in which historical and natural forces operate. The poem is spoken by an objective, observing voice; no "I" or "we," as victim, enters this poem. Yet objects are arranged with telling absences to achieve a clear emotional relationship which in the end generates and earns something like discursive wisdom. Hugo takes the scene and place as a text to be teased toward extrapolation of larger truths. In many of his poems he tells us to "Remember." When he does not say it, he means it, for by his poems he sanctifies and resurrects life. In consequence, his tone is typically somber and on occasion turns preacherly. In fact, this poem is a kind of guided tour through failure that is still wild with possibility and we note that the speaker appears to move intimately here while the poem shows us that he is removed, controlled. Yet he is not unengaged. This speaker moving through the world of the degraded and the real is performing the hypothetical test that is the critical act of Richard Hugo's art. He intends quite simply to know, to see what is real and what is not, what remains and what degrades.

Richard Hugo, in spite of his reputation for pessimism and worse, is a relentless optimist whose examination of the symptoms of personal and communal disintegration has tended to disguise his search for permanent, healthy, and reliable values. He resists rather than cultivates despair and degradation. But he must know experientially, and must express, the full defeats of life if he is to do more than present false pictures of the Netherlands. For Hugo the imagination seems to be a transforming power to create and transfer to his readers a tragic sympathy which leads to joy and freedom. That freedom and joy is inevitably equated with home and home's various trial landscapes. In his search for home there is always a dialectic of voices: one speaker is the squint-eyed realist our grandmothers praised for having feet on the ground, the concluding voice of "1614 Boren"; the other voice is the dreamer to whom all remains mysterious, unknown, alive, and expressive of secret vitality. In effect, it is the dreamer who cannot leave the picture of the Netherlands. Hugo refuses ever to resolve this dialectic and thus he presents us with no clear answers that may be gleaned from the *Selected Poems*, but rather takes the role of both voices in dramatic contention through poem after poem. It will seem heretic to some, but I think that Hugo is not, finally, a narrative poet but a philosophic (and imagistic) poet whose debates are those of the contemporary American spirit, debates primarily of hypothesis and question. Another poem of landscape, this time from the second collection, *The Death of the Kapowsin Tavern,* will suggest what I mean.

PORT TOWNSEND

On cliffs above the town, high homes disdain
what is not Victorian below
but Indian or cruel. A plaque declares
a chapel older than the town.
(Many worship God before they're born.)
The Keystone ferry sails without a car,
a passenger, not even trailing gulls.
The pulp mill shoots bad odor at the sun.

Arriving here is feeling some old love—
half a memory—a silly dream of how
a war would end, a world would settle down
with time for hair to gray before you die.
The other half of memory is sight.
The cliffs will hold another thousand years.
The town is rotting every Sunday night.

A novel fakes a start in every bar,
gives way to gin and talk. The talk gives way
to memories of elk, and elk were never here.
Freighters never give this town a second look.
The dead are buried as an afterthought
and when the tide comes glittering with smelt
the grebes have gone to look for meaty ports.

Another way of naming Hugo's great theme is to speak of dispossession. Here everything seems kicked out, cut off, harried away. Notice how the poem *feels* like something has been happening. But where is the beginning middle end sequence of events? Because of his peculiar intensity of language and the way he fills his lines with vivid imagery, we sense narrative progression when we are in fact in the presence of spatial description. "Port Townsend" is another landscape suggesting the presence of civilization (read failure) and the wilderness, and a presence of each in contention. Hugo's poems are perhaps best seen as Bosch-like panoramas which he composes out of compressed narrative statements. For example, "high homes disdain" means nothing literally but that in this visual perception some homes are above others and their obvious expense can be seen. But Hugo implicates a social ordering that feels continuous. Below these homes are the homes of everyone else: "Indian or cruel." *Indian* particularly invites into the poem the entire history of western treatment of native Americans, the original homeless among us. Notice that having invoked the image of housing to suggest divided societies and practices, Hugo does not extend or amplify that image but jumps to another, the historical plaque, and then to a discursive comment in the form of a black joke. Immediately, then, he shifts our eyes to a ferry, to the absence of the usual foraging gulls, and then to a polluting mill. There is no event, only a viewing. The second stanza is analytical, not progressive. The final stanza is speculative and symbolically exemplary. This is "every bar" and we are not in any one of them where the silence is hard to break and when, once broken, the talk is of what exists only elsewhere. The poem concludes with an image of natural process which is itself an absence: the grebes which feed on decay and garbage are also missing in this scene. This is a portrait of home as it really is, the emptiness of emotional dispossession. Such a landscape remains Hugo's primary ground through all of his poems, but let me leave this momentarily and note how "Port Townsend" is typical in other respects.

Hugo's poems have undergone only slight changes in style in the nearly thirty years the *Selected Poems* represents. His music has always been insistent and derived from Anglo-Saxon sonic practices. He loves a strongly stressed line, usually three to five stresses, whose density and intensity is always willing to risk overwhelming the ear. The quality of his sound is ordinarily determined by frequent alliteration, blunt monosyllabics, interior sound repetitions, jammed and nervy phrasings, and a syntax which alternates an extended weaving with a terse statement. He deploys images as if they were sequential flashbulbs, almost too quickly for absorption. Yet he surrounds these images with commentary that frames as well as shifts them for perception. And over the course of a book, he repeats and modulates his imagery until it becomes a coded language. His quirky placement of adjectives begins as apparent registration but usually alters to an ethical, moral, historical, or social observation. His lines function vertically, horizontally, and collectively to create description, pointing, and meaning. He has been said to write a boredom of iambics. Above all he operates stanzaically, as if by paragraphs, using stanzas for changes of perspective, voice, and subject. His stanzas balance the alternating long and short sentences which, with his fervent stresses, accomplish his jumpy and recognizable style. He does not trust very much the music of white space. He is, in words, and has always been a meat and potatoes man. "Port Townsend" shows each of these characteristics as clearly as any of his later, more well-known poems.

Having spoken of so much in Hugo that is typical, obsessive, characteristic, and, perhaps, predictable, I do not wish to leave the impression that I agree with a scattering of critics who find him a monotonous poet. Truly, he writes a lot and a lot of what he writes comes demandingly in the same cadence and with the same strategies. If he is a predictable poet it is well to remember that his subjects and his subthemes are also predictable: weather, oceans, rivers, stars, the evidence of failure and love and death, bars, drunks, the dead, and that dominant impossibility of getting home, a quest which begins in self-consideration as well as in definition of the visible world. For Hugo, this quest is the act of search and revelation and, though it helps to be aware of his strategic techniques, ultimately his interest is in revealing the truth more than in verbal acrobatics.

"Quest for a self is fundamental to poetry," Hugo writes in his collected prose, *The Triggering Town*. But one doesn't find a misplaced self like a favorite fishing rod. The self, like a poem, is a created and then discovered organism of values, definitions, attitudes, and gestures. Donald Hall says that landscape is important to our poems because it represents the place and time when we felt connected, reinforced, and freed in the world. But the contemporary, fluid self is apt to be removed from that communal definition. Values and objects alike float in disregard. But Hugo holds to those old values suggested by a homelife and is compelled, as an exile, to ask: what matters? what is reliable? what endures? what do I really feel? I have said that his poems are hypothetical tests, spatial descriptions, not narratives; yet in the aggregate the poems tell the singular story of the self seeking its nature, its convictions, its reality. This is the zigzagging search for home, a home which at times appears to be the wilderness of Nature, at times the society of bars, at times the sleepy afternoons of remote towns in the West. No matter what his announced subject in a poem, it is only a triggering subject for this self-search which might reveal the true home. That is, Hugo's search for the self is the ancient quest for identity in the face of ever-assertive anonymity.

For Richard Hugo, the quest for self and the quest for home are virtually synonymous and are the act of survival that is as necessary as it is temporary. If it were possible to draw a paradigmatic figure for his poems, such a figure would show an oscillating process of men who find themselves in places that ought to have provided support for the struggling human spirit and did not. The men themselves vary according to the roles Hugo assigns them, being clowns, drunks, fishermen, lovers, madmen, travelers, etc., but they are all the self dispossessed. They waken as from a hallucinatory sleep and observe a landscape that is suddenly as readable as a sacred text. Often they feel they have come near home and sometimes believe they have reached it. Inevitably they are disabused and sent back to memory and dream where the journey, and the self-creation, must begin once more. Hugo has developed for this experience a poem which requires an energetic and nominational progression of statements which will be altered, questioned, negated, and restated within a single poem until that construction feels complete and unified. In his first two collections the makers of these statements are usually to be found beside western American rivers, in bars, or at the site of decaying towns. In the third collection, *Good Luck in Cracked Italian,* the speaker is a more autobiographical Hugo, an ex-World War II bombardier who has returned to the Italy he bombed and then occupied. In whatever disguise, as fisherman or comrade or traveler, the man at the center of Hugo's attention continues to observe, to state, to seek his way home, as he does in stanza two of "Montesano Revisited":

> You never find the road. You pass the cemetery,
> military, British, World War Two and huge.
> Maybe your car will die and the garage
> you go to will be out of parts. The hotel
> you have to stay in may have postcard shots,
> deep focus stuff, of graves close up
> and far off, just as clear, the bright town
> that is someone's grave. Towns are bad things happening,
> a spear elected mayor, a whip ordained.
> You know in that town there's a beautiful girl
> you'd rescue if your horse could run.

"You weave home to homes you'll never own," Hugo says in "Cantina Iannini." The search is more intense and obvious in this collection than ever before and with his vigorous and hypothetical statements Hugo replays more intensely than ever the scenes of harm and abuse out of which the self is continuously forming. In an interview in the *Ohio Review,* he said: "The poem is always in your home town but you have a better chance of finding it in another. . . . In a way, all towns you look at are your home town." And in what may be seen as a blueprint for all his work, "Assumptions" from *The Triggering Town,* he says "I am an eleven-year-old orphan." It is more than a casual remark, for it suggests the stunted growth that follows from division from the self's source of growth and maturity. All the towns of Italy that Hugo visits and all the wonderfully obsessive places of his poems—Klallock, Kapowsin, Tahola, Maratea, Missoula, Silver Star, Philipsburg, Ten Sleep, Wisdom—are stages upon which Hugo plays out his dual quest. They are not intrinsically important to the particular poem he writes but rather are stations on the map of his progress, a progress that is the spirit's as much as it is in any poet of our time. Indeed, Hugo is fascinated with maps and they recur throughout his work because they spatialize what would otherwise have to be a linear and narrative progression. But his *home* does not lie on any map. It exists inside language alone, in poems, so that language itself becomes not merely the referent of what is real but the literal container and shaper of what is real. To invite all those places into the poem is, therefore, to give them a chance to live, to exercise their values once more in the life of the speaker. This in turn allows the speaker to test his evolving self. In *The Triggering Town,* Hugo writes, "To feel that you are a wrong thing in a right world should lead a poet to be highly self-critical in the act of writing." Of course he means poets ought to feel humility. But he also means that the opposition of communal values and the self's values may lead to home and all that that means. It may lead to a proper vision. It is worth remarking here that this attitude separates Hugo from many of his comtemporaries. For them the world is usually wrong, while Hugo imagines himself wrong and the world the victim of his transgressions. Indeed, the underlying conviction of Hugo's vision is that home, which waits only in the imagination, cannot be reached precisely because men continue to violate the spirit. That is, they do not relive to the point of understanding and even forgiveness the acts and moments of their dispossession. But this is exactly what Hugo does in his best single volume, *The Lady in Kicking Horse Reservoir,* as the following stanza from "Montgomery Hollow" indicates:

> Birds here should have names so hard to say
> you name them over. They finally found
> the farmer hanging near the stream.
> Only insect hum today and the purple odor
> of thyme. You'd bet your throat against
> the way a mind goes bad. You conquer loss
> by going to the place it happened
> and replaying it, saying the name
> of the face in the open casket right.

It is that journey to the place which Hugo believes might allow a wrong self the chance of getting right that his characters continually undertake. Such figures are, reductively, the haves and have-nots. They form a rough society of the beautiful, the rich, the blonde, the sexy on one hand and the ugly, the poor, the lonely, the frustrated on the other. Hugo's women tend to be extremes of happy mothers or girls gone mad. His men tend to be domineering officials (mayors, cops, etc.) or Hemingwayesque survivors. But though he portrays a society of belongers and outsiders, the only finally safe and sanctified characters are those who possess vision and courage. He frequently causes such men to be fishermen, and he is not unaware of the fisherman's traditional role as a quasi-religious art figure, a visionary. In "Plunking the Skagit," from his first collection, he says of them:

> These men are never cold. Their faces
> burn with winter and their eyes
> are hot. They see, across the flat,
> the black day coming for them
> and the black sea. Good wind
> mixes with the bourbon in their bones.

These are survivors. They gather in bars and cantinas within the fellowship of shared vision and frontier virtues: courage, loyalty, self-reliance, tolerance, affection—what one expects from home. Bars become, as in "The Death of the Kapowsin Tavern," recognizably home as well as "the temple and our sanctuary."

But getting right, for Richard Hugo, is not, as it may seem, merely a matter of cultivating a romantic reentry into the companionship of bars or even the solidarity with Nature which seems so much a part of his vision. One cannot fail to see that in the end the picture he hangs on the wall is not a pastoral ideal at all. If towns represent one kind of dispossession and anonymity, Nature is an even more implaccable anonymity and it is alien to man. In *The Triggering Town* Hugo writes: "I've found anonymity to be wonderfully seductive. Something pulls some of us back from that tempting disappearance." That something is art. Those who pull back most are those who achieve vision, who learn to value the mysteries of existence, what Hugo calls the "unknowns." Hugo's art, again, requires his spatial depiction of dense reality in order to suggest rather than consecutively follow the journey of the self away from anonymity and toward a substantial existence. Hugo wants to depict the life of the spirit not in mystical phrases and leaps but in the most realistic terms he can manage, a spiritual realism very like that of a Bosch or Brueghel.

It is this spiritual realism which causes Hugo to construct a coded vocabulary. If his tones are usually mournful and celebratory, his words are verbs and nouns jammed together with emotional weight and telescopic accuracy. Who describes death better than Hugo, saying "the long starch of his side begins"? Again, in *The Triggering Town,* Hugo speaks of his intention: "You are after those words you can own and ways of putting them in phrases and lines that are yours by right of obsessive musical deed. . . . Your words used your way will generate your meanings. . . . Your way of writing locates, even creates, your inner life." He believes that language is indivisible and organic, that the vitality of life depends literally on the power of words to re-new, re-view, and re-say what would otherwise invisibly degenerate, decay, and disappear into anonymity. Readers of Hugo's poems well know his symbolic code of colors, of dominant grays, the continuous use of wind and cold and north to suggest the forces of dissolution and death, the vitality and deception implied by beautiful waters and grasses and trees, the chilling evidence of minimal survival portrayed in abandoned buildings, rotting farm implements, polluted rivers, girls turned to barking dogs. All these, used repeatedly, form the vocabulary of what he calls "the world / of black dazzle" which only the essentially wild, essentially visionary self can heroically resist. Or, it may be, understand passionately enough to express in poems we must learn to read not as discrete successes or failures but as the long and continuous reading of the landscape of the spirit which is the great accomplishment of this *Selected Poems.* This is the act, as Hugo describes it in *The Triggering Town,* of "receiving, responding, converting and appropriating," an act of scavenging, reviving, of holding on, sticking, using the world, of surviving. He reminds us in his poems that though we are in harm's way if we are alive it is nevertheless our glory and our responsibility to live according to the values that most enhance each other's being. That is to say, Hugo returns us to man's ancient dream of the free and vital self in a home community of selves. That is precisely the point of that abandoned picture in "1614 Boren," just as it is the paradox at the heart of the American experiment in nationhood.

Hugo is a particularly American poet in his insistence on the independent self's survival and the need of a home community for self's definitions. Perhaps it is clear by now that I think we most understand his art by viewing him as a player of roles, not as a self-revealing *misérable.* His exaggeration of himself as the most offensive social outlaw proceeds from his need to dramatize the deeply fundamental American dream (and paradox) of individuality and communal identity. He testifies to what Americans have believed to be humanly decent and permanent as well as to what we break by ineptness, ignorance, greed, and malice. He has the spirit of Melville and Warren in telling us how dark a thing man is. His poems depend upon his own hard self-accusations: he drinks too much, he wastes himself, he lacks courage, he is fat, ugly, uneducated, unsophisticated, inferior, an orphan. Who among us isn't all that? Who isn't a wrong thing in a right place? And who doesn't carry imagination's dream of getting right, that particular fervor of our national mission? Here is what Hugo says of his art of the self in "Galleria Umberto I":

There's no metaphor for pain, despair.
It's just there. You live with it, if lucky
in a poem, or try to see it, how it was
under this dome roof with children dead,
the stench of death blown at you
off a sea we should have asked for wisdom
by a wind we still should beg for tears.
In all our years, we come to only this:
capacity to harm, to starve, to claim
I'm not myself. I didn't do these things.

But Hugo's real genius forces him to say, "I did lots of things and I'm myself / to live with, bad as any German." So are we all. And that is why Hugo says, "An act of imagination is an act of self-acceptance."

I suppose that some readers will take it odd that I have not made here my list of the best and worst poems in Richard Hugo's *Selected Poems.* Well, the mountains are there from "1614 Boren" to "Degrees of Gray at Philipsburg" to "Missoula Softball Tournament." Many favorites are eliminated, left for an inevitable collected poems. I think, too, that it ought to be said that Hugo has two additional collections waiting for publication. There is little point to making lists around a poet I imagine to be as important and substantial as Richard Hugo.

And if my way of looking at Hugo's poems seems odd, it will appear outrageous to claim that he is a tragic poet in the manner of Yeats, yet I think his poems derive their resonance from the irresolvable confrontation of dream and fact whose dramatic embodiment in strongly musical language releases the human spirit to joy. Though his hobnailed lines throb through the gray towns of despair, Hugo is neither cynical nor pessimistic, nor even solipsistic. If there is any lingering connection with his teacher Roethke, it is that insistent search for joy in the revelations of the least things in this world, for he knows that only there do the truths remain and only the true poet can draw forth those small songs of enduring vitality. In spite of all his protestations of fear, inadequacy, and degradation, Richard Hugo does not and will not shrink from the risk of being thought a sentimental fool. For him the poem is neither a sigh for silence nor a crafty toy, but the necessary exploration of simple and inexhaustible love that is freedom. As he puts it in "Letter to Matthews from Barton Street Flats":

And we return to the field of first games where,
when we find it again, we look hard for the broken toy,
the rock we call home plate, evidence to support our claim
our lives really happened.

The tragic poet of joy is a paradox but not an impossibility. In the debris and folly of human history imagination finds that picture of hope on the wall of "1614 Boren" because it put it there, because imagination and song are the homes which sanctify those virtues without which we are less than men. Hugo conquers loss by finding in the world the continuing evidence of love, beauty, courage, fidelity, forgiveness, and passion. He helps us to know and possess our lives. In "Montgomery Hollow" he writes:

> To know a road you own it, every bend
> and pebble and the weeds along it,
> dust that itches when the August hayrake
> rambles home. You own the home.

Those who watched the Pittsburgh Pirates survive to take the 1979 World Series know the will, determination, and style personified by windmilling Willie Stargell. Richard Hugo is that kind of man and poet. Over seven years ago I drove 163 miles to hear him read his poems before a large audience. Afterward he asked for questions and a young woman, her voice breaking, asked, "Mr. Hugo, what do you think of yourself?" I thought Lord, he won't, he can't answer that. For more than an hour he tried, just as he has tried to say what he thinks in thirty years of poems, a poetry that is as bear-blunt and shufflingly endearing as he was that day. Mostly, he said, he thought of himself as a carrier of hope. In *The Triggering Town* he writes: "Hope for what? I don't know. Maybe hope that humanity will always survive civilization." Civilization, many of us are always saying, is what we lack. Hugo knows better, knows that this is the anonymity which buries the fierce individual, and knows that the poet does not speak to crowds but to the single beleaguered spirit. This is the speech of survival that is like a drumbeat.

I met Richard Hugo after that reading. He was not, as I expected, mobbed by adoring fans. My wife and I alone accompanied him to his motel room. We did not talk of great issues or great poets. Instead we watched a World Series game punctuated by his running chatter and wisecracks. Here was a man of uncommon humor and passion, a man who ate a half-gallon of ice cream as if the child in him, the orphan, had always been denied that pleasure. Coming to see him, I had felt like a wrong thing in a right world, a feeling that none of us are ever quite without. He joked to make me feel right. He said, "You drove 163 miles for me? I wouldn't go that far for Yeats." He has been going farther than that for all of us and his *Selected Poems* is the map of his passage. Any reader who cares about poetry will do what is necessary to get Hugo's *Selected Poems* and his *Triggering Town,* books which tell us, "Storms are spotted far enough / to plan going home and home has fire."

The Man from White Center

■

Richard Hugo, widely considered the preeminent poet of western America, proclaimed "those words you can own . . . by right of obsessive musical deed" (*The Triggering Town*). His subject was the American orphan, himself, refracted by scenes, people, weather, objects, and creatures. Reading him is like browsing through secondhand shops with Wallace Stevens and Ernest Hemingway, chanting the mute histories of each cracked mirror and dented spittoon. Hugo felt and voiced the unprivileged, inarticulate world. His poems, although they are rarely outright narratives, tell the tale of the American search for identity and knowledge from the underbelly. One might say of him what he wrote about President Kennedy: "He was not afraid of what we are." His is sometimes clunky, plodding poetry, but his collected work is a surprising, remarkable song of courage that penetrates inner landscapes. In *Making Certain It Goes On: The Collected Poems of Richard Hugo*—a welcome, stubby, wandering, and final collection—Richard Hugo, like Thoreau, earned the right to look any man in the face.

To Hugo poetry wasn't ethical or moral commentary in lines, but every poem was an instruction. To him the poem was life's harsh music learned in the school of hard knocks. He saw man as cruel, hurt and hurting, incapable of much improvement, and ill-prepared for the little wisdom he can cull from the elements that doom him to the loss and oblivion Hugo called "north." He said it plainly in the early poem "Duwamish No. 2":

> When the world hurts, I come back alone
> along the river, certain the salt

of vague eyes makes me ready for the sea.
And the river says: you're not unique—
learn now there is one direction only—
north, and, though terror to believe,
quickly found by river and never love.

Against this implacable condition, Hugo set himself to witness what mattered—the struggle to survive with intense feeling, pell-mell energy, utter and immediate honesty. He tried to put that survival in every poem, believing

You conquer loss
by going to the place it happened
and replaying it.

He went continuously home—to all the American homes, as he would have said, we had and never had.

Fatherless and abandoned by his teenage mother, Hugo was raised by elderly, severe grandparents in White Center, Washington, then a semirural, poor suburb of Seattle. Enforced churchgoing left him feeling he owed something, spiritually dunned all his life. Shy, awkward, and isolated, he believed himself not only the cause of his ill fortunes but also unregenerately weak, worthless, and ever "a wrong thing in a right world." He grew up admiring local toughs for their violent courage. He extended this admiration later to sardonic movie stars, detective heroes, and British Royal Air Force flyers, who seemed to have a stylish, right manhood. He feared, hated, and coveted girls and compensated by making himself a skilled baseball player, fisherman, and dreamer. His tutelary spirits appeared early and never abandoned him—waters, sky, hills, ocean, fish, birds, and drunks. All meant unimpeachable and continuous acceptance, private dignity, and sweet, if unrecognized, belonging.

He had been writing poetry nearly forty years before he named his home directly in "White Center" with an address to his dead grandmother whom he loved:

It all comes back but in bites. I am the man
you beat to perversion. That was the drugstore MacCameron
flipped out in early one morning, waltzing
on his soda fountain. The siren married his shrieking.
His wife said, "We'll try again, in Des Moines."

And the people of White Center?—"Men cracking up or retreating. / Resolute women deep in hard prayer." Like MacCameron's wife, Hugo determined to split.

He got out to become a twenty-one-year-old bombardier stationed in Italy in 1944. He became the hero he had dreamed, but the tough life was catatonic fear and boredom punctuated by hellish missions, crashes, the death and madness of comrades, and the oblivion of booze. Twenty years later he would go back and write the poems in the volume *Good Luck in Cracked Italian* which said:

> Home's always been a long way from a friend.
> I mix things up, the town, the wind, the war.
> I can't explain the drone. Bombers seemed
> to scream toward the target, on the let-down
> hum. My memory is weak from bombs.
> Say I dropped them bad with shaking sight.
> Call me German and my enemy the air.

Back in Seattle after the war, Hugo took two degrees from the University of Washington and worked for the Boeing Aircraft Company where he was repelled by the suppression of feeling in his colleagues. He also studied with Theodore Roethke and learned how to let his own secrets cry aloud. He was reinforced by the presence in the city of other poets—David Wagoner, James Wright, Carolyn Kizer, Kenneth O. Hanson, and others. He married. At forty, he quit his job and lived for a year in Italy. He returned to teach at the University of Montana. He was divorced. For years he lived a deep shame, drowning it in small-town bars like the one in Dixon about which he wrote, that let him write, "Home. Home. I knew it entering" and "Five bourbons / and I'm in some other home." Or he'd climb into his convertible and go hard for delight:

> The day is a woman who loves you. Open.
> Deer drink close to the road and magpies
> spray from your car. Miles from any town
> your radio comes in strong, unlikely
> Mozart from Belgrade, rock and roll
> from Butte. Whatever the next number,
> you want to hear it. Never has your Buick
> found this forward a gear.

John Updike's Rabbit would have understood Hugo's running, and his American Buick. He was on the road for home. Lord, how he looked! I can think of no poet whose verbal and emotional odometer laid on so many miles. His finest individual books, *The Lady in Kicking Horse Reservoir* (1973) and *What Thou Lovest Well Remains American* (1975) are psychic maps that end in the secret, splendid places we now call "Hugo's." He took us to Silver Star, Wisdom, Ovando, Ten Sleep,

Camas, and Bearpaw. He rested at waters named Kicking Horse, Pishkin, Sweathouse, Napi, Lone Lake, Taholah, and Drummond. In *The Triggering Town* (1979), a collection of his prose essays, he wrote: "Take someone you emotionally trust, a friend or lover, to a town you like the looks of but know little about, and show your companion around the town in the poem. . . . You know where you are and that is a source of stability."

He was looking for what he called the "knowns" and, as if his readers were his companions, he was our guide to the permanent, passionate, not yet completely civilized, not entirely homogenized life where we might confront and survive degradation, shame, and deterioration. Whether it was a bar, grassy bank, or a night softball field, he ran to a place of communion where one might be abused, hated, or loved, but not ignored or anonymous. There one could wail, know names, dance, maybe find women, at least find music and howl back at "weather, that lone surviving god." He took us to see the cruelty, rage, oppression, and debris of a town and spirit in "Degrees of Gray in Philipsburg." Here all defeats seemed fused in that "ancient kiss / still burning out your eyes" and the world loomed so bad that death appeared seductive in the guise of a lifelong prisoner. Hugo wasn't running toward that. He was running for his life. "You tell him no. You're talking to yourself. / The car that brought you here still runs."

He found his aggressive ring-tailed roaring voice early and never abandoned its drumming iambics or his stark and alliterative sentences that account for so many unusually memorable, epigrammatic lines, such as "We were renegade when God had gills." And he favored quick cinematic cuts, quirkily placed adjectives, and stanzas that function like chapters in fiction. His fulcrum was the hypothesis: "Say your life broke down." He called his way of writing *style* and named its character "the adhesive force." This adhesive force, he wrote, "will be your way of writing." It was, in Ezra Pound's formula, "uncounterfeitable." Unlike most of his contemporaries, Hugo did not seriously alter it in successive books. His form was right for what he wanted—intensity, immediacy, and verbal velocity, the panoramic and the telescopic. He made the poem a state of mind and a force field. Yet he felt it wasn't enough.

In the poems in *31 Letters and 13 Dreams* (1977) he extended and relaxed his usual line and he admitted prose elements. It is impossible to convey in a review how much information, story, joke, gossip, vitality, and, often enough, sheer prattle the book carries. We learn about his wartime hip injury, his interest in civic referendums, his experience with whores, loneliness, barbers, offended bar owners who read about themselves in his poems in *The New Yorker,* and the final payment of his mortgage (due in 2001). He eats, drinks, fishes, cruises, and chatters about Isaac Bashevis Singer, Herbert Gold, Milton, Keats, Mr. Chips, C. C. Rider, and Perry Mason.

After that book appeared he asked me if I thought it was a mistake, recognizing, I think, that its slack structure, garrulous personality, and huge appetite were so at odds with the coolly corseted tastes of academics and their journals. Flattered that he asked, I nevertheless said it was a mistake. Now, when I read "Letter to Goldbarth from Big Fork" where he writes, "Dear Albert. This is a wholesome town. Really. Cherries grow / big here and all summer a charming theater puts on / worthy productions," and drones on like a state brochure hack, I think I was right. But I was wrong. It matters that a poet's work should create a large, unified, and resonant image of man. That is why poets have written the sequence poem. *31 Letters and 13 Dreams* is Hugo's version of John Berryman's *Dream Songs,* Robert Lowell's *History,* and William Carlos Williams's *Paterson.* If Hugo's music is more the honking and wheezing of a one-man band than we might wish, the image of a man bearing himself with relentless introspection, intelligence, courage, and withering good humor is one we haven't yet ceased to need.

Though he would never be a serene poet, his collected poems show Hugo turning toward a calm peace that would mark his best work in *White Center* (1980), *The Right Madness on Skye* (1980), and in the twenty-two new poems of *Making Certain It Goes On.* Perhaps he had merely loved the world hard enough and long enough to accept its worst. Perhaps it was growing recognition by a public which gave him no major prizes. Perhaps it was his marriage to Ripley Schemm, who loved him as, after all, he deserved. In "To Women" the man who put music in the north wind now could write of his adversary, "You start it all. You are lovely. / We look at you and we flow."

Among the new poems in the collected poems Hugo was still driving, looking, and naming. If we had not noticed before that his great gift was the elegy, we see it now in poems about Anthony Ostroff, Thomas Wolfe, Zen Hoffman, and the Confederate graves in Little Rock. Two of his best poems are here—"Salt Water Story" and "Here, but Unable to Answer," the only poem which unequivocally addressed and celebrated his father.

There is also one that ought to make granite weep. Long after they were young comrades, Hugo and James Wright fondly called each other Ed Bedford, after a surly tavern keeper they'd met when the Wrights and the Hugos had once vacationed together. Each could laugh at the Bedford in the other, and also love him. In "Last Words to James Wright" Hugo is flying to New York for a poetry reading, remembering his great friend whose courage in poetry and struggles with alcohol, depression, and cancer had been exemplary. Why should we not hope for a gray town and a clear river where the poets wait and speak with such honor as this poem confers upon us all? I like to think of James Wright, perhaps Roethke and others, watching with affection and dignity as Richard Hugo shuffles forward, unslouches, and reads through to the pain, the anger, the forgiveness, the unbreakable linkages of his poem's last stanza:

> Ed Bedford, you bastard, you died.
> What a chill. We circle the Statue of Liberty.
> I feel no liberty at all on the final approach.
> I feel a little drunk and a lot more empty,
> like passing through some unknown factory town
> knowing it must be home.
> Be glad of the green wall you climbed across one day.
> Be glad as me.
> I forgive you, Ed, even if I did swear never.
> What's a lie between Eds? What's one more dirty river?

Richard Hugo died in 1982. He did not doubt his poetry would go on. It will.

James Wright: That Halting, Stammering Movement

■

William Carlos Williams, the original "in the grain" American writer, was not a misguided provincial in his passion for a native language. He raged against Eliot's refusal to employ the sufficient and various strengths of American English because he believed the possibilities for an American poetry could not be achieved through an appropriated language. Williams believed in the poet who would "make it new" in spite of critics who would equate new with crude. James Wright is such a poet, especially in the final poems of *Collected Poems* and *Two Citizens.* Wright proposes for us the simple, though in practice still radical, idea that there is a language and a poetry adequate to express the pathetic yearning of our age—and a tenuous consolation based on moral values.

Wright's critics have been strident in their opposition to his newer poems. Gerritt Henry thrashed *Two Citizens* for a language that was "painfully plain and undistinguished" and then lumped Wright into a complaint against American poets who would play Huck Finn, saying: "Like so many 'in the grain' American writers (the book is prefaced with a passage from Hemingway), Wright is afraid to completely commit himself one way or the other, or to (what is taken to be) European high style and artificing."

The argument against an American poetry which posits the alternatives of an acceptable primitivism or a continuity of the sophisticated European is not new. Noah Webster, Emerson, Whitman, Williams, and others have confronted it. Whether it is better to write (if not to *be*) something other than American is both a political and artistic question which was reinforced by Vietnam and the violent sixties. Our best and worst poets turned away from militarism, homegrown impurity, and American language. We looked for answers not where Williams counseled, but in the poetries of Europe, South America, and Asia.

James Wright and Robert Bly were among the first poets of the contemporary generation to translate widely and then write a poetry influenced directly by translation. Obviously affected by the German, the French, the Spanish, the Russian, and the Chinese, both poets moved away from poetry as an artificial, nonconversational artifact and toward a poetry of lyrical speech characterized by naked epiphany and political engagement. If the poetry they created was not Eliotic English, neither was it Main Street American. It retained a goodly degree of European high style and artificing. The internationalizing effect on American poetry, difficult as that is to gauge, is widespread and positive. Yet it also enhances the superficial notion that the American language, if not the American, is inherently inferior. A great intelligence is never comfortable with superficiality and, in consequence, James Wright has turned back to a language "in the grain" whose one purpose is to cut through deadly mannerism. In "She's Awake" Wright says:

> It was easy.
> All I had to do was delete the words lonely and shadow,
> Dispose of the dactylic hexameters into amphibrachs.

That is, to cut through language which prevents recovery of what is loved, such as Emerson Buchanan, an uncle who is "one half-hendecasyllabic, / And almost an amphibrach." To fail to find that plain language, as Wright says in "Emerson Buchanan," means: "I try and try to hear them, and all I get / Is a blind dial tone."

Wright knows that his citizens, all of us, can scarcely help being citizens of the world as well as of our root-place. But vital poetry begins and ends at home. Americans are an openly affirming people who have believed in making realities of absolute ideals, dreamers whose despairs are exaggerated by such initial optimism. Wright insists that the most fundamental nature of poetry is its affirmation of *possibility*, exactly the root characteristic of the American dream. His new poetry is an aggressive reaching for and embracing of that possibility. In *Two Citizens* poems begin in the embrace of France, Italy, Yugoslavia, Bach, Dante, Horace, and Lu Yu, but translate themselves into American language relentlessly seeking transparency. Ironically, Gerritt Henry suggests an accurate figure for Wright: at mid-career he is achieving equipoise by balancing extremes in painfully plain language whose fidelity is to the old dream.

What many have thought sudden in Wright's new poetry is an evolution. His early work is well known for its polish and predictability. Hayden Carruth has written: "Wright's early poems recall exactly those years of the late 1940s, the time when we had an ideal music running in our minds." *The Green Wall* (1957) and *Saint Judas* (1959) remain admirable examples of what Ransom called music and verse texture. Yet, in retrospect, we can see embryonic forms of Wright's more innovative work: the flashing personal voice, the semisurreal imagery, the epiphany, the accruing myth of Christ-Everyman in the Hell of Ohio, and especially the plain idiomatic speech woven among tones of Frost, Eliot, and Edwin Arlington Robinson. This idiomatic speech dominates *Two Citizens* and is neither arbitrary nor revolutionary; it is a crafted language reflective of a people and a time suspicious of ideal musics and unwilling to yield to silence.

We badly understand Wright to take this language's blunt and garrulous simplicity as a lapse in poetic control or richness. Indeed it is a pendulum swing away from Modernist impersonality as well as those fifties' codes of decorum. It is language undressed, apparently, stripped of stylizations, forms, metric and sonic mannerisms, a language trying to be so transparently healthy that it appears to have skidded beyond poetry to bald statement and blatant proselytizing. I think, however, that Wright's effects are deliberate and that we must engage in cautionary *seems*. Wright is no less an artificer than he ever was. He tells us much when he says, frequently, that his master is Horace, a poetic innovator. Another master, one Wright rarely alludes to, is that angel of narrative, Charles Dickens, for whom the writer's task is to create literal worlds which both absorb and change a reader. Such masters insist that the *real* is attained only through the most realistic, the least artificial artifice.

It has often been said that Wright's middle books showed him breaking from his artificial early work, a partial truth. With *The Branch Will Not Break* (1963) he began to abandon English devices of the metaphysical. But a paradox, for example, is useful without Donne's clothing. It may be turned, as one turns a prism, until it provides contrast without logical rhetoric. Bly and the Chinese showed Wright this possibility. In the sixties Wright's poems became assertive, skeletal, exotic as they rejected his laboriously traditional voice. "Lying in a Hammock in William Duffy's Farm at Pine Island, Minnesota," a poem which catalogued a brilliant, peaceful landscape, ended with the controversial last line, "I have wasted my life." It was not artificial or unearned. It did not entirely abdicate the ideal music of paradox and tension created by a net of counterstraining ironies and logics. The poem is a skeletal paradox built on irony. The last line nails one argument against the poem's other argument, resulting in a blunt, factual effect possible only through high artifice.

Both artifice and statement, however, mean to convince. The difference is in the force employed. Any poem of faith and assertion is a paradox. Wright's use of paradox is not historically important except as it shows a recognition of complexity, which is truth, not available to flat statement. The truth, we say, is multiple and absolutes are at best relative. Paradox recognizes the contrary and irrefutable truths of opposites. It is one way to search for moral absolutes, but its use need not be limited to a poem's internal mechanics. There is also the paradox of poems set in polar opposition so that a book becomes a self-reflexive process, as *Two Citizens* is. Here "A Poem of Towers" is paired against "To You, Out There (Mars? Jupiter?)" in order to achieve a full respect for truth's complexity. The first poem is a positive, lyrical, intuitively achieved vision of a singing world at momentary unity. Wright says:

> and my love
> Leans on my shoulder precise
> As the flute notes
> Of the snow, with songs

and the poem's movement leaps. The second poem despairs of disconnection from God in plodding, rational, and sarcastic language. It imagines the same "nobility of dreams" though people are now

> Alone in the griped cold, hopelessly longing
> To pray to someone whose name
> Is Streisand.

This is a world of "pubes and inner arms" where "You will not find God." Both poems lean at absolutes but together approach the possibility of balance and complexity that is not emotional gush but the wage of intelligence. (It is beneficial to think of all of Wright's books in such a relationship.)

A third way to approach the possibility of truth is to realize a transparent language. That is impossible but skilled use of artifice may come close. For Wright, artifice is only as important as the end it serves and that end is the poem of equipoise where the truth may be held in the moment, the poem that is made possible only by the simultaneous employment of poetic equipment from the past and a language of immediate human vitality. In this regard I believe Wright may be approached, if not explained, through his connection with a poet more recent and less expected than Horace or Dickens or Robinson. In 1959 Wright reviewed Robert Penn Warren's remarkable *Promises* and wrote: "In effect [Warren] has chosen, not to write his good poems over again but to break down his own rules, to shatter his words and try again to recreate them, to fight through and beyond his own craftsmanship in order to revitalize his language at the sources of tenderness and horror." If words, unlike glass, may not be wholly reblown, it is still Wright's task to recreate language so long as it remains less than transparent, so long as artifice has not escaped artificiality.

While it is wrong to suggest that Wright has imitated Warren and of only marginal importance to worry over poetic influences, what Wright praises in Warren coincides in time and development with Wright's own interests. From the early sixties to the present no subject more concerns Wright than language, the way in which we know and experience reality. In "The Offense," one of the last poems in *Collected Poems,* he writes:

> Hell to me was a girl whose lonely body
> Needed me, somewhere, to be lonely with her.
> Hell to you was the difficult, the dazzling
>   Hendecasyllabic.

The insistence on Hell, that moral abstraction, as more than a linguistic trick lies at the heart of a poetry trying always to define reality with the force of revelation. Wright knows exactly what he wants and does not want to create:

> The kind of poetry I want to write is
>   The poetry of a grown man.
> The young poets of New York come to me with
> Their mangled figures of speech
> But they have little pity
> For the pure clear word.

By *Two Citizens* Wright's insistence on that clarity has created a language that is, to casual attention, stripped of poetic device. It is *apparently* nothing but the emotional effusion of one incapable of restraint.

Yet Wright's language is neither happy accident nor chaos come again. Language in the twentieth century is severely suspect. If it makes reality, it also distorts reality. Villanelles, sestinas, sonnets render atomic violence as remote artifacts. Burning Asian children are not contained in alexandrines. Of the Polish poet, Janos Pilinszky, Ted Hughes has written, "It has often been said that words, for his generation, were given an abnormal testing. Their experience screwed up the price of such terms as 'truth' and 'reality' and 'understanding' beyond what common language seems able to pay." All that language seems capable of doing is to state personal abjection for many who, like Pilinszky, would write, "I am alone, orphaned of everything." And everything is orphaned from everything. Hughes on Pilinszky might well be Hughes on Wright: "This loneliness is something more than a cosmic experience. It is a metaphysical state. It is intimately connected, in all Pilinszky's poetry, through sexual love, to the pathos of the created world, where trembling creatures still go uselessly through their motions, in a radiant emptiness. This loneliness is separated from the nearest other creature as the flesh is separated from any form of consolation. The real presence of that other creature, in fact, would be the presence of salvation." Wright's long-evolving myth of the exiled, wandering alien who is the human analogue of Christ is also Pilinszky's pathos and invokes the same suspicions of language. But Wright has gone beyond Pilinszky. His two citizens, James and Annie Wright, have recreated love, which is to say salvation or consolation. Annie Wright is both sexual and spiritual presence, a presence which requires of James Wright a new language to leap across the metaphysical loneliness and the radiant emptiness. Such a language must reaccommodate the absolutes priced out of poetry, must return poetry to a witnessing of the truth beyond pathos.

Language, for Wright as for Warren, will make only superficial poetry if it is disengaged. It must not stand between and frustrate a possible connection between poet and audience. Therefore, Wright works to stimulate a conversational idiom which is, nevertheless, an illusion of greatly shortened distance. It remains a system of organized symbols on a page, inert and closely manipulated, but with an identifiable human voice speaking urgently of urgent matters. As Dickens's had, Wright's language croons, curses, sings, whines, giggles, fawns, shouts, demands, coos, and drones. Such blatant wrenching of poetry grates on many ears in our age of monotoned lyrics and Wright considers that, too:

> If these lines get published, I will hear
> From some God damned deaf moron who knows
> Everything.
>
> "At the Grave"

But poetry as a parlor game, however skillful, will not suffice for Wright's intention, which is *a gathering* and *an embrace.* When language exists as poetry it is true, it witnesses and celebrates the right human condition, it affirms the nature of the Good. Language conceptualizes and expresses the Good, but it also mortifies and obscures and hides the Good. Language can be effective in evil ways. Such simple nouns as *nigger* or *dago* have an effect but the effect is usually dehumanizing and that is exactly what poetry opposes. An active poetry, therefore, may have to resort to wholesale recreation, including new words. Wright speaks of:

> my love and me wandering silent in the breeze
> Of a strange language, at home with each other.
> Saying nothing, listening
>
> To a new word for mountain, to a new
> Word for cathedral, to a new word for
> Cheese, to a word beyond words for
> Cathedrals and homes.
> "I Wish I May Never Hear of the United States Again"

Language, as Wright implies, is both home and cathedral, a way and a place of belonging, thus of possibility. And in possibility lies the dreamed moral life. Wright's chosen speech forces the reader to confront the lack of transparency in his own language and thereby, perhaps, to know again what *poetry* means. If Williams was correct about the validity of the American language in poetry, then Wright has more than willful self-authority behind his saying "The one tongue I can write in / Is my Ohioan."

But what exactly is the "Ohioan" in which Wright's poems are grounded? Here again the link with Robert Penn Warren is especially helpful. In the review-essay of *Promises,* that collection which marked Warren's own turn to a different poetry, Wright speaks with close attention and clear admiration about a dislocated syntax, an orchestral suspension of phrasing, a direct and earthy colloquial idiom, and a fuguelike weaving of formal and informal. After *Saint Judas* Wright began to evidence the same characteristics. In his criticism of *Promises,* Wright did not engage in citing "beautiful" lines and felicitous phrases; he was little concerned with metric patterns, choosing instead to examine the way in which Warren's language architecture supported a poetry of human truth. Wright admits quickly that Warren's language is eccentric and accepts it, thus rejecting the poem as seamless artifact. He concludes that *Promises* is written in the poetry of a grown man who cannot flinch from the contemporary paralysis of will and spirit nor yet live with it. What is important in Wright's judgments is the clear and early recognition that his language, like Warren's, belied his sense of reality. Warren had had to grapple with an eccentric speech to express his own frustration and in that speech Wright saw possibility. This is not to say that Wright grew out of Warren, only to suggest what Wright was approaching and revealing as he read Warren. The poetry of a grown man did not have to be the honed abstraction which participates in a kind of international drone.

It might, as it had for the Chinese, be a kind of powerful and direct statement, though such a statement would have to recognize the simultaneous beauty and horror which truth is. In Warren, Wright saw the possibility of a wrenched language which had accommodated the oppositions a grown man understands.

Wright wrote of *Promises,* "The poetic function of the distortion is to mediate between the two distinct modes of tenderness and horror." And this was an "extreme exaggeration of a very formal style." That is, it was high artifice pushing toward immediate reality. Wright, as well as Warren, had had his lessons in artifice from Ransom and his poetics were well steeped in Latinate composition. He had, therefore, full knowledge of where Warren's poetry had been and a clear sense of where it was going:

> I propose the hypothesis that one can hear in the poem two movements of language: a strong formal regularity, which can be identified with a little struggle, but which is driven so fiercely by the poet that one starts to hear beyond it the approach of an unpredictable and hence discomforting second movement, which can be identified as something chaotic, something very powerful but unorganized. It is the halting, stammering movement of an ordinarily articulate man who has been shocked. The order and chaos move side by side; and, as the poem proceeds, I get the feeling that each movement becomes a little stronger, and together they help to produce an echoing violence in the syntax. . . . It is the exaggerated formality with which a man faces and acknowledges the concrete and inescapable existence of an utterly innocent (and therefore utterly ruthless) reality which is quite capable not only of cursing him, but also of letting him linger contemplatively over the sound of his own bones breaking.

Wright's poetry, like Warren's, has become of necessity a halting, stammering movement whose function is to mediate between horror and tenderness, whose distortions and polarities represent an exaggerated formality that is quite simply trying to reawaken the reader's moral consciousness. His language is designed to display but, also, like a Virgilian guide, to go beyond the Sartrian nightmare of pathos. "Ohio Valley Swains," a poem of hideous cruelty, suggests the language and the figure of the poet hugely shocked. The poem begins "The granddaddy longlegs did twilight / And light." The speaker is fumbling backward in memory to recover an ugly scene where a girl is violated by local thugs and the speaker is sent helplessly away:

What are you doing here, boy,
In cherry lane?

Leave her alone. I love her.

But, the poet says, "They knocked me down." He is denied help at "That tent where the insane Jesus Jumpers / Spoke in their blind tongues" and the "railroad dick" responded to his plea by saying "you go on home, / And get out of this." Speaking in precise, almost hallucinatory fragments the poet works by immediate accretion. When he repeats "here comes Johnny Gumball" the effect is terror unmitigated by time and it is the present tense we notice in "Guido don't give a diddly damn."

What marks distortion in "Ohio Valley Swains" is the lack of clear time demarcation, the nightmare-memory, the savage irony, the direct address of the speaker to the rapists over time and distance, the immediacy of a long-concluded violence. The speech is brutal, blunt, filled with swearwords ("The bad bastards are fishing"), and so tautly truncated that narrative is remote. The girl is, in fact, never present. Having taken this tour of Hell, Wright does not become meditative but an angry defender of innocence with a language to match:

You thought that was funny, didn't you, to mock a girl?
I loved her only in my dreams,
But my dreams meant something
And so did she,
You son of a bitch,
And if I ever see you again, so help me in the sight of God,
I'll kill you.

Such language as Wright has come to employ is distorted, however, only in comparison to an expected poetic. It is not far from a poetry of common speech and, as such, it is vulnerable to glibness. Glibness is a form of sentimentality and sentimentality leads Wright to monotonous verbal tags such as *shadow, good, clear, lovely, secret,* and especially *lonely.* But is this sentimentality? What Wright has to say of "the pure clear word" suggests something else. Hughes's comment on Pilinszky's loneliness also leads elsewhere. No word seems more abused by Wright than *lonely.* But why did Wright, in an essay on his craft in *American Poets in 1976,* cite the following passage from a letter by the poet Bill Knott:

I'm so lonely I can't stand it. Solitude is all right.
It's not the same thing. Loneliness rots the soul.

Perhaps when Wright uses *lonely* he is not whining about personal misfortune, but is using a code word to trigger a reader's sense of the greater decay in the citizenry. Such code words inform Wright's personal and poetic vocabulary and are so used that they do not always mean the same thing, nor even what we expect them to mean. They are an attempt to redeem language, to make it clear.

Such an attempt leads to a poetry of great risks and risks invite poetic disasters. Indeed, the attempt, while laudable per se, matters only in so far as it succeeds more than it fails—and Wright does fail in *Two Citizens*. "The Last Drunk" is tediously thin. "Love in a Warm Room" is a paradox without the tissue of mystery that often makes Wright's poems explode. The first stanza of an otherwise marvellous poem, "Prayer to the Good Poet," suggests how Wright's meaningful distortion may dissolve beyond control:

> QUINTUS HORATIUS FLACCUS, my good secret,
> Now my father, a good man in Ohio,
> Lies alone in pain and I scarcely
> Know where to turn now.

The breathlessness of "scarcely" and the repeated "now" mean to gain emotional intensity but are excessive. This excess combines with an impatience to produce gratuitous arm-twisting in "Emerson Buchanan." "On the Liberation of Women" and "Hotel Lenox" are both weakened by a gushy rapture. And for a poet of Wright's power, language can also go limp, as it does in "You and I Saw Hawks Exchanging the Prey":

> They are terrified. They touch.
> Life is too much.

If such complacent and inert language does appear in Wright's collection, it is nevertheless the exception and ought not to obscure the more characteristic and functional vigor of the better work.

Wright views language as an almost organically active moral agent. It will not infinitely suffer abuse and shameless manipulation. Our government described the human carnage of Vietnam in numerical terms that were indistinguishable from stock exchange reports; citizens slept through the drone. Yet, ultimately, the jargon of "body count" became the ugliness it truly was. Nixon convicted himself in his slurs against Blacks, Jews, and intellectuals. Wright believes that language eventually strikes back at its abuse because the moral offense grows too great for bearing. Nowhere is it more morally aggressive than in poetry and

Wright's attempt to revitalize language hopes to make poetry cut sharply for the truth and the good.

Pilinszky's experience in Poland and our own in Asia suggest part of why contemporary man is suspicious of absolute terms. Ideological fervor has too often meant barbarous destruction. As citizens of pathos, we have no connection to a significant vision of possibility. Too often this means an abdication of art's venerable function, the affirmation of the antipathetic values which humans have ceaselessly recognized as necessary for emotional, individual, and communal health. This abdication yields up intelligent consciousness in art; art becomes the panderer of sensation, then sensationalism, which is to say either no vision or a vision of nothing. The danger of absolutes is in all or nothing. Is an imbalanced art really art? Pope's warning about "a little learning" keeps its edge.

Yet consciousness need not lead to cynicism or to Laputan sterility any more than absolutes must lead to rapture. Wright demonstrates that poetry must mediate between tenderness and horror, recognizing that both are true and real, as it makes its way toward morality. This is not a fortune cookie moralism tagged in the poem, but a working out of a comprehensive vision and a matching language. Wright, like Warren, understands that the will to change begins in confronting the self and turns to communion with and celebration of the Good in society. This Good, simplistic though it may sound, is Love, a love that despairs of its inability to comfort the hurt and the suffering. To despair of achieving an ideal, say a moral existence, is not the same thing as the denial of its possibility. Wright believes in a possible consolation inherent in language and poetry which balances love and horror, mind and emotion, Latinate and vulgar. The authority for such a vision is the love offered gratuitously to Wright by all of his muse-women, from the prostitute Jenny in all his books to his wife Annie, who radiates in the poems of *Two Citizens*. Annie is Pilinszky's "real presence" who makes vision possible, who makes mediation a progress.

The absolute toward which Wright's vision continually moves is the moral dream of self and society in love. Wright defines it in "The Art of the Fugue: A Prayer":

> And me there alone at last with my only love,
> Waiting to begin.
>
> Whoever you are, ambling past my grave,
> My name worn thin as the shawl of the lovely hill town
> Fiesole, the radiance and silence of the sky,
> Listen to me:

Though love can be scarcely imaginable Hell,
By God, it is not a lie.

Here Bach and Dante are, by God, warrantors of love's truth and absolute value. In Wright's "Prayer to the Good Poet" Horace has the same function and Wright knows his poetry must try to achieve the solidity and clarity of these visionaries.

Wright has been called a dark poet, a poet of pessimism and disbelief. He is not. He is a religious celebrant who cannot avoid the darkness engulfing the human spirit but who, in the Romantic tradition, always brings the quickening light of poetry to that darkness. *Two Citizens* is a denial of dark's permanence, an affirmation of the Good possible even for Judas, Jenny, Mary Magdalene, those sinners and sinned-against in one body. For Wright such figures are human paradigms and his continual effort is to afford them love and speech. To do so is to save himself from the nightmare of pathos. Wright's myth of creation and redemption from human cruelty is based on the single absolute which allows the self to grow toward recognition, acceptance, and consolation. Love is the only possibility for reconciling ourselves to ourselves and to the world.

Love and reconciliation actually construct the vision of *Two Citizens*. Wright's effort in these poems is always to draw together his ambitious dream of renewed possibility with a language that halts and stutters in a local passion. "Ars Poetica: Some Recent Criticism," the first poem in the book, is a kind of Genesis which not only forecasts the evolving progress of each poem but also provides a thematic point of origin. In its savage humor, the poem is a curse against America, that country which has subverted the Good. But America has also been the birthplace and residence of the great moral dream of possibility and liberty. In this way the poem is a love poem and a powerful lament. The final section of the poem reveals the poet's as yet unresolved ambivalence:

When I was a boy
I loved my country.

Ense petit placidam
Sub libertate quietem.

Hell, I ain't got nothing.
Ah, you bastards.

How I hate you.

As children we love indiscriminately. With maturity, we lose innocence. We gain frustration, bitterness, and hatred, which is a form of love. If we cannot reclaim love that alone leads to morality, then perhaps sword-rattling can help as a kind of electric shock therapy. Perhaps an aggressive poetry can reveal our cruelty and ugliness.

"Ars Poetica" weaves a narrative spiced with the poet's terse comments on the nature of tenderness, horror, the blind self, poetry, and language. It tells the story of Wright's Uncle Sherman and Aunt Agnes, the woman he did not so much love as "he fell in with." Agnes, who went mad, was the source of all tenderness and knowledge in that country of Wright's youth. The two of them are prototypical Americans, metaphorical citizens analogous to the Wrights. If "Ars Poetica" is a love poem for the lost possibility of America, it is also a poem of love for Agnes, who becomes another of Wright's muse figures acting out a redemption:

> The goat ran down the alley,
> And many boys giggled
> While they tried to stone our fellow
> Goat to death.
> And my Aunt Agnes,
> Who stank and lied,
> Threw stones at the boys
> And gathered the goat,
> Nuts as she was,
> Into her sloppy arms.

Cruelty, violence, madness, and an ineradicable compassion are the facts of Agnes's American life. It is easy but fruitless to read this poem as a folktale of eccentricity in belligerent Ohio, for the event serves primarily as a base for Wright's reflections. Agnes, the citizen lost in Hell, participates helplessly in the violence yet maintains an ability to love. The scapegoat, which cannot escape, suggests Wright himself, torturously caught between tenderness and horror, and the "plot" is a searing parody of the American dream. But how is this a statement about the art of poetry or a response to "some recent criticism"? Perhaps Horace best answers, saying "It is not enough for a poem to be beautiful: / It must have something to get at the reader's mind," which is to say a proper poetry must engage matters of substance. The substantive matter for Wright is how not to be lost in pathos, or what to believe in. Agnes's story allows Wright to say what is missing as well as what makes the old dream hollow, the American lies:

Reader,
We had a lovely language,
We would not listen.

I don't believe in your God.
I don't believe my Aunt Agnes is a saint.
I don't believe the little boys
Who stoned the poor
Son of a bitch goat
Are charming Tom Sawyers.

I don't believe in the goat either.

If the old dream is only a sham of nightmarish and relativistic values which leave us nothing to believe in outside dogmatic and maddening absolutes, what possibility remains except the Hell of a perpetual hatred and hurt? Wright's answer is an immediate and very accessible poetry of love:

I gather my Aunt Agnes
Into my veins.
I could tell you,
If you have read this far,
That the nut house in Cambridge
Where Agnes is dying
Is no more Harvard
Than you could ever be.
And I want to gather you back to my Ohio.

Here "Harvard" is a synecdoche for the kind of language which obscures the old dream that Ohio was. If the local and mythical reality of Ohio is now Hell, it was once love's reality and may be, in poetry, regathered. Possibility, as always, exists in the imagination driving forcefully toward recognition, acceptance, and consolation. In "She's Awake" Wright says:

Lying myself awake,
I imagine everything terrible in my own life,
The hitchhiking drunk, the shame of knowing
My self a fool.
Bad friend to me.

Wright does not say he remembers, but that he *imagines* for, like Stevens and Williams, he is inventing what will suffice for love's renewal.

Indeed, the obsessive direction of Wright's poetry is toward a sense of communion between the deepest self and that exiled other which might bring the possibility of redemption. Love, Wright's poems discover, exists as the achievable consolation which can re-member, rather than dismember, the world's body. In the final poem of *Two Citizens,* "To the Creature of the Creation," he writes, "You are the world's body." And in "Son of Judas," the poem which links this book with Wright's earliest work, he says, "I've discovered my body that was alive / After all." Wright's essential argument is, therefore, that though one cannot blink away the forces of dissolution and death one may oppose them in a healthy and angry imagination which can turn the oldest connections good. Consequently, the poet's function is more than discovery, it is a fathering of the moral community. In "Prayer to the Good Poet," Wright links himself, his father, and Horace in a continuity of poets struggling to know and understand love:

> More than love, my father knew how to bear love,
> One quick woman a dark river of labor.
> He led me and my two good brothers
> To gather and swim there.

Without ignoring the recurrent figure of the woman as the suffering source of love's birth, we see that Wright suggests the problem is not only to know that love exists but also to know what to do with it, a question that poetry must answer. Of Horace and his father, Wright says, "Some people think poetry is easy, / But you two didn't."

That the poetry of communion and possibility is not easy underlies Wright's demand for a pure, clear language and a constant gesture of embrace. Warren has said in "Caveat" that "every man / Is a sort of Jesus" and this has always been Wright's figurative stance. To be exiled is to live in the strange truth of an alien language that is all sound and to be driven back into the most basic language of one's self, to the most basic understanding of one's own reality. Thus, facing home ground in *Two Citizens,* Wright says in "I Wish I May Never Hear of the United States Again":

> In Yugoslavia I am learning the words
> For greeting and goodbye.
> Everything else is the language
> Of the silent woman who walks beside me.

The language of love begins in silence and in the simplest words, and it creates everything between beginning and end. To love implies the knowledge that love ends, because death is inevitable, and that suffering may not be escaped. Yet love and language have the power to deflect pain and, in art, to create imaginative consolation. The wait for such a consolation and the frustrating fear it might not exist, however, explain Wright's anger.

But anger is not what *Two Citizens* comes to. Again, Warren provides a touchstone in his poem "Waiting," which tells us "You will have to wait. Until it." At the heart of Wright's poems is a plea for patience which is the prelude to possibility. After Wright tells us in "Prayer to the Good Poet" how Bennie Capaletti refused violent revenge for an insult and how his own father learned to outwait the ugliness that is "A bitter / Taste of one body," Wright pleads for the extension of this lesson:

> Easy, easy, I ask you, easy, easy.
> Early, evening, by Tiber, by Ohio
> Give the gift to each lovely other.

And in an elegy for his teacher, "In Memory of Charles Coffin," Wright says,

> All right, you said: Ben Jonson said
> Give Salathiel Pavy one
> More chance, and give yourself one more.

Perhaps no poem in *Two Citizens* more tenderly and dramatically presents what Wright is after than "The Old WPA Swimming Pool in Martins Ferry, Ohio." Here, in a scene from America's Great Depression, the men of the Work Projects Administration have dug a swimming pool instead of the usual graves and it becomes a baptismal font:

> No, this hole was filled with water,
> And suddenly I flung myself into the water.
> All I had on was a jockstrap my brother stole
> From a miserable football team.
>
> Oh never mind, Jesus Christ, my father
> And my uncles dug a hole in the ground,
> No grave for once. It is going to be hard
> For you to believe; when I rose from that water,
>
> A little girl who belonged to somebody else,
> A face thin and haunted appeared
> Over my left shoulder, and whispered, Take care now,
> Be patient, and live.
>
> I have loved you all this time,
> And didn't even know
> I am alive.

Assuming once again the role of sinner (theft) and innocent (Christ's bearing of man's sin), Wright establishes his connection with all men, those "uncles," and goes into the ground for them. But this time, as a second Christ, he ascends to accept the wisdom of the most living, a little girl whose love is lifesaving and absolute. "Be patient, and live," she tells him, and in that simple knowledge Wright sees the secret of what was always good about himself, his country, and the human. A poem as conversational as an anecdote, at times harsh and vulgar, one which begins in fear and anger and asks the question "What the hell is this," turns to a prayer of celebration.

The circling movement in "The Old WPA Swimming Pool in Martins Ferry, Ohio" represents the largest movement of *Two Citizens,* the turn from despair to possibility, which is also the turn from Europe to America. This movement is countered by an internal movement whose rhythm is a pendulum swing between opposites, whose result is an orchestrated tension between the forces of destruction and the forces of affirmation. Wright's use of a distorted language, his code words, his blunt gouging at the reader, his rhetorical questions, his acrimonious petulance, his fusion of a Dantesque Hell with a local and industrial Ohio landscape, all operate in search of a poetry whose function is to release us from pathos and self-hatred. In "Names Scarred at the Entrance to Chartres," such a poetry is reduced to American names scrawled against Death "whose genius it is / to remember our death on the wet / roads of Chartres, America, and to forget / Our names." But even names, Doyle, Dolan, and Wright, are possibilities seeking the power to know an absolute which can contradict Death's absolute. And even in the complexly halting and surging rhythms of *Two Citizens,* a book of wandering, there is finally a moment of rest, a truth which shines through all darkness.

In "Bologna: A Poem about Gold" Wright offers another prayer, this time over "the heavy wine" and "the glass that so many have drunk from." Wright speaks of himself as having "come forth / Golden on the left corner / Of a cathedral's wing," which is a wonderful synthesis of an emerging butterfly and Christ's resurrection. Life in all ways begins with love and the golden wine of Bologna turns James and Annie Wright to celebrants at communion:

> White wine of Bologna,
> And the knowing golden shadows
> At the left corners of Mary Magdalene's eyes,
> While St. Cecilia stands
> Smirking in the center of a blank wall,
> The saint letting her silly pipes wilt down,

Adoring
Herself, while the lowly and richest of all women eyes
Me the beholder, with a knowing sympathy, her love
For the golden body of the earth, she knows me,
Her halo faintly askew,
And no despair in her gold
That drags thrones down
And then makes them pay for it.

To live in pathos and alienation is the greatest horror, what once was called the worst sin, but neither reason nor righteous saint nor any poetry remote from the humanness of a Mary Magdalene will answer despair. What is needed is "love / For the golden body of the earth" in which there is the possibility of a moral life where some things are not relative, but simply are. It is art's task to imagine and understand what these things may be in and out of artifice and the poet's task to find the inexhaustible secret of hope. As Wright says in his recent poem, "Cold Summer Sun, Be with Me Soon":

And all I wanted to do was write something that you could
Understand.
Just as Dr. Williams said.
For his own good.

The great poets are always those who have suffered in our stead, who have become the mythical heroes of love descending into netherworlds and returning with the good news of possibility and a language vigorous enough to shake us from lethargy and the abuse of our dreams. In his poem "Redwings" Wright tells us, "It turns out / You can make the earth absolutely clean." It isn't easy, it may not be done without pain and shock, and there are no guarantees, but for his own good and the good of all of us this is what the poet must attempt. To live at all we must reclaim the old dream of possibility, the dream of love's reality which Wright insists on in his poem "The Art of the Fugue: A Prayer" and in the journey of *Two Citizens:*

Whoever you are, ambling past my grave,
My name worn thin as the shawl of the lovely hill town
Fiesole, the radiance and silence of the sky,
Listen to me:

Though love can be scarcely imaginable Hell,
By God, it is not a lie.

May Swenson: Perpetual Worlds Taking Place

■

May Swenson's *New and Selected Things Taking Place* collects nearly thirty years of her remarkable poetry. At sixty, she may well be the fiercest, most inquisitive poet of her generation; certainly few are more brilliant or more independent of mien. Her poems, through six collections since 1954, are characterized by an extreme reticence of personality, an abundant energy, and an extraordinary intercourse between the natural and intellectual worlds. She has always been as formal as poets come, demonstrating early and late a skilled employment of traditional verse as well as a passion for invented patterns. There are two central obsessions in her work: the search for a proper perspective and the celebration of life's rage to continue. Her poems ask teleological questions and answer them, insofar as answers are ever possible, in every conceivable poetic strategy: she writes narrative, catalog, image, concrete, interrogatory, and sequence poems (often mixing these in single poems). Her language is generally sonorous, remarkable for its Anglo-Saxon stress, alliteration, extensive word fusions, and a devotion (now declining, it appears) to rhyme. She has made language an instrument for pursuit of ideas, but always ideas discoverable only in the things of the experiential world. She believes, apparently, that the world functions according to some hidden final purpose, and furthermore that a right apprehension ultimately reveals a Colridgean interconnectedness of all parts. A section from "Order of Diet," an early poem, suggests her belief and her cadences, both essentially unchanged though refined:

Ashes find their way to green;
the worm is raised into the wing;

the sluggish fish to muscle slides;
eventual chemistry will bring
the lightning bug to the shrewd toad's eye.
It is true no thing of earth can die.

Nothing so excites Swenson's imagination or reveals her poetic investigation as that image of flight. In poems about airplanes, birds, insects, and especially space exploration, she celebrates the joy of flight. Motion is both her subject and her image, being life itself. Flight, however, rarely means escape; it is her means for exploration, penetration, for travel to and through the world; it is what humans cannot naturally do ("light pierces wings of jays in flight: / they shout my grief") but what becomes the passage toward and into vision. In this book's oldest poem, Swenson wrote "all that my Eye encircles I become" and risked an Emersonian cartoon. Vision, seeing, looking, recording are so pervasive in her poems that one almost forgets how active she makes all the senses in the service of penetrating surfaces. Flight is not only the revelation of human bondage, it is also the vehicle of imaginative and intellectual possibilities. As she writes in "Distance and a Certain Light," speaking of her poetics, "No contortion / without intention, and nothing ugly." Never a poet of ennui or cynicism, though often a poet of elegaic grief, she believes that all is beautiful if seen properly: "Rubbish becomes engaging shape— / you only have to get a bead on it." And:

From an airplane, all
that rigid splatter of the Bronx
becomes organic, logical
as web or beehive.

In her later poem, "Flying Home from Utah," her angle and distance of vision produces what seems a purely descriptive record of geometric shades and shapes but this macrocosmic vision ("it becomes the world") is partial so the long-distance view is shifted to a microscopic look at a single leaf and she concludes:

One leaf of a tree that's one tree of a forest,
that's the branch of the vein of a leaf

of a tree. Perpetual worlds
within, upon, above the world, the world
a leaf within a wilderness of worlds.

Swenson's emphasis on flight and perspective, always in the context that "earth will not let go our foot," extends from her conception of the primary tension of existence: "The tug of the void / the will of the world."

By will she means the rage to survive and flourish which is continually contested by absence, death, and the void, hence "Though devious and shifty in detail, the whole expanse / reiterated constancy and purpose." Swenson's effort has been and is to make felt the nature of that purpose. In another early poem, "Snow in New York," she wrote:

> a magic notion
> I, too, used to play with: from chosen words a potion
> could be wrung; pickings of them, eaten, could make you fly, walk
> on water, be somebody else, do or undo anything, go back
> or forward on belts of time.

"October," a new poem, shows she means to fly into the world, not out of it. Here she emphasizes the search for vision, not its verbal contrivance:

> Stand still, stare
> hard into bramble and tangle,
> past leaning broken trunks,
> sprawled roots exposed. Will
> something move?—some vision
> come to outline? Yes, there—

Swenson, however, seems not to have come to any definitive identification of a teleological purpose. She has found or accepted no answer except her intuited conviction that all is interconnected and rooted in love. Her temperament, always religious and never orthodox, causes her to caution, "I do not mean to pray." Yet her newest poems seem prayerful, perhaps in the increased awareness of the void's tug which makes her note, "Too vivid / the last pink / petunia's indrawn mouth." More acutely now she feels what age reveals, "the steep / edge of hopelessness," and writes more intimately of what's been loved, family, flowers, landscapes and seascapes, birds, and vibrant colors. Perhaps no poet since Wallace Stevens has so reveled in colors; they name poems, accrue into image patterns, are ingested as objects. For May Swenson, life is motion and color. Yet the colors of new poems are slightly less brilliant, are the colors of seasonal decline. Staring into the bramble thicket, she writes, "Better here / in the familiar, to fade."

If Swenson's new poems are more attentive to the inevitable void, she remains at least as interested in chronicling what is happening as what has happened. Her sixty-two new poems evidence still a vigorous curiosity, a compulsive meticulousness, and a passionate sense of life which forces us toward poetry's accomplishment, renewed vision. She has plenty to write about, including Navaho rugs, bison, rodeos, western mountains, the sea, swamps, income tax, fashion, Georgia O'Keeffe, baseball and football, an outhouse, parents, a junkyard dog, Mormonism, Nanook the Eskimo, and an aviary of birds (there can hardly be a poet who has written more about birds or about more birds!). And writing of July 4th fireworks, she says:

> And we want more: we want red giant, white dwarf,
> black hole, extinct, orgasmic, all in one!

Dedicated as they are to angles of vision, avoiding autobiography and personality, Swenson's poems necessarily emphasize structure—sometimes to the point of mannerism. Often enough they possess a wonderful lyricism that celebrates, but primarily they nominate and this occasionally leads to an annoyingly indiscriminate series of similes: a thing looks like this. Or this, or this. This mannerism reveals a kind of "scientific" attitude in her work, an attitude also marked by often esoteric and technical terminology—not in itself a problem though it helps create the impression of a dispassionate stance when there is passion present and a need to show it. Swenson's reticence may sometimes mean the difference between a powerful experience and no experience, as in riddles or dry humor. Indeed, one of Swenson's characteristics is a wry wit which sometimes trails off into whimsy, into the glib and clever. For me she has too strong a willingness to keep work marked by visual puns (particularly from *Iconographs*), work less felt and sustaining than contrived and biodegradable. Such work does disservice to her significant accomplishment, though some "readers" will doubtless applaud her gamesmanship and experimenting. For them, here is a stanza of "MAsterMANANiMAL":

> ANiMAte MANANiMAL MAttress of Nerves
> MANipulAtor Motor ANd Motive MAker
> MAMMAliAN MAtrix MAt of rivers red
> MortAl MANic Morsel Mover shAker

Swenson's interest in this sort of visual wordplay extends to poems carved in zigzags, curves, a snail's shape (among others), and multiple, often opposed, columns of print. Sometimes charming, sometimes bitingly effective as in "Women" and "Orbiter 5 Shows How Earth Looks from the Moon," the poems too often depend on a gimmickry that wears quickly thin. In "Look," for example, a poem about two people before a mirror, the right hand column of print uses a form of "look" twenty-two times, and one wants as much as anything not to look.

Neither are all of Swenson's more traditionally executed poems free from excess that may be attributed to her high and democratic spirit. She betrays a tendency to telegraph conclusions in some of the image poems. In "The Solar Corona" the sun's enormous ring becomes a pizza that:

is 400 times
larger than the moon.
Don't burn your lips!

Here, we can only say Ouch! And we cringe when in a love poem, "Poet to Tiger," she writes, "You put your paws in your armpits / make a tiger-moo." Because there is a strain of the highly impressionistic in this eclectic poet, there is a scattering of poems of which the closest readings scarcely dislodge either subject or meaning or both, so that poems such as "Written while Riding the Long Island Rail Road" and "O'Keefe Retrospective" remain interesting and baffling.

Any collection as rich and massive as this one must have, however, its weaknesses and I would hope they do not obscure the book's dominant strength. Swenson's voracious imagination makes her an extremely social and adventurous writer who turns poetry into a living, if idealized, human speech. From previous collections she has trimmed more than fifty poems and has reordered most of what remains, in effect creating not merely a collected poems but a freshly ordained and perpetual world of poetry. Among the new poems I would cite for their excellence "Bison Crossing near Mt. Rushmore," "Staying at Ed's Place," "The Willets," "That the Soul May Wax Plump," "Scroppo's Dog," "October," and "Dream after Nanook" in particular. Among the previous collections there is such an abundance of splendid, welcome old friends that it is impossible and nearly invidious to choose for citation, but to demonstrate Swenson's inventiveness, her power, her conviction in the right to be free and wild, I offer these stanzas from a favorite early poem:

Watching you they remember their fathers
  the frightening hairs in their fathers' ears

Young girls remember lovers too timid and white
  and I remember how I played lion with my brothers
  under the round yellow-grained table
  the shadow our cave in the lamplight

Your beauty burns the brain
  though your paws slue on foul cement
  the fetor of captivity you do right to ignore
  the bars too an illusion

Your heroic paranoia plants you in the African jungle
  pacing by the cool water-hole as dawn streaks the sky

and the foretaste of the all-day hunt
is sweet as yearling's blood
in the corners of your lips
("Lion")

If Swenson sometimes generates consternation and dismay, that fault is born of a poetry urgently trying to tell us that everything matters, a poetry so affirmative that we cannot escape knowing we matter. Even random reading here produces surprise, delight, love, wisdom, joy, and grief. May Swenson transforms the ordinary little-scrutinized world to a teeming, flying, first creation. Bother such words as great and major—she is a poet we want in this world for this world is in her as it is in few among us ever. I have been told she hasn't a great readership. Not in size or, perhaps, intensity. Too often we accuse our poets of inattention when the fault is in ourselves. That she deserves readers as intense, as scrupulous, as intelligent, and as rewarding as May Swenson is seems to me as plainly true as the continually unfurling world of her *New and Selected Things Taking Place*. Twenty years ago she wrote of her relationship with the reader and called it "the lightning-string / between your eye and mine." The first poem in this eminent new collection reengages that paradigmatic image and serves better than any reviewer's words to introduce what she does and who she is.

A NAVAHO BLANKET

Eye-dazzlers the Indians weave. Three colors
are paths that pull you in, and pin you
to the maze. Brightness makes your eyes jump,
surveying the geometric field. Alight, and enter
any of the gates—of Blue, of Red, of Black.
Be calmed and hooded, a hawk brought down,
glad to fasten to the forearm of a chief.

You can sleep at the center,
attended by the Sun that never fades, by Moon
that cools. Then, slipping free of zigzag and
hypnotic diamond, find your way out
by spirit trail, a faint Green thread that
secretly crosses the border, where your mind
is rinsed and returned to you like a white cup.

Louis Simpson: A Child of the World

■

In 1967, M. L. Rosenthal, in *The New Poets,* described a number of poets he found to have some tenuous connection with Robert Bly's *The Sixties* and said of them: "this group, which includes Robert Bly, Donald Hall, Louis Simpson, James Wright, and James Dickey, is seeking to affect the aims of American poetry." If that sounds like an ominous and card-carrying cartel, one can only say that Rosenthal deserves high marks for a half-correct prescience. Though I think it is arguable that American poetry had *aims,* clearly the poets have affected the nature and direction of the art. Whether it was the bottle and filler of traditional verse or the "I-like-Ike" hypocrisy of "all's right with the Republic" that stung such poets into a conviction that poetry was not what it ought to be is for scholars to sift and weigh as is their wont. We know the poets wanted something that wasn't coming up on the Wurlitzer. They wanted something personal though, with obviously differing opinions, they were inclined to refuse mere personality with its eccentricities: postures, fantasies, self-deceit, solipsisms, hermetic escapisms—all those soapboxes of assertion which publicly seemed to have no more real authority than the monkish sign-carriers of doom in so many cartoons.

More than two decades have passed since the first books of these poets appeared and while it is still unclear that any of their names will name the literary age to be described in anthologies years hence, no serious reader of poetry can be unaware that each has affected not only what American poetry is but also what it might be. If it is impossible to think of Bly, Hall, Simpson, Wright, and Dickey as conspirators of one mind, it is nevertheless true that together they have created the poetry of a surfaced, examined, and revitalized inner life, a life not simply of the mind but of the personalized mind. They have been noisy, exuberant, truculent, testy, and necessary—like many children in a house too small. Of Rosenthal's appointed group, perhaps the quietest and least public and even least affective on younger poets has been Louis Simpson.

A practicing Christian would surely remind me here that the least shall enter Heaven first and a good case for that could be made on Simpson's behalf. In the end it is not going to be noise or influence that matters, but the durable quality and scope of achieved art. No one of that grouping seems to have so steadily and honestly gone on creating a credible and shareable vision of life in this world, in these times, more than Simpson has. It is, of course, not necessary to reduce the value and accomplishment of another poet to praise Simpson. I have no wish to do that. I only say that the poetry of Louis Simpson seems to me extraordinarily beautiful and complex, that it demonstrates an engagement with the vicissitudes and antinomies of American life in the 1960s and 1970s that is equal to the best we have, and that it may even possess a greater, quieter power of staying because it is extremely accessible. Accessible, yes, but scarcely without the deep resonance and luminosity of an imaginative intelligence whose reach is inward and outward, vertical and horizontal at the same time. Quoting Goethe, Simpson has called himself "the child of the world in the middle." In his seventh collection, *Searching for the Ox,* Simpson has extended that middle world beyond the prophets right and left, creating a remarkable vision of fundamentally human ground upon which, sooner or later, we all must stand.

Louis Simpson's poetry is marked by its steady development in two directions. From the beginning he has wanted a synthetic vision, hence his attraction to Whitman, which would discover and fix the true nature of human existence and which, moreover, would reaffirm traditional and timeless values of the human as social and responsible creature who might, nevertheless, intuit some binding, beyond-reason force. He has been, therefore, a consistently moral and ethical poet. Not, I insist quickly, a moralistic poet, one who writes a poetry that bends our ears with a prefabricated polemic. He has not been a ferocious preacher in the manner of Bly, but he has been a kind of conscience in the way of James Wright. And, like Wright, Simpson has always found himself equipped with an ironic voice, a disposition toward a poetry of steely intelligence which would play Mercutio to a poetry of romantic moaning in the dark bushes. It is this second strain in his poetry which accounts for his frequent humor, satire, social comment, good citizenry, and, ultimately, the evolution of his mature poetic style. Simpson has come far from that ideal music of the 1950s. His language now, as Randall Jarrell would say, is often clear enough even for cats and dogs. He has come to a certain unfashionable narrative base, to a poetry that unabashedly employs the devices of prose fiction. But not, it should be noted, to the fashionable prose-poem, for he appears to believe he can still detect a valuable difference between poetry and prose, a difference that is marked by the continued prominence of such tensions and ironies as are generated by the contending of mind and heart under equal pressure.

Louis Simpson has made a poetry out of ourselves who want mystical unity, harmony, and escape from the almost unendurable brutalities of the world; but he has also made it out of ourselves who are grinning realists, who know that escape from the difficulties of being human, especially in poetry whose function is to help us be more human, serves the forces of brutalization and division. Simpson has never forgotten, moralist and artist as he is, that a poem must have an audience before it is a true poem, that such a poem is a bridge to somewhere and to someone. His poems, therefore, are always testing their own authority and reality—they are always having to prove their right to exist—for he has wanted what he has increasingly created, an art which speaks in plain language about subjects experienced in a social world of ordinary people. He says, "I have a sort of Wordsworthian vision: a picture of a very ordinary human being who is also highly intelligent and likes to read poetry; he is the one I write for. This man knows what a garage looks like, this man knows what a milk-bottle sounds like on the back porch in the morning." Simpson does not aspire to mass pablum, however, but to a total and authentic communication through art, a speaking that is both deeply personal and broadly human. He says: "Total poetry, like the total human being, must include so-called rational as well as irrational states—the poem must be logical as well as unpredictable. Images that move us do so because they are connected to logical thought processes which we all share. They are connected to the psyche of the author and an understandable feeling, or idea if you prefer, underlying the poem. Poetry in which there are no dream states is trivial, but dream images may be trivial also when they are produced by automatic writing, without a necessary direction by the psyche of the poet."

More than his contemporaries, then, Simpson has searched for a poetry which would not be content with either a fabric of associational images and an esoteric mysticism or a poetry of received ideas and rational discourse. Though his early work demonstrated the traditional, literate, and neatly cadenced character of late Modernism, there was also a strain of fresh diction which was not decorative figuring but muscular nomination. He moved away from the poem *bien fait,* closer to that diction which James Wright called the "poetry of a grown man." Increasingly he has employed rhythms and organizational units which parallel actual human speech, knowing it was this speech which would allow the resonance of both personal and mythic, or psychic if you will, depths. This direction has meant a reliance on image juxtaposition that has seemed to some critics to keep him in lockstep with Robert Bly, but he has never been truly illogical or surreal. While others have gravitated toward hermetic languages of utter personality, toward European modes of the fabular, toward anecdotal journalism, Simpson, like Wordsworth, sought a dialect of the actually spoken. He has told stories in a parabolic speech of local roots. It is no accident that he has often praised William Carlos Williams. It is as if he had believed everything in the phenomenal world might speak if the right plain language could be wrestled to the purpose. The risk, and he has sometimes succumbed to it, has been a loss of tension, a flattened music, a prose. The gain has been that widened world of experience which is not *merely* personal, which is never gamesmanship or buffoonery, which is recognizably diverse, contradictory, mature, and immediate. He has come to a poetry that, as he says, "ad dresses itself to the human condition, a poetry of truth, not dreams . . . [that] depicts human actions and the way we live. Poetry must express the reality behind appearances. . . . This poetry will frequently be in the form of a narrative. Not a mere relation of events, but a narrative of significant actions."

It is Simpson's insistence on "significant actions" which has led him to reject the poetries of tonal effects, assertion, dream fragments. Such poetries, apparently, do not provide enough of the objective life. They do not, arguably, cause poetry to help provide designs for healthy living based on historical values such as love, pride, piety, responsibility, etc. The drive toward a literature (I do not think Simpson would find that word offensive) of moral and ethical service must employ but go beyond the eccentric collisions of image, just as art goes beyond anecdote. Simpson wants to look *through* the events and language of the common world to what he has intuited: a kind of changeless reality. He says, "The happening, or the mere field of events, is very little. . . . The real problem of fiction is what is the significance of these events?" That is, what good will these arrangements of word and action, these reflectors of reality, do for anyone? The evident answer is that appropriate actions appropriately arranged, and memorably, will allow a reasonable reader to experience the extrapersonal continuous world. Simpson is neither a poet of the deep image nor of the personality. Like Whitman he contains many selves who go adventuring within the letter *I*. Some of them see synthesis, some of them see division.

Searching for the Ox contains less than half-a-dozen poems which are not remarkable for motion, for this adventuring. Here someone is always walking, wandering, motoring—engaging in a ruminative movement which observes people, landscapes, circumstances, the thingness of community. The first poem, "Venus in the Tropics," begins "One morning I went over to Bournemouth," and we are immediately placed by a gesture characteristic of the collection. There are no obscurities, no psychic or metaphoric flights, no elaborating descriptions, only an action that takes us from a closed world to an open one. In this event we hear the story of Peter, Simpson's name for a character created out of the memory of himself as a boy. It is an initiation story in which Peter discovers ugliness through American sailors, the gauds of city life, prostitutes, and the unknown humanity of his family. Protected from such worldly "truths" by his relatives and driven back to his Caribbean home, the boy remains isolated—but through his memories we learn what subtle changes come in the first growth of vision. The poem also provides certain vital images which recur in Simpson's poetry:

> I sat by the pool at Bournemouth
> reading *Typhoon.*
> I had the pool all to myself,
> the raft, the diving boards, and the rings.
> There wasn't a living soul.
>
> Not a voice—just rustling palm leaves
> and the tops of the coconuts
> moving around in circles.
>
> In the afternoon a wind sprang up,
> blowing from the sea to the land,
> covering the harbor with whitecaps.
>
> It smelled of shells and seaweed,
> and something else—perfume.

The poem's invocation of Conrad does two things: it sets youth's early vision of simplistic hero-dreaming as a base against the book's drive toward maturity and it evokes a master of moral and ethical inquiry. The last two stanzas also invoke Ernest Hemingway's "Ten Indians"—whose concern is with sexual and ethical initiation. Simpson's poem, of course, generates greater compression as it works more in the direction of archetypal rather than rounded experience. His intention is to lead us to that "perfume" which may make the whole curvature and complexity of sexual knowledge, its joy and pain, suddenly visible.

Simpson's echoes of Hemingway and Conrad derive from his wish to create a language of precise nomination in which appearance and reality, with minimal intrusion by the author's personality, stand in subtle but bright opposition. Events in the world, after all, do not ordinarily come with a gloss, though they are not less meaningful for that. The poet's task in his arrangement of words is to release meaning.

Simpson's second poem, "Dinner at the Sea-View Inn," suggests Hemingway's "Hills like White Elephants" and is, essentially, a short story of dialect and scene. Peter, now a young adult, has had dinner with Marie and her parents. He and Marie go for a walk during which he wants to tell her something of his perceptions about how things are in the world:

> "When I was a child," said Peter,
> "I used to think that the waves were cavalry . . .
> the way they come in, curling over."
>
> She said, "Is that what you were in,
> the calvary?"
>
> He laughed, "Calvary? For Christ's sake. . . ."

The literate and sensitive young man recognizes the irony of Marie's mistake. He is reaching for an image of vitality and motion and she has transposed it to an image of death. Marie is offended, yet Peter understands it has been, somehow, a moment of insight for him. Returned to his apartment, he begins to see how the moment and the event reveal the bittersweet flow of life:

> Lying in bed, hands clasped beneath his head,
> listening . . .
>
> to the stopping and starting of traffic
> in the street five floors below.
> And the opening of the elevator,
> and the sound of feet going down the corridor.

All of the poems in the first section of *Searching for the Ox* are such moments of maturation and recognition. As Simpson writes, "all the voyage would be inward" and in "The Psyche of Riverside Drive" Peter visits his old professor of literature who tells him that "the visible world was a dream." Once Peter would have believed that but now he knows that "there is a difference between dreaming and waking," though false art and weak intelligences may blur the difference. Confused now, and feeling betrayed, Peter abandons the counsel of his professor and seeks "the solidity / and resonance of the sidewalk under his feet." He has become the proto-American, dreamer and pragmatist, an exile in his native land. Now he falls back to the first language of perception: feeling.

> There is always some passionate race
> that has just arrived in *America.*
>
> And a fragrance, *pimienta,*
> the wind brings over the sea.

In "Lorenzo," Simpson's Peter has become a fledgling writer, another sort of exile, and the experience which initiates is that of visiting novelist Harry Ascham on *his* island, of entering the metier of D. H. Lawrence and "Tom Eliot"—all exemplars of the tradition into which he hopes to fit his individual talent. He moves from first awe to the sad recognition of what a pitiful and magnificent thing is the man who would write:

> Sitting among the stones
> I listened to the dry leaves rustling
> and thought of a poet's life.
> *Genus irritabile vatum.*
> Because he longs for Beauty
> with man he grows enraged.

Speaking in Eliot's tones Peter sees Eliot as the dry leaf no young man quite expects to become. He would be a susceptible prophet on whom nothing is lost, with sensitivity and glamor, a universal wayfarer among angels. Yet there is Ascham, an example of the plain, sad end most writers come to. But also there is Lawrence "bending his neck to the yoke / of local speech and custom . . . / whatever smells of the earth." Or is this Ascham that Simpson describes? Simpson has tried to be so clear in contrasting the failed and the worldly successful writer that one can't quite tell who is who. Perhaps the implication, for Peter, is that any writer is a little of both.

Simpson called the first section of this book "Venus in the Tropics" in order to indicate the tangled and initial confusion of love at its sources. He calls the second section "The Company of Flesh and Blood" to suggest a further movement into the social world. Peter is now "five years in publishing" but has discovered little of the inner life's intuited connection with the visibly shabby life around him. He must now learn, if his engagement is to be with art rather than publishing and commerce, to go beyond the surface. He encounters a manuscript which frames for him his feelings of both discontinuity and isolation as well as a sense of communal identity. He writes, "Words are realities. They have the power / to make us feel and see." Echoing the Romantic manifestos as well as Conrad, it is a bluntness which any aggressive young editor might bridle at, yet the manuscript, those words, changes Peter's life; it turns him from publishing to writing. Peter undertakes the writer's mission, a mission that is not entirely attractive since there must be nothing marginal about it. The true writer stands outside the superficially committed who are but people with the one story of their lives, just as he is most essentially outside the more ordinary society. In "The Stevenson Poster," Simpson reveals what Peter will give up for art: a lucrative job, comfortable circumstances, expensive possessions, various political stances, all the illusions of normal prosperity and happiness—for the educated and upwardly mobile young people. Instead, with luck, he must apprentice himself to the imagining and creation of character and truth. He must become a messenger of the true news. At best, he may feel he is not "missing out on life." With this choice, he begins to read "a deeper significance / into everything," not manipulating the world, but allowing the world to reveal its perpetual and significant speech. This starts with his reading of the manuscript written by a paranoid woman—which, as it reveals a distorted, divided reality, he rejects. Peter has begun to look both *at* things and *through* things in "The Hour of Feeling," a poem Simpson identifies as an advance in his art because it marks the discovery of love, the power through which inert phenomena achieve meaning. In consequence, Peter makes further discoveries. He had thought significant art required an excess of emotion to the point of illness ("You have to be mad, that's the catch") but learns it requires feeling tempered by labor, steady attention, intelligence, and self-argument:

> I sit down to write . . .
>
> An hour later the table is covered
> with words.
> And then I start crossing them out.

The remaining poems of section 2 dramatize the refusal of glib and received public truths and show the artist asking of each thing and each event: "What is it to me?" By structuring his collection in the quasi-plot form of a fictional and spiritual autobiography, Simpson brings his reader into the progress of his own mind, though without a single indeterminate *you* of address. Effectively, he forces us to look for ourselves, as Conrad has said he would make us *see*.

Perhaps because of his intention to create a poetry leavened with ideas, Simpson has provided a preface to his collection and in it he tells us, of his third section, "Poems in the third part are more meditative; they are about a way of life." These seven poems are dense narratives but their story lines seem less important than a substructure of imagery drawn from Zen Buddhist writing, an imagery which creates an architecture of knowing. In "Chimneys" a speaker walks to a cliff overlooking a harbor and describes the far shore. The posture of exile has become the posture of inbetweenness. In "Cliff Road" this posture is extended to a line of fishermen "surfcasting, in absolute silence" at the New York seashore. Exemplary figures, both Platonic and literal,

> "Two fishermen, wearing straw hats
> that conceal their faces. They look Chinese.
> The boat in which they sit seems to be drifting
> on images—of the shore, with trees
> and a white cloud standing over."

These fishermen, described in "The Sanctuaries," are only images in the speaker's mind, not literal observations. They are reminiscent, too, of Yeat's Chinamen who stare at the "tragic scene" with their serene, gay eyes. What is important here is that Simpson has been building a single, vital pattern of imagery—of the sea, water's thoughtlike movement, shores, and that sifting, imagining observer who stands nowhere really, or stands midway between a human landscape and that yearned-for other shore. Because we most immediately know the physical, Simpson shows us the sea through acute sensory images: we see, we smell, we hear, and this leads into the untouched depth of memory where the self, or selves, resides. In a poem from his earlier collection, *Adventures of the Letter I,* Simpson shows his intention:

PORT JEFFERSON

> My whole life coming to this place,
> and understanding it better
> maybe for having been born
> offshore, and at an early age
> left to my own support . . .
>
> I have come where sea and wind,
> wave and leaf, are one sighing,
> where the house strains at an anchor
> and the salt-rose clings and clambers
> on the humorous grave.
>
> This is the place, Camerado,
> that hides the sea-bird's nest.

Listening to the distant voices
in summer, a murmur of the sea,
I seem to remember everything.

Simpson recalls love's promise in the tropics, that Eden, and recalls a time before division from place, people, and continuity. He seems indeed, in his assumption of Whitman's expanded personality, to contain all history, all human events, all emotion. Ironically he stands on the ground of promise which he had described in "Lines Written near San Francisco" and "the land / The pioneers looked for, shading their eyes / Against the sun—a murmur of serious life." Simpson's careful working of image patterns means to suggest the internal and the external life is one, and is always a journey. Consider what he is attempting in the light of this passage from the *Manual of Zen Buddhism* (D. T. Suzuki, Grove Press): "What is *Paramita?* This is a Sanskrit term of the Western country. In T'ang it means 'the other shore reached.' When the meaning (*artha* in Sanskrit) is understood, one is detached from birth and death. When the objective world (*visaya*) is clung to, there is the rise of birth and death; it is like waves rising from the water; this is called 'this shore.' When you are detached from the objective world, there is no birth and death for you; it is like the water constantly running its course: this is 'reaching the other shore.' " In Zen, the "other shore" symbolizes great wisdom. We are at liberty to examine the connection of Simpson's poetry with Zen vision since he has told us that the third section of the book defines a way of life and since the book's title is taken from Zen writing.

"Searching for the Ox," the title poem of the fourth section as well as of Simpson's collection, is obliquely related to a series of ten oxherding pictures by Kakuan Sji-en, a Zen master of the Sung dynasty. The pictures seem to be a visual parable of the process by which man moves from an ordinary unenlightened state of the spirit (the condition of dualism or division) to the state of Buddha in which he experiences and exists in what is called, variously, the Essence, Oneness, Suchness, etc. It is extremely difficult for me to discuss this mystical process, having no experience in Zen understanding. (Yet if the poem is successful it must have an accessibility to those who haven't Zen knowledge, though perhaps it will be richer for those who have it.) Zen writing says, however, that one reaches Buddhism only when one makes no assertive definition about it. For example, "When one attains this stage of realization, seeing is no-seeing, hearing is no-hearing, preaching is no-preaching." Or, again, "The Essence is neither in the world nor of the world, nor is it outside the world."

The idea is that a man is betrayed by the assertions of his mind so long as he is disconnected from the Essence. Discontinuous, he is said to be "astray" and thereby will be fooled by a false vision of dualism. The first portrait in the oxherding series, "Searching for the Ox," carries this gloss: "The beast has gone astray, and what is the use of searching for him? The reason why the oxherd is not on intimate terms with him is because the oxherd has violated his inmost nature. The beast is lost, for the oxherd has himself been led out of the way through his deluding senses. His home is receding farther away from him, and byways and crossways are ever confused. Desire for gain and fear of loss burn like fire; ideas of right and wrong shoot up like a phalanx" (D. T. Suzuki, *Manual of Zen Buddhism*).

Interestingly, this picture contains no ox while the cover portrait on Simpson's book contains no man and features the ox. In the Zen series the ox is the symbol of man's spirit-soul-connection with Buddha. The man in the parable has to track, find, tame, and ride the ox. When this has happened, both man and ox disappear into the "serenity of non-assertion." Inner and outer life are fused, continuous.

Simpson's "Searching for the Ox" is divided into five parts. In section 1 we hear the speaker has "the one face that will listen / to any incoherent aimless story." We are told "There is something in disorder that calls to me / Out there beyond the harbor," and that caller is the far shore of great wisdom. But the speaker tells us of his discontinuity:

> I have stayed outside and watched
> the shadow-life of the interior,
> feeling myself apart from it.

Section 2 contrasts this intuited inner life with the public disciplines of "engineering, law" which dominate contemporary life and generate enormous but superficial power. These the speaker rejects, saying "They will send me off to Heaven / when all I want is to live in this world." Section 3 appears to suggest that all disciplines which take us out of this world are distortions; it says, "The search for the ox continues." Section 4, reinforcing the need to live by the inner discipline, says, quoting Cavafy, "As you have wasted your life here in this corner / you have ruined it all over the world." There follows a tableau of social life which is continuous in the things and the people of the world. In the fifth section Simpson directly approaches, for the first time, the Zen portrait:

> Following in the Way
> that "regards sensory experience as relatively unimportant,"
> and that aims to teach the follower
> "to renounce what one is attached to"—

in spite of this dubious gift
that would end by negating poetry altogether,
in the practice of meditating
on the breath, I find my awareness
of the world—the cry of a bird,
susurrus of tires, the wheezing

of the man in the chair next to me—
has increased. That every sound
falls like a pebble into a well,
sending out ripples that seem to be continuing
through the universe. Sound has a tail
that whips around the corner;
I try not to follow. In any case,
I find I am far more aware
of the present, sensory life.

I seem to understand what the artist
was driving at; every leaf stands clear
and separate. The twig seems to quiver
with intellect. Searching for the ox
I come upon a single hoofprint.
I find the ox, and tame it,
and lead it home. In the next scene
the moon has risen, a cool light.
Both the ox and herdsman vanished.

There is only earth:
in winter laden with snow,
in summer covered with leaves.

Simpson now appears to have entered the parable in order to express apprehension of a singular life, the inner and outer made one. Choosing to live well within the vicissitudes of this world but rejecting "desire for gain and fear of loss," he will not yearn for another shore but attempt to turn more intensely the light of the mind to the shore where he stands. Simpson has placed himself in a Keatsian circumstance and he has realized that to have crossed—even in the assertions of the imagination—to that other shore would have been to lose the chance to become more human. Extrapersonal visions are, he seems to feel, both escapist and without truth. His conclusion suggests that his poetry will be the act of knowing better the ordinary reality of life. Or does it?

I have said that Simpson's ironic second voice prevents him from the lyrical assertion which is not tested by felt experience. Why has he told us that the twig quivers with intellect rather than feeling? And why is it that "the ox and herdsman" have vanished rather than the "ox and I"? Is it possible there is a countermovement even to the Zen mysticism? One of the great strengths of Simpson's poetry, to my way of thinking, has been his refusal to accept an unearned vision of transcendence. In the final poem of *Adventures of the Letter I,* he wrote: "And now we talk of 'the inner life', / And I ask myself, where is it?" Having been a geographical orphan who was compelled to argument with his adopted country, Simpson is, similarly, an orphan of belief. He argues with himself about what may be believed. He is not, I think, a Zen believer but is merely using an imagery which may help to make visible certain values which must be true, primarily that life is good and that art helps us to "prove" it so. It is not that the inner life is less beautiful or necessary than jacket copy says it is, but that the kind and quality of that life is as complex and hard to know as external life. In his poem "Big Dream, Little Dream," based on a Jungian description of the Algonyi tribal belief, Simpson examines the power of the big (some would say racial, some would say archetypal) dream to produce images which might be translated into human action. All images are not wonderful; some may be dangerous. In his poem, the American president has a big dream "and before you know it there is war." Unless I am far off the mark, Simpson is suggesting that it is the artist's moral responsibility (which is a function of the quality of his intellect and his feeling fused in art) to be certain of the effect and value of the images he summons from the inner life. In 1974, Simpson said in the *Ohio Review:* "There is a belief that poetry must be only about the 'inner life'—anything else is not poetry. The effect of this poetry is to reduce poems to a few lines, the barest perception. I once heard someone speak of the works of one American poet as 'ghost poems,' and indeed what is going on at present in some sectors is a Ghost Dance. The cure, I think, is by means of drama and narrative to bring into poetry the feelings people have for one another. Nothing can come of the feelings they have, or say they have, for darkness and stones."

Simpson would, doubtless, argue that there is no division between the inner and outer life except for those who have gone "astray" and would argue that what poetry must do is find a direct and clear way of making this life, its Oneness, as fully visible as it was in whatever tropics we came from. He says, "People want the sights and sounds of life; they ask for life in poetry. They ask for bread, but instead they have been given stones." Putting aside the frustration and despair common to all poets, Simpson's idea of a missing sustenance in poetry is emphatic. In the final section of his book the poems are dramas of loss both witnessed by and consoled through art. They are also poems of search and of momentary joys in this world.

Simpson does not give us gratuitous harvest of bread, but he does give art's recognition of the life right under our noses, a portrait of ourselves. The plot of his collection is that ultimate search for the names of men, for realities. In the events, the actions, the momentary actors we are, what we do is to seek the ox of our spirits. We would not have it tamed exactly, but would see it and know it steadily for awhile. This search allows for a dramatic meditation on the nature of being and, implicitly, for ethical discrimination. Simpson's poems lead us to the sanctuary of the self where each one must stare at the wall, an act the Zennists call Pi-Kuan ("abandoning the false and embracing the true")—which is one of two ways of entering the Path to the Essence. The end of mature vision is surely balance, is knowing. In "The Shelling Machine" Simpson writes:

> In turn, I have changed the machine.
> No one else would have stopped to look at it—
> certainly none of the people
> who work there every day in the field.

The act of looking is the act of Pi-Kuan and everything in the world, most especially those intricate machines which are people, is the wall we must stare at. Look hard and with love, says Louis Simpson, and there is the knowing which gives us pleasure, hope, instruction, and—for the artist—images of courage. Simpson finds the trail of the ox even in a poker game. Here is my own favorite from *Searching for the Ox,* a blessing:

THE DALED

> Across the room the night city editor
> has turned his face toward me
> with a curious, mild stare.
> Waiting for copy . . .
>
> Later in the evening there will be a crowd
> at Jack's. Discussing sports . . .
> Some old codger holding forth—
> what His Honor said to the Commissioner.
> And there will be the usual four.
>
> According to an ancient fable
> there are thirty six "hidden saints."
> It could be the tailor, the shoemaker,
> it could be a Regular Army Colonel—

as long as there are thirty-six
the world will not come to an end.

Also there are the Daled—four newspapermen
who are always playing poker.
As long as this situation continues
God will hold back the final catastrophe.
"What's that? It sounds like water."
"Wait a minute," says Shapiro.
"We're here to play cards. Whose deal is it?"

"I'll see your five," says Flanagan,
"and raise it."

So the game goes on
from week to week. I have known them to begin
late at night when everything is silent
and to play right through till dawn.

Sylvia Plath: The Electric Horse

■

We know her. How odd it is to say that of a poet dead nearly two decades. It is certainly not the Truth, yet we feel we know her and in important ways it is the truth to say we know her. For many readers Sylvia Plath is still the phosphorescent ingenue of contemporary American poetry, not a woman who would be now on the edge of fifty, a woman whose children are nearing their majorities. She is, almost, *the* American woman poet, yet she is featured in British anthologies of their poetry. No one knew Sylvia Plath less than she knew herself but *The Collected Poems* is, I think, beyond anything else the record of her struggle to know herself, which was the struggle finally to accept the self she was beyond all choosing and posturing. That is why we know her. If we do not really *know* her poetry, her prose, her letters—in the sense that one means when one has immersed oneself in another's written life, or even in the sense of the scholar who has "mastered the canon"—we continue to speak of her as if we do know her. At parties, in lectures, in conversations we invoke her name to describe a kind of poetry. Sometimes it is in derogation, sometimes in admiration, and lately as the name of a place, mostly unpleasant, we had to pass through. No one who invokes her name feels compelled to explain who she is. Or was. Can we really say *was* about Sylvia Plath? None of the women now writing poetry in America could have written as they have, not quite, without the example of Sylvia Plath. If they breathe poetry, they breathe that which has Plath in it.They may not know this, may not actually know her poems, are unlikely to know her. Because these days her absence is more pronounced than her presence, they may know her glancingly but not wholly. Still Sylvia Plath's presence abides in the ways any contemporary poem gets written, in what is possible, what is assumed, and most especially in the conviction that the self and its myths—their constructions and sources, evidences, spoors—are the only true and inevitable subject for the poet.

Reading *The Collected Poems* straight through on a gray fall day, after a week of dipping in and out of it, I am astonished to discover this poet is not the Plath I have vaguely remembered, the Plath I have called *interesting,* that epithet, when students jittery with their fresh discoveries of her have asked what I think. So caught up in this cranky, beautiful, maudlin, neurotic, soaring book am I that I have rummaged the shelves to read those critical assessments of contemporary poetry which I have casually acquired out of a mild intention to read them someday. I discover what I did know: she has become a critical industry, the subject of all manner of intense speculation. There is even a book whose purpose is to set at rest the burning question of whether she is the creator of her ex-husband Ted Hughes or the creation of that poet. Everyone, it appears, has had to have a say about her. No index is complete without her name. There is much talk of the Plath myth, many sincere assertions that this essay and that study will penetrate the myth and lay bare the real Sylvia Plath: here she is obsessed with love, there she is a hatemonger; her trouble is men, in spades; she is schizophrenic or depressed. Robert Phillips, in *The Confessional Poets,* says, "In the act of committing her confession to paper, she was committing her life to death." I bet Robert Phillips wishes he hadn't said that. I think it is balderdash. Doubtless there is good and even sufficient passion in all the speculative muttering her poetry has engendered but most of it seems little more than a snipe hunt. She can't be explained away. Maybe we feel if we can't explain her we can't explain ourselves. We all feel we know her.

Yet if we know her, clearly we haven't a clue. Rummaging through my books, I keep returning to her *Johnny Panic and the Bible of Dreams* and to her *Letters Home.* But my hand will not stay long from *The Collected Poems*—and not because I make any attempt to correlate the poems with the prose and the letters—because the poems are just there like members of our family, the suspicious members. This book is the record of a life. That is an ordinary thing to say but not less true for saying it. Her life in most respects is ordinary, even typically American. Yet it is like the life of a crowd all at once, only a special, enormously talented, complicated, hyper-hungry crowd. In that crowd the real Sylvia Plath will not stand up, quite. Perhaps we may be self-generous enough to say we are that crowd and through her poems we almost see ourselves. This is why we know her and don't know her.

Flip Wilson, the black comedian, has told us, "What you see is what you get." But is it what we want? How do we know what we want? Did Sylvia Plath know? There are as many answers to that as there are dissections of her poetry. Her selves wanted different things, with varying intensity, and maybe her great struggle was the attempt to manage those selves. At any rate we shall see, no one can doubt, a surf of reviews, views, studies, and reappraisals, and if the smugness is not too thick we may learn something valuable. But we can learn better from the poems. They have stung me as never before and they compel me to talk, too, about who Sylvia Plath is, whom I knew so little until *The Collected Poems.*

Many of us spend, and have spent, our literal and literary lives well outside the New York-Cambridge corridor and we just can't fully understand the young woman Sylvia Plath was, the woman who seems so desperately to have wanted the coinage and spoils of the eastern life. Smith and Wellesley colleges, the starlet writer for *Mademoiselle,* meetings with famous writers and teachers, a Fullbright to England's Cambridge University, publication not merely of a first collection of poems at age twenty-eight but a truly significant book, publication before that of poems in magazines which would bring her eastern certification—this was some of what she wanted and got. Where the roads diverged she took the intellectual one, the well-traveled one. But it wasn't enough. She wanted to be perfect, a new Keats. She says in "Cambridge Notes," written at twenty-four, "I too want to be important." And she adds, "By being different." Even in the boonies we understand that. Only she by god did it.

Yet, I think, Sylvia Plath also wanted another eastern road, one that she denigrated as the scribbling young intellectual. She wanted to be very pretty, charming, well-dressed, well-heeled, well-loved, well-married, the kind of young woman who shimmers early on and goes sadly, painfully soft in John Updike's fiction. She wanted to be an intellectual Junior Leaguer. That, too, is a kind of perfection. And it is hardly different from the dreams of most young Americans, excepting eastern idiosyncrasies. Out here we may not seek exactly the objects of her desires, but the desire is something we know all too well. We recognize that in her physical ache to achieve the "perfection" of status she would attach to publishing in the "right" magazines. She says, "*New Yorker* rejection of poems may smack me in the stomach any morning. God, it is pretty poor when a life depends on such ridiculous sitting ducks as those poems, ready for editors' grapeshot." Sylvia Plath, too, could be "shot down." She wanted the perfect life, fame, fortune, glory, love. To what shall the heart be given?

Her wanting turns so scary at times that in "Cambridge Notes" she writes herself a homiletic reminder: "PS: Winning or losing an argument, receiving an acceptance or rejection, is no proof of the validity or value of personal identity. One may be wrong, mistaken, a poor craftsman, or just ignorant—but this is no indication of the true worth of one's total human identity: past, present, and future!"

She wanted to be a good girl, a good woman. That sort of corn pone was something Plath had to chuck out to be the poet she was destined to be. Maybe she never had a choice; maybe her only choice was to learn to ignore the self that was a good, conscientious soldier. By now I may have fabricated entirely some words I *think* I heard the writer Shelby Foote say twenty years ago. I think he told George Garrett's class that he would stick into the oven the head of any wife who got in the way of his book. I was young, appalled, angered, and confused. Weren't writers noble citizens? Perhaps Foote meant that metaphorically, if he said it. But there is Faulkner saying any number of old ladies might be sacrificed for Keats's "Ode on a Grecian Urn." All the necessary do-gooders in society, including those inside us, may very well *understand* what Faulkner and Foote mean, but they do not know it as the obsessive writer does. This writer is bound to the relentless pursuit of perfection, and perfection changes so that the pursuit is both endless and increasingly insular. The perfectionist ceases to care about the conventional world and then the stakes go up. Failure often becomes the poet's fear and a looming companion. This is why when Sylvia Plath has six years of incredibly intense writing behind her at the age of twenty-nine she says in "Context" that "The poets I delight in are possessed by their poems as by the rhythms of their own breathing." Ted Hughes talks about this in the fine introduction to *Johnny Panic and the Bible of Dreams:* "It was only when she gave up that effort to 'get outside' herself, and finally accepted the fact that her painful subjectivity was her real theme, and that the plunge into herself was her only real direction, and that poetic strategies were her only real means, that she suddenly found herself in full possession of her genius—with all the special skills that had developed as if by biological necessity, to deal with those unique inner conditions."

This change of life sounds easy enough. It sounds as if Plath matured enough to select the life of the artist and abandon all other dreams of perfection. But it was not so. In *Letters Home* there is ample evidence of the girl who wanted to belong back home even as she panted to live in Yeats's old London flat. She is sincerely devoted to seeing Mr. Hughes has the wifely support which will make him a great man even as she notes, dazzled, all the great men and women she is meeting. Her letters show you a young wife and mother in curlers, surrounded by diapers, frenetic, trying to be a perfect maiden, trying to control the insurgent writer in her. I keep thinking that had she lived she would be sporting L. L. Bean finery and Sperry Topsiders. No, it wasn't an easy change which would allow her to isolate the self that wrote the poems at the expense of those others. Sylvia Plath had given her heart to nothing but the *idea* of perfection, not the practice of perfection. But she had no choice about that. She was a writer, however she might make poems that were stages upon which her other selves kept trying out. The maiden she wanted to be was constantly losing to the poet she was and she knew it. She says it in "Spinster":

> And round her house she set
> Such a barricade of barb and check
> Against such mutinous weather
> As no mere insurgent man could hope to break
> With curse, fist, threat
> Or love, either.

Though we might think so, she would not find it ironic that six years after "Spinster" she is writing about *kindness* when she says abruptly, "The blood jet is poetry, / There is no stopping it."

During those six years Plath had learned to write what would be her poem, the poem which was unlike any other, the poem Ted Hughes and others call the Ariel poem. I like it that this poem takes the name of her horse, the horse she is hell-bent on in a predawn ride that is all fluid feeling: "Stasis in darkness. / Then the substanceless blue / Pour of tor and distances." Nobody ever rode a horse exactly like that, then she did. She not only rode it, but as the physical meld of the images shows she became it in blood and hoof and stride and foam. When she calls what this comes to "The dew that flies / Suicidal, at one with the drive / Into the red / Eye, cauldron of morning," it is not suicide that interests her but the ebb and surge of passion. It has to be sexual and has to feel total. Plath did not, of course, come to the Ariel poem without labor. *The Collected Poems* shows as none of her single volumes does the chorus of voices she had been hearing: Stevens, Ransom, Roethke, Eliot, Hardy, Hopkins, some Frost and Robinson, of course Shakespeare, even a little William Carlos Williams, and not a little Emily Dickinson. They were mostly the hard chargers, the stress makers with swift, clattering boots. Ted Hughes may have been responsible for reinforcing this direction but Plath's pre-Hughes juvenilia proves she was no sweet singer ever. Evanescence wasn't enough for her; she had to be the flame and the radiance, the electrical horse. She came close as early as 1956 with "Street Song" and "Black Rook in Rainy Weather." She failed often and often had partial successes but on such an ambitious scale that it seems unfair to compare her with most younger poets. In time she wrote more than her share of poems which altered ordinary reality for the rest of us, "Lady Lazarus," "Cut," "Death & Co.," "The Moon and the Yew Tree," "Daddy," "Blackberrying," and one of my favorites, "Among the Narcissi." There was that brief tour de force "The Munich Mannequins," where she wrote, "Perfection is terrible, it cannot have children." She meant that perfection is barren because it is absolute. She also meant the perfectionist should not be allowed to have children because they will be neglected. One of the most finely terrible poems was the last one she wrote, "Edge," which begins "The woman is perfected." Ted Hughes has spoken of the true poet's need to lay hold to the power circuit of the universe, a metaphor for the life that is in poetry as well as the life that poetry is. There are not many willing to pay the toll for that power. Sylvia Plath's *The Collected Poems* is a record of how she learned to ride that electric horse, sitting, then trotting, then galloping, finally becoming the current, the motion itself. *The Collected Poems* is that shimmering change, a gothic fairy tale with the properties of dry ice: it keeps, it burns, it lives.

Poetry became Sylvia Plath's life. It did not kill her except where it failed her. The record of these poems, 224 written after 1956—many in amazing jets that come one after another on the same day—and 50 written before 1956 (selected from 220 plus, Hughes says in his introduction), is the drive toward fusion of herself and poetry, a life she meant to perfect as deliberately and single-mindedly as Yeats had. There will be many arguments down the road about what, if anything, Plath perfected and a lot of talk about poets killing themselves. They don't have to kill themselves for art, but they won't amount to much without a killing drive. Moreover what does it matter how she died? I don't know why she killed herself. I don't care. And I don't think it helps us to know the value of her poetry when we hear the sort of gibberish that is in "Ariel's Flight: The Death of Sylvia Plath," by N. J. C. Andreason, who says: "The death of Sylvia Plath seems to have resulted from a complex interaction between personal conflicts, the strain of her creative drive, and recurrent psychiatric illness—three factors that hovered over her life and struck with vicious energy during its last months. The role of each of these must be examined and weighed. The weight of the evidence suggests that psychiatric illness must be implicated as the primary factor." Suppose we knew without a doubt what caused her death? What does that change? It will not explain nor can it alter the poems. It is a perverse logic which begins with the fact of Plath's suicide and works back to find the poems as scripts of illness. Poetry kept Sylvia Plath alive; her poems are ectoplasmic with the will to live, to be as right as poetry can be, to be unequivocally, seriously, perfectly the voice of the poem as magical as a heartbeat. That is a burden no poet can bear forever, and it surprises any poet who bears it at all. Plath knew this in the end of "Poppies in October":

> O my God, what am I
> That these late mouths should cry open
> In a forest of frost, in a dawn of cornflowers.

Maybe Sylvia Plath wanted too much life. We shall be likely to think that is something peculiarly and sinisterly American. We have lots of psychiatrists and psychocritics to tell us what happens when you want too much, too fast, and how you can get into corners where even the walls accuse you. But the Faust myth tells us how little new there is under the sun. And it breaks our hearts every time. It will be a hard heart that doesn't break at Sylvia Plath's story. I do not mean that we ought not, as we will anyway, sit before this book as before the open casket of one we loved and swap the prickly, picky stories and assays and conjectures and lies—good and bad—by which we keep alive the dead. I mean she tried to stay alive. And she did keep alive. The poems, famous and unknown, brilliant and blurred, show us that. They have made it possible for others to know and to enter the poem's struggle for life. Sylvia Plath cannot be blamed for all the weird, silly, decadent poems that followed her any more than the Beatles can be blamed for Wendy and the Spasmodics. Or whatever. Her dying may have been a failure greater than ours but is not her life somehow also greater than ours? More intense, closer to the heat? We know her because the shape of her words contains the shape of our lives. In a poem written during her thirtieth year, during the month of her death, she calls words "Axes / After whose stroke the wood rings, / And the echoes!" She was letting us know, as she had known for some time, that the chips could fall where they might. Perfect or not, she was a poet. She would be nothing else so long as the lightning kept striking, as Jarrell might have said. That is what I feel in *The Collected Poems*, the crack and sizzle of lightning that Mrs. Shelley invited down to create life. We can no more turn away from Sylvia Plath than we have been able to escape the unnamed creature we, not Mrs. Shelley, dubbed Frankenstein and Monster, the monster we persist in regarding as Death. If you think you know Sylvia Plath, read her again. For the first time.

The Strength of James Dickey

■

James Dickey, as a self-defined poet of "The Second Birth," has always been committed to discovering and exploring "his own uniquely human segment of the common consciousness" and to developing "a characteristic style suited to express his discoveries" (*The Suspect in Poetry*). To an unusual degree Dickey's critical prose illuminates his poetry and while he has attained to a style that is, as Pound says, "uncounterfeitable," Dickey's description of Robinson Jeffers speaks volumes about the poetry Dickey has published in the decade of the 1970s:

> Surely he provides us with plenty to carp about: his oracular moralizing, his cruel and repellant sexuality, his dreadful lapses of taste when he seems simply to throw back his head and howl, his slovenly diction, the eternal sameness of his themes, the amorphous sprawl of his poems on the page. The sheer power and drama of some of his writing, however, still carries the day despite everything, and this is not so much because of the presence of the Truth Jeffers believes he has got hold of but because of what might be called his embodiment of that Truth: Jeffers's gorgeous panorama of *big* imagery, his galaxies, suns, seas, cliffs, continents, mountains, rivers, flocks of birds, gigantic schools of fish and so on.
>
> (*Babel to Byzantium*)

In subject and in style and in appetite, Jeffers has influenced Dickey. Perhaps the single and profound difference is that Dickey has also and always lived in the social house, sometimes comfortably, and his poetry has consistently described a man's oscillating journey from that house to the field life of Nature. Behind this imaginative travel has been the conviction that man is everywhere the powerless stranger, a specter of himself, and the further conviction that through moments of electric, or energized, union with the world a man might become a heroic messenger to his kind. His problem has been to contact the power circuit of the universe and turn headlong for joy where "all things connect and stream toward light and speech." Before visions of exhaustion and language gone static, opaque, or habitual, many poets have turned quiet minimalists. Dickey, from the beginning, chose not merely grandeur, but the grandeur of failure always exhibited by the monomythical Hero: his best poems imply comedic and courageous resolution but end before the dominance of the indifferent universe. His style has progressively altered to demand a full fronting of poem and reader within the context of the failed power search whose aesthetic kinship is Romantic, revolutionary, and especially American.

Dickey's *Poems 1957–1967*, often as good as American poetry has gotten, shows the slow and steady development of the dense, drummingly cadenced poem that was intensely personal and privately imagistic in statemental lines alternately composed of kinetic verbals and mystic assertions with the present tense. There was throughout this selection a reliance on narrative, or linear progression, though narrative is often sacrificed for poems of contemplation. There are, in fact, not many poems which do not achieve a tenuous balance of story and meditation. Typically, Dickey shows movement from early poems overwhelmed by the lushness of sound to poems in which narrative and a hypnotically gorgeous texture of phrase blend to produce poems of hallucinatory clarity and amazing power. Consider the following stanzas, for example:

> Fog envelops the animals.
> Not one can be seen, and they live.
> At my knees, a cloud wears slowly
> Up out of the buried earth.
> In a white suit I stand waiting.
> ("Fog Envelops the Animals")
>
> I thought I saw the still sun
> Strike the side of a hammer in flight
>
> And from it a sea bird be born
> To take off over the marshes.
> ("At Darien Bridge")

Indeed, to my mind there are too many exceptional poems in *Poems 1957–1967* to cite the exemplary ones, but readers might compare "The

Heaven of Animals," "Pursuit from Under," and "Encounter in the Cage Country" with any poems written in the last thirty years. They will, I think, be seen to possess sustained originality and excellence. Too, readers will find in them, within the framework of narrative, Dickey's identification of the poet as the Chosen Man whose mission was always two-dimensional: to operate as the monomythical warrior for individual vitality and fertility and to personally transform a man's enervated selves to cohesive unity by engaging the infinite through finite actions and moments. H. L. Weatherby has clearly shown Dickey's attempts to exchange the spirit of humanness with recipients in the nonhuman natural world. This exchange represents Dickey's imaginative attempt to make a true connection to the continuous energy of the phenomenal and animal world; its way is the way of both prayer and poetry which seeks otherworldly vision. In "Approaching Prayer" Dickey goes into his dead father's attic, a kind of temple, where he literally puts on his father's hunting sweater, a pair of spurs for his father's gamecocks, and the head of a killed boar:

> Nothing. Perhaps I should feel more foolish,
> Even, than this.
> I put on the ravelled nerves
> And gray hairs of my tall father
> In the dry grave growing like fleece,
> Strap his bird spurs to my heels
> And kneel down under the skylight.
> I put on the hollow hog's head
> Gazing straight up
> With star points in the glass eyes
> That would blind anything that looked in
>
> And cause it to utter words.

The critical response to Dickey's poetry has been to point out emphatically his storytelling and his beast-vision. This has, I think, masked an equally powerful and characteristic side of his work, his attempt to dramatize the social house. I mean Dickey's attempts to consider what contemplative states of being may be available to the man who lives, as most of us do, in the ordinary suburbs. Because Dickey's wandering hero is dominantly engaged in motorcycling, hunting, flying, climbing mountains, or making love, we perhaps fail to observe that this figure is inevitably a prisoner. His act of the mind—the act of contemplation—is to know "Identities! Identities!" ("Mangham") as a kind of horizon he will never reach. Or, if it is reached, a horizon which leaves a man not energized but once more the prisoner of illusion. Experiential reality, Dickey has been at some pains to show, is no more inherent in vivid and memorable portraits of aerial combat than it is in mathematics contemplated as language. James Dickey's poems have been as much sorties in epistemology and ontology as in the spoors of the dark woods. That Dickey is, like most Southern writers, divided in his loyalties to the self as macho realist and the self as intellectual explains much about the deceptive surfaces of his poems. Because the search for the energizing Truth was always doomed, as the intellectual Dickey knows, he has been a poet for whom "the embodiment of that Truth," or the development and the refinement of style, was very nearly all there could be.

Dickey's vision of becoming an animal, like Keats's wish to become a nightingale, was always doomed. That road foreclosed, the form of the poem need not be. The history of contemporary American poetry will record massive movement toward conventionally open styles. Ginsberg, Warren, Wright, Lowell, Roethke, Simpson, Dickey, and others have been accused of abandoning something like an ideal music for an inferior form. This argument is not resolvable because it masks political, economic, and cultural arguments metastasized to aesthetics. All we can really ask, must ask, of a poet is that his poem in part and in whole give pleasure, be durable, and lead us to better know what we dimly intuit as the reality of life. As contemporary poets began to feel in the late 1950s and early 1960s that inherited verse forms were sealing them off from realized experience, preventing the poem from answering its contemporary function, they moved from verse repetitions to repetitions of image, phrase, and symbol. For Dickey this meant the form of "The Fiend," "Falling," or what he has called a "shimmering wall of words." It was a form identified by long lines and sweeping periodic sentences in which the single poetic line carried truncated and whole his earliest two-, three-, and four-stress statement-lines. For example, here is Dickey's first draft of a few lines from "The Fiend," as shown by the manuscript in the Washington University Rare Books collection:

> Walking moodily, head down, a worried accountant,
> And he is gliding up among
> The seagreen light of its branches,
> The inside light, the light flowing out,
> Floating out, and turning the tree
> Into something with a light of its own
> Flowing back in through the window.
> He prowls the air outside
> Along the limbs, and finds her

Talking on the phone, chewing gum.
He can wait; he lives
On imagination, and on
Invisibility. The wind sways him softly; she must sleep.
He stands idly, legs crossed,
On a limb, his eyes coming out in a curve
Around the bole, everything in his pockets
Rigid with purpose. She gets up; he follows her along the limb
Into another room.

These lines appear as follows in the published form of "The Fiend":

He has only to pass by a tree   moodily walking   head down
A worried accountant   not with it   and he is swarming
He is gliding up the underside light of leaves   upfloating
In a seersucker suit   passing window after window of her building.
He finds her at last, chewing gum   talking on the telephone.
The wind sways him softly   comfortably sighing   she must bathe
Or sleep.   She gets up, and he follows her along the branch
Into another room.   She stands there for a moment   and the. . . .

Dickey has printed his lines for opportune enjambment and he has moved to include complete actions within the gap-punctuated sentence. Clearly, James Dickey understood graphics as well as Charles Olson. With "May Day Sermon to the Women of Gilmer County, Georgia, by a Woman Preacher Leaving the Baptist Church," Dickey had taken this variation of his form to its extreme and every subsequent poem has shown a gradual return to more conventional lineation. (Though the recently appearing poems of *Puella,* his next collection, indicate this may not hold true.)

Oddly enough, Dickey's formal evolution was away from narrative's temporal progression and resolution and toward spatial experience, which consists in spite of talky rhetoric in image and symbol density. Poetry is the flow of the mind to a large extent and is intrinsically spatial; it seeks circularity and simultaneity. Dickey's hero-journey linearly tries to organize what is spatially presented, the Truth of emotional complexity and psychological depth. At his extreme in "May Day Sermon" Dickey had moved as close to cinematic poetry as possible, seeking dimension and action through what remained an oral and intensely stressed convention, the rhetorical poetry of the sermon. Dickey's formal oscillation parallels that earlier myth of oscillation between field and house and, without being at all judgmental, we can see the analogues of the energized man and of the power of poetry from Beowulf to Jekyll and Hyde to television's Incredible Hulk. (The same mythical impulse lies behind the Million-Dollar Man, the Bionic Woman, and all other superhuman figures.) Dickey's progression as a poet, that is to say, has been Faustian: from lyric toward epic, to novel and film, with the final choice of mindless explosion or retrenchment to a controlled art. The figure Dickey created for Robinson Jeffers, the poet howling and tearing at words like a hungry dog, has often enough been himself. It is precisely this Faustian progress that *The Zodiac* (1976) enacts, its dying poet driven to exclaim:

> But I want to come back with the secret
> with the poem
>
> That links up my balls and the strange, silent words
> Of God his scrambled zoo and my own words
>
> and includes the
> earth
>
> Among the symbols.

The Zodiac is a poem about fear and estrangement and what poetry can do to make felt "The star-beasts of intellect and madness." Dickey's preface tells us this is "the story of a drunken and perhaps dying Dutch poet who returns to his home in Amsterdam after years of travel and tries desperately to relate himself, by means of stars, to the universe." Organized in twelve zodiacal and seasonal panels, occurring within a period of time as controlled and symbolic as Leopold Bloom's, and being an approximation of the dying poet's mind-flow mediated through Dickey, with intrusive commentary by Dickey, *The Zodiac* is not a narrative progression except as the poet-hero's madness implies the eternal story of "connecting and joining things that lay their meanings / Over billions of light years," or the madness that comes of failure and fear. Nature, in *The Zodiac,* is either the meaning of stars or their deadness. Dickey's oscillating journey, in the poet's "story," is now between the failure of everything on earth (history, time, love, home—all betrayals) and whatever, if anything, the distant stars are saying. In this sense *The Zodiac* is entirely self-referential and everything to which the poet responds leaves him aware he is only a prisoner of illusion. His darkness reigns.

The Zodiac seems to me important as an impressive failure and as a transitional poem for Dickey. Its failure is partly caused by the absence of narrative and hence an absence of event which might generate the storm of emotional rhetoric and partly caused by the artificial organization of zodiacal panels which remain static and shed little, if any, of the Pythagorean aura of divine immanence. Drunk not only on *aquavit* but on cosmological abstractions, Dickey's poet is harassed by images of Time in both the world-city and in the "Peaceful-sea-beast-blue" of universal space—but his life in time is a failure and an imprisonment. He has no life in or out of the world and his homecoming is the occasion to ruminate, while attempting to write, on all the great unknowns. But why this apparently diseased and world-bruised symbolic man should particularly constitute a window into some universal reality, or how, is never quite clear. For all the poem's tortured anguish and virtually hacked-out-alive language, it has the feel of ideas sketched hugely but neither dramatically nor clearly. There is simply no sense that the emotional progression comes to a rest except that the poet sits writing a prayer for "the music / That poetry has never really found." No one will ever regard that as a worthless prayer; nor will anyone, I think, ever imagine that Dickey has been less than the most intense searcher for that music. But the expression of the poet's wish is a pitiful substitution for a credible and unified ending to this poem. Lacking necessity and motion, failing to coalesce around the secret it aspired to claim, *The Zodiac* turns Dickey's spatial organization into spatial occupation. The poem rambles in space and fills up space. On the other hand, there is so much plainly good and true writing in the poem that I am tempted to feel it is impertinent to cavil. Ignoring the poet who writes "He polar-bears through the room" is sometimes all you can do before ghostly luminosity, the sheer screaming silence, the gentle wonder of vision when

> He looks sideways, out and up   and there it is;
>   The perpetual Eden of space
>   there where you want it.

If *The Zodiac* suffers from Faustian explosion, Dickey's newest collection does not, or not on the whole. This is perhaps because ten of the poems in "The Strength of Fields" section of the book by the same title were published by 1973 and are, in character, continuous with the style appearing late in *Poems 1957–1967* and in *The Eye-Beaters, Blood, Victory, Madness, Buckhead and Mercy* (1970).These poems are not walls of words but they avoid such conventions as a continuous left-hand margin, stanzas, repetitive line-lengths, and consistent punctuation. Ordinarily such matters have little to do with what poetry essentially is, but Dickey calls our attention to them to insist he is working less with narrative than with spatial suspensions of states of being. In fact, there is little new in these fourteen poems, but that does not compromise their general excellence. In all of them we find Dickey's obsessive and linking image patterns of water, flight, evasion, ascent, descent, the ghosts of the dead, and mythopoeic animals, though Dickey's metaphoric transformation with the beast-world is remarkably absent. Dickey seems, since *The Eye-Beaters,* to locate his poems more firmly in the social and public house of human society and the genesis of the energized man finds its most dramatic moments in sexual epiphanies and the remembered dangers of war. At age fifty-eight, Dickey's vision of heroic glory remains intact but the Melville-like dark abysm against which the powerless man contends has come, like the military drums of his neighboring Fort Jackson, closer to the living place. Still, Dickey's problem in *The Strength of Fields* (1977) is:

> how
> To withdraw   how to penetrate and find the source
> Of the power you always had

especially when all one's best strengths and efforts have revealed that icily indifferent universe of *The Zodiac.* It is possible now, I think, to argue that that pattern of oscillation in Dickey's poetry was also an oscillation between a tragic anguish and a comedic joy. Where earlier Dickey's vision of connection and resolution seemed dominant, perhaps the product of a war survivor's faith in the future, his poems now stand in the present of "death-mud shaking" and they increasingly look backward in great despair.

Dickey's title poem,"The Strength of Fields," believes nevertheless that we "can all be saved / By a secret blooming." In this poem, as in his earlier poetry, Dickey skates the thin ice of fear and trembling, courageously and believably assuming the role of the Chosen Man doomed to bring back from the psychic underworld the secret of life's fertility and renewal. There is no dramatic occasion or plot beyond the presiding ghost of the monomyth's rite of passage but the poem has the force of the private man's public declaration of faith in the earth and the dead who speak to us through "the renewing green" and "the homes of men." Straight through Dickey speaks with the power of a man who has seen beyond the surfaces of things and, hard as it is for me to say it, he redeems us.

Each of the thirteen other poems in Dickey's first section aspire in one way or another to be acts of redemption. "Root-Light, or the Lawyer's Daughter," the tightest of them all, is an epiphany of passion's beginning, a kind of folk religion's "Image / Of Woman to last / All your life" as she was once seen diving into and rising up from the St. Mary's River. This poem's reverent excitement matches the sexual aura and jittery magic of "The Voyage of the Needle," in which a man taking a bath remembers himself as a child who learned from his mother the "scientific trickery" that would allow a sewing needle to float. "Remnant Water" alone returns Dickey to the animal world. In this case, he witnesses the death of a pond. As if an extension of the last, dying carp (and Dickey's readers will note the poem's relationship to Dickey's earlier elegy, "For the Last Wolverine"), Dickey is the shamanistic genius of the place. His words alone can redeem "my people gone my fish rolling" and his mission is "Suffering its consequences, dying, / Living up to it." It is fair, here, to point out that Dickey's poems have always required great leaps of faith on the reader's part and such a faith in his dramatic illusion is still necessary to take seriously the tribal godhead who mourns a pond. But Dickey is, I believe, convincing in such poems as very few are.

Also among the poems of this section are five poems of war experience. Dickey had, in his journals, once called this collection *War Embrace* but he rightly recognized that this would have been both a misleading and constricting title. Each of his war poems is a kind of latter-day redemption of those lost not to war deaths but to war's betrayals of ordinary human responsibility. None of the poems glorify combat; however, in the context of the soldier's unanswerable introspection which asks "O why / In Hell are we doing this?" each poem seeks to celebrate those who passed through the valley of death with human distinction, which is to say committed acts of fearful evasion and bright courage. "Camden Town," which may be the best of all of Dickey's war poems, shows a cadet pilot's training flight, the fear which causes him to hide under his instruments so that his ship becomes a Flying Dutchman until he gathers himself and swings the ship "East, and the deaths and nightmares / And training of many." It is not too much to say that with these poems James Dickey reminds us that all war survivors may be psychological and emotional flying dutchmen. Soldiers, it ought to be remembered, have not always chosen to fight but have been chosen to fight by the country to which they feel complex and necessary loyalties. Not since Randall Jarrell has there been an American poet who has written well about soldiering, that area of human experience which is almost unshareable for the individuals who survive it. No one currently writing poetry writes about war as well as James Dickey does. We are always living in a time of rattling sabers, now louder and now softer, and one has only to read these poems to comprehend the huge psychic wound of war, a debt really and one whose amortization is endless.

Two of these poems, however, are superior to anything in *The Strength of Fields*. They are "False Youth: Autumn: Clothes of the Age" and "Exchanges." The latter poem takes the form of an interlineated use of lines of poetry by the dead Joseph Trumbal Stickney, thus creating a sort of dialogue between the words of Dickey and those of Stickney. Dickey likes this sort of "contest" or dialectic motif; it is responsible for the "Dueling Banjos" theme to the movie version of his novel *Deliverance*, for an interesting and eccentric review-debate he imagined between himself and Randall Jarrell, and for the form of a number of previous poems. In "Exchanges" there is not the animal-man form of transformation, or exchange, which Dickey frequently employed early in his career. Rather the poem constructs juxtapositions of what we give and what we are given of value in our lives. In *Sorties* (1971) Dickey said of this poem: "I have got in some of the current preoccupation with the environment, as well as a good deal about Los Angeles, nature, space exploration, and damn near everything else except Vietnam." We cannot say of Dickey, he is too modest. The poem imagines Dickey and a lover sitting atop a Pacific cliff at Zuma Point where, he recalls, "we sang and prayed for purity" while they are surrounded by smog and oil-slick. In changes of time that shift like his guitar Dickey reveals to us that his lover has died, she who had gone with him to watch the Apollo moon shot. Where now, the poem appears to ask, is the dead place—that far shining rock of the moon or this "deadest world of all"? Orchestrating "ballad / After ballad" of what he calls "Appalachian love" with Stickney's vision of "*The last of earthly things / Carelessly blooming in immensity,*" Dickey creates a vision of death grinding against the life necessarily celebrated by "all those / *Of the line of wizards and saviors.*" Dickey imagines that the Apollo moon exploration may very well signal "the quality of life / And death changed forever" as some kind of new dimension of being beyond Cartesian reality may have happened. But, he says, "Nothing for me / Was solved." All we have ever asked of poets is to insist on life and often enough that is what they redeem from the chaos of experience and words. In "Exchanges" Dickey has done that.

In spite of the general and significant accomplishment of *The Strength of Fields,* this book has some pronounced disasters. "For the Running of the New York Marathon" reminds me of Dickey's early and uncollected "The Sprinter's Mother." It is a bathetic and sentimental grabbing of the cosmic hand-mike to proclaim they also win who only show up and trot. It is not to be doubted that Dickey, once again the war survivor who said that serving in World War II was like being on a great football team you knew couldn't lose, regards the mass of runners as tangible evidence of democracy's virtues but the naive enthusiasm of a Richard Simmons in poetry is sheer corn. A similar failure, with better moments, is "For the Death of Vince Lombardi," a poem which demonstrates by implication Dickey's formidable power and a singular weakness.

Ostensibly Dickey hovers near the hospital deathbed of the cancer-riddled legendary football coach. This is the speech of one hero paying homage to another's manly courage, pride, passion, and sacrifice. Lombardi, who was by frequent published testimony revered and hated by his players, said, "Fatigue makes cowards of us all." That is an enormously compassionate and valuable perception. But Lombardi also said, "Winning isn't everything. It's the only thing." This is true in the combat of nations, even true in personal self-defense. It may be true in business but in sport it is only ugly. Was Vince Lombardi a tragic hero or only a George Patton without a war? There is every opportunity in "For the Death of Vince Lombardi" for a great elegy of interrogation, for a contemporary psychological drama, for a grand resolution. Dickey seems to have had such a poem in mind, but there is mostly only a lot of huffing admiration. There is no dramatic occasion out of which Dickey's oracular moralizing *must* arise. Dickey is, therefore, just gratuitous when he says, "Did you make of us, indeed, / Figments over-specialized ghosts / Who could have been real / Men in a better sense?" Because Dickey begs the questions of who "us" is, what "real men" are, and what a "better sense" might mean, such writing smacks of superior postseason banquet bouquets.

Dickey should know this poem's weakness as well as anyone, for his splendid poem "The Bee" (*Poems 1957–1967*) does exactly right what "For the Death of Vince Lombardi" does wrong: it dramatizes human weakness and the necessity of manly virtues. There, a middle-aged father has to summon long untested emotional and physical powers, taught to him by his ex-coach Shag Norton, to redeem a son frightened into traffic by a whirling bee. Dickey knows he will, and in fact does, hurt the child that even so he may be unable to save—when he tackles the child and drives him to ground beyond passing cars. When Dickey writes, "God damn / You, Dickey, dig," all the force of education, love, and art demand just those words. When he writes, "Drive, *Drive*" in the Lombardi poem the words are only habitual rhetoric. Dickey's powerful vision of the Viking death and life of every man is tragically real in "The Bee" but it is only sententious in the conclusion of the Lombardi poem: "We're with you all the way / You're going forever, Vince." Dickey has given us no occasion to make *felt* the idea that the hero's importance is not merely the fact of his death but is, or ought to be, his lifelong defeat of the spirit's sickness in each act of courage. Lombardi forced fatigue to strength and fear to an energizing vision. On his best day Dickey has been Lombardi's equal. On such a day Dickey would have cut this poem.

Fourteen poems comprise the second half of Dickey's book and are titled "Head-Deep in Strange Sounds: Free-Flight Improvisations from the UnEnglish." Each poem carries an acknowledger such as *from, after, near,* and hails such poets as Montale, Aleixandre, and Paz. These are, apparently, what he called "misreadings" in *Sorties*. In a limited edition of these poems published by the Palaemon Press, Dickey says in a preface:

> With these poems I hope to bring the activity previously known as translation into a realm toward which the changing of a poem from one language into another has seemed to move ever since the Chinese renderings of Ezra Pound. The poems in this book do not pretend to any sort of literalness; they are free-ranging. My motive for taking such liberties as I have done with the originals is simply the fact that I have chosen to take those liberties; each poem is as much of my own invention as it is of the concept and execution of the poet who first initiated it, and in some cases the poem is more mine than his.

Whether these poems are regarded as translations, imitations, or mutations, all continue to work with Dickey's theme of the heroic Energized Man and all are, in style, radically discontinuous with Dickey's characteristic poetry. They are short, terse, and intensely imagistic of body though written mostly in long, gap-punctuated, and spatially dispersed lines. There was always a surreal quality to Dickey's poems and it is emphatic in these poems. If there is a precursor to this work, it is *The Zodiac* and its heightened dream of vitality surrounded by disease, death, and doom. Each poem feels like a parable but is not, being essentially a kind of nakedly psychic speech, studded with image clusters, that blurs both dramatic occasion and public accessibility. "Low Voice, Out Loud" is a familiar plea for sexual intensity: "Let us go back into the immense and soft-handed double / Fire-bringing ignorance." Dickey has ever been a writer of nervy consciousness who would like, at certain times, to get as shut of consciousness as the most mindlessly rutting animals. "Nameless" is a statement about evil, good, and beauty. "Math" continues Dickey's long fascination with pre-Socratic philosophy and the mysticality of language. "Small Song," "Poem," "When," and "A Saying of Farewell" are rages against the imprisonment of death. A number of these poems seem to me so impenetrable as to prevent anyone's knowing what they are about.

Perhaps the best of this new brand of Dickey poem is "Purgation," which is addressed to the ninth-century Chinese master poet Po Chu-yi. It describes the emotional season for "wildfire" and renewal. The poem is a stunning and wonderfully gentle lyric, as a few lines will show:

> My ancient friend, you are dead, as we both know.
>
> But I remember, and I feel the grass and the fire
> Get together in April   with you and me, and that
> Is where I want to be
>   both sighing like grass and fire.

I cannot help feeling that these poems from the UnEnglish and Dickey's *Strength of Fields* "carr[y] the day despite everything," as Dickey said of Robinson Jeffers, but not merely because of the embodiment of *his* Truth. No, it is because he returns us to our most deeply longed-for lives, and he shows us those lives in motion, as few are gifted to do. There are changes in James Dickey's poetry: a deepened sense of mortality and fragility, a less frenetic impatience with the constraints of form, and a joy less the result of making literature than of setting the large visionary personality against fear and trembling. No one was ever a greater lover of poetry, of the sheerness of passionate sound and the honesty of feel that poetry makes our first and last way of knowing the labor that life is. No one has tried to demand more of art as the ungulled and absolute measure of individual experience. Dickey's strength, the force of this book, is that he is not a poet of argument and has never tried to be one. He has been and he remains a poet who turns the world "tall / In the April wind." To live with some kind of meaning and purpose that might translate into joy, to sing life into permanence and glory—this has been James Dickey's accomplishment. He says what that can mean for all of us in one of my favorite poems:

FALSE YOUTH: AUTUMN: CLOTHES OF THE AGE

—For Susan Tuckerman Dickey

Three red foxes on my head, come down
There last Christmas from Brooks Brothers
As a joke, I wander down Harden Street
In Columbia, South Carolina, fur-haired and bald,
Looking for impulse in camera stores and redneck greeting cards.
A pole is spinning
Colors I have little use for, but I go in
Anyway, and take off my fox hat and jacket
They have not seen from behind yet. The barber does what he can
With what I have left, and I hear the end man say, as my own
Hair-cutter turns my face
To the floor, Jesus, if there's anything I hate
It's a middle-aged hippie. Well, so do I, I swallow
Back: so do I   so do I
And to hell. I get up, and somebody else says
When're you gonna put on that hat,
Buddy? Right now. Another says softly,
Goodbye, Fox. I arm my denim jacket

On and walk to the door, stopping for the murmur of chairs,
And there it is
hand-stitched by the needles of the mother
Of my grandson   eagle riding on his claws with a banner
Outstretched as the wings of my shoulders,
Coming after me with his flag
Disintegrating, his one eye raveling
Out, filthy strings flying
From the white feathers, one wing nearly gone:
Blind eagle but flying
Where I walk, where I stop with my fox
Head at the glass to let the row of chairs spell it out
And get a lifetime look at my bird's
One word, raggedly blazing with extinction and soaring loose
In red threads burning up white until I am shot in the back
Through my wings   or ripped apart
For rags:

Poetry.

Part IV

■

An Honest Tub

Passion, Possibility, and Poetry

Notes on Responsibility and the Teaching of Creative Writing

Beagling

Heroes of the Spirit

An Honest Tub

"All art is the disengaging of a soul from place and history. . . ."
W. B. Yeats

■

It was Christmas day. A rare snow had fallen, maybe three inches, and had covered the hundred or so work-boats berthed in the small harbor. We had shoveled and scraped it off the *Peter Liss*. Now, piled in Billy Carmines's Volkswagen, we headed home. We were sweaty and loose, sipping a communal bottle. Billy was lying about vicious cheaters who ran buy-boats. (A buy-boat is a floating wholesaler, a middleman between those who catch seafood and those who retail it.) I, who knew nothing about watermen and their boats, listened like a child, though already I saw Billy had slipped into the lie. Just the night before I had caught him, drunk as I had been, in a story about a winter so bad that his Uncle Luke had got ice on his washboards thick enough that he'd taken out his prick to hammer it away. Now Billy swore that his father, Peter Liss, who sat glum and small between bottle and windshield, had once put-a-wish on one particularly unscrupulous son of a bitch whose buy-boat had immediately sunk.

"Oh shit," I said in the back seat.

Peter Liss swiveled his turtle head around the edge of the seat and said, "You go to college, too?"

Sometimes late at night, reading, I think about Peter Liss, especially when I read the Anglo-Saxon poems I love. "The Wanderer" says:

The forms of his kinsmen take shape in the silence;
In rapture he greets them; in gladness he scans
Old comrades remembered. But they melt into air
With no word of greeting to gladden his heart.

What lasts? The answers to that are about all any writer's words try to tell him. His books are the answers he allows the reader to overhear. "The Wanderer" tells us that "All the foundation of earth   shall fail!" But later in his poem, to buck up his courage, he says "Good man is he   who guardeth his faith." A writer is after knowing faith in what. Or who. Joseph Conrad found faith in wretched Kurtz, who had an idea, who was an idea to T. S. Eliot—one gone wrongly out of the world when the hollow men marched in. Eliot and Conrad, like the Wanderer, knew Kurtz's idea made him one of those who were "men enough to face the darkness." His idea, or illusion, gave him character enough to hope for dignity, for life beyond mere survival. Kurtz and his writers got this illusion from a people and a place. The illusion was an obligation, to the dead and the living, a responsibility for the life and the place that continues after us. Flannery O'Connor says about place that "The writer operates at a peculiar crossroads where time and place and eternity somehow meet. His problem is to find that location." The writer who imaginatively claims a place as the foundation for vision knows something about the illusions by which it is both possible and necessary to live. That knowledge isn't so easy to come by but when the writer has it, he has, it appears, his obligation, his subject, his influence.

Regionalism, like free verse, is a self-evident lie. The regionalist can't get beyond strict image. The writer of place can't help reaching through image to vision. The vision he wants is not an accurate representation, for example Rockefeller's Williamsburg, but a living identity, a character, the image lifted to the level of symbol but made powerful, active, and affective because it is in a *felt* place. His right ground is memory's space and time, not geography's fact. His place is more emotional than literal because it supports and is supported by the illusions of living men. And the dead, as well. His place is not precisely real, which is why Wallace Stevens wrote that "The genuine artist is never 'true to life.' " Later Stevens says, "a poem would be nothing without some meaning. The truth is that meaning is an awareness and a communication." This meaning is the obligation of the writer of place, as it is not for the regionalist.

The only community a writer is really interested in, unless he has both eyes on critics or dollars or both, is the community of character, that man or woman in action and in spirit attaining as near as possible to nobility before being ignobly crunched by the adversity that is inescapable. This writer doesn't give a damn about accurate geography or what place critics attach his name to. He cares only how useful a place is in penetrating to and through the illusions men can live by. For him, character in place is meaning. He measures himself as part of what lasts by how well and truly he attends to or abuses that faith.

That we do not last, hack critics, sociologists, and suffering professors have been telling us for a very long time. That we are entries, numbers, digits in life's little ledger is supposed to be a discovery of Modernism. Either we have no values or the values we have are archaic. Or impotent. What we have got, if anything, are illusions. Apparently we don't have to lose, like King Lear, kingdom and daughters to see the abyss before and around us. We just have to listen. They'll tell us, especially the pale critics, we're just tiny illusions orbiting aimlessly in the Big Illusion. And as illusions, we have illusions, what might otherwise be called convictions, principles, values, ideas. These, many suppose, matter less than a writer's handling of the poetic line or the inevitable movement of plot.

The writer of place is not so cerebral. He imagines a man's life has shape and meaning and that his purpose, imaginatively, is to try to separate what a man thinks he is from what he knows he has been from what he desperately hopes he can be. He can do this only image by image, illusion by illusion, driving toward an awareness of and a communication of the obligations that are meaning. Robert Penn Warren's "History is what you can't / Resign from" may say all that can be said about what has formed the abiding obsession and influence of any writer. Perhaps what he most cannot resign from is the tale of one man who occupies the writer's chosen place and who becomes the active intersection of human illusions the writer knows he cannot ever fully understand but which he may dramatically possess. If he can communicate this man's being in a place, as Conrad makes us aware of Kurtz's relationship with primeval Africa, then he can communicate the history of men and the price a man pays to be one of those who are "men enough to face the darkness." Just so Kurtz becomes the price Marlow pays. It may be old-fashioned and portentous to believe it, but the writer I have in mind believes a man and a place last because he wills it, because he will not let it be otherwise. The discovery of such a man, in the memory or the imagination, gives the writer a lever with which he knows he can pry open the earth for the secrets of the dead. His obligation, that tricky word again, is to spend a lifetime deciphering and communicating those secrets. Only fools understand this to be nothing more than the registration of eccentric local color. That is, the writer of place seeks to know what it means to be, as Conrad, Faulkner, and Hemingway are forever saying, "one of us."

My first poems, and in some ways all I have ever written, are about the watermen from Poquoson, Virginia, a people and a town of which I was entirely ignorant until they hired me as a high school teacher of French and a coach of football. I was then twenty-two years old. My first, self-published, chapbook of poems was called *Bull Island,* the native name for Poquoson. In the world of my mind the lower Virginia waterman has become indistinguishable from the Anglo-Saxon wanderer. I regard him as mythic brother, father, and silent poet. Of him I know two things clearly: I will never understand him precisely and I cannot resign from trying to understand him. Yet, for me, he is not a type but a man and his son, two without whom I doubt I would ever have written at all. Were I to attempt this meandering speculation about their lives, their place, and art, both Billy Carmines and his father Peter Liss would, with vile and crusty affection, ridicule me for my fancy *idears.* How I love saying their word and hearing the *endearment* so unconsciously built into its corrupted form! Plain men and halves of one whole to me, they liked to think they had no idears, but they are the one idear that has got into me and that I have been trying to communicate since the day we buried the boat.

Peter Liss Carmines was dead, that was the main thing. He had been dead for two weeks, had been duly and properly put in the Methodist ground. The church accountants marked his ticket paid. I stood at the dock with his sons Billy and George, still unaware I was about to be part of something that would change my life. We were preparing to bury Peter Liss's boat. The sun was yet low ahead of us but the heat was intense, the humidity like invisible plaster. When you grow up in this climate you learn to move slowly. Breathing sometimes feels like whispering with your head in a bucket. But we moved even more gravely than the heat required.

I was an ignorant teacher in the high school where Billy's wife taught, where he had gone to school and had also taught. We partied together. They had already introduced me to the woman I would marry. I knew brother George, but not much. Billy was a junior high school principal now, a keeper of discipline, and George was what his problems grew up to be, a half-ass bar brawler and drifter. Both had been off and on watermen, like their father, but neither could stand up to the grinding labor, loneliness, and sad wages, unlike their father. If George hadn't happened to be unemployed again he would have been in Florida.

"Hot as shit," Billy said. We'd climbed aboard the *Peter Liss.* Billy knelt at the engine and tried to make a rusted cable fast to a car battery he had lugged along. Both brothers were grieving, though neither ever much got on with their father. There was none of the usual chatter about bluefish, booze, pussy, boats, or what one had forgotten more of than the other would ever learn.

I sat on the flat sheet of plywood nailed to the twenty-footer's stern, the cull-board on which a waterman culls oysters from empty shells. I looked south at Langley Air Force Base, across Back River, where a morning mist floated as pretty as you please. George, arms crossed and surly, leaned against the port washboard. The cigarette hanging from his lips made him look like James Dean. We all wore white T-shirts and faded jeans. Billy and George wore the waterman's tall rubber boots that had a red trim just at the knee. These were hard to find but you could get them at Rooster Smith's general store. Rooster kept decades of insults and credit in his head. He raised his son, Clyde Russell, with that credit in his head too, and the names of families and histories to go along. I had on white Converse low-cuts.

Billy worked at the engine until his shirt grayed with sweat. Finally the Lathrop sputtered and caught. I watched him adjust this, open that, close the other, working in a patient sequence. If he needed help, he didn't ask for it. George never offered any. There were bleaching crab fins all over the deck, without smell now, and a pair of pliers rusted to the wood. This boat hadn't sailed in some time.

The Lathrop died. Billy repeated the sequence and got it going. It never did, as a bad novel might say, roar to life. Slowly, reluctantly, belching and farting, dying down to be goosed into yet another shudder, it sounded about like the clunker that Humphrey Bogart so memorably nursed in *The African Queen*. We eased away from the pier.

The sun was now turning everything the color of lemon, even the stacked crab pots that look like they are made of chicken wire but are not. To starboard the tower on which the first American astronauts had trained stood high over Langley, for all the world a child's giant erector set abandoned in a backyard. Lyndon Johnson, quite objectively it was said, had thought the astronauts would do better in Houston, which is Texas. Local people said they had been screwed out of their future, meaning their payrolls. Peter Liss and the other watermen had said nothing. Maybe they hadn't noticed.

Once Peter Liss had sailed up this river to fish his crab pots. A crabber sets out maybe eighty pots over a mile of water. Each pot is daily baited, sunk to the bottom, marked by a rope and a Clorox bottle float, and then returned to daily so the crabber can lift the forty-pound pots one by one and take off his catch. Sometimes he'll sell crabs to a warehouse; sometimes he'll eat them. Ordinarily crabbers work deep channels. Peter Liss worked this river because he was old and it was safe water. He worked it also because he had done just that for more than fifty years. This day he was stopped before the first pot. The Coast Guard man said nobody could fish. Lyndon Johnson was visiting Langley. Lyndon Johnson was a man even Peter Liss had to notice.

Lyndon Johnson didn't know, Liss may have told us but probably did not, that the goddamn crabs would drown and rot in the cage; or that these crabs were all he and Miss Homer, his wife of more than fifty years, would have to eat that day. He probably didn't say that Johnson and his frigging moonmen had got flat in the way of a life that he hadn't known to be interrupted even by the German U-boats that used to surface at midnight and send in the bodies of dead American seamen, a way of life for these descendants of English fisherman that existed before the first white man heard of the Pedernales. But I remember Liss telling about the Coast Guard pistol easing down on him because he had said *something*. Of course, as Liss noted, that wasn't the first time. Now I watched that tower, eerie, dead as Lyndon Johnson. Dead as Liss, too.

We headed at the sun, toward the Chesapeake Bay. Off to the right was Hampton, Buckroe Beach, and Phoebus, the setting for William Styron's *Lie Down in Darkness*. I had read about Peyton Loftis and the Warwick Country Club while in college. It had seemed very real. We began to swing west around Plum Tree Island. The Air Force used Plum Tree as a bombing range. Sometimes they'd made little mistakes. I remembered Peter Liss describing kin that had been blown out of the water. He fished the same spot next day. We started across Egg Island Bar.

Liss had told Billy where to take the boat. By car it was only ten minutes from his house but we were riding in a forty-six-year-old heavy-bellied lady that took ten minutes to go fifty yards, if she felt like it and didn't quit. She quit just onto the bar. And kept on quitting. She stalled better than Proust. I almost believed she was resisting. Patiently, Billy coaxed her ahead. For the first time I began to understand he was, truly, a waterman. There was about him now a grim dignity. He simply *fit* what we were doing. I knew he was what was called, locally, a wild hair. He was the only man I'd ever known who had commanded a Coast Guard cutter and who, on his last active duty day, had, accidentally one supposes, run her full tilt into the Guard Headquarters dock at Portsmouth, shattering every window for three floors. The secretaries applauded him. I've bounced through gales in rowboats with Billy, my fingernails sunk into the pine planks, running wide open for no reason. I've gone with him up winding canals full of sunken hulls, skimming at almost fifty miles per hour with only a slice of moonlight on his teeth. He scared the shit out of me and I don't think he knew I was even there. Only himself against the night, the water, and himself. As I watched him fool with that engine I could see Liss doing the same thing year after year.

Billy had read William Warner's Pulitzer-Prize-winning *Beautiful Swimmers: Watermen, Crabs, and the Chesapeake Bay*. Very few watermen have. Billy knows how beautiful that book is, how close to righteous Warner is. He also knows that Warner has only written about the upper Bay. *Swimmers* doesn't touch the watermen from Hampton, Yorktown,

Poquoson, or Gloucester—all less than fifteen miles apart, men who think themselves entirely different according to their place. Well, they aren't very different. They make a living from crabs, oyster, fish, clams, whatever they can take. They love their boats like a cowboy loves his horse, only they wouldn't say so. They don't talk about it. They become it, are connected to the water and to a heritage by that workboat. Billy sent me a letter some years ago in which he describes what I didn't know that burial day about a waterman, his boat, and his idears:

> *Boat*
>
> His boat was a reflection of his personality. She was always shabby but well painted & coppered. She was built of bull pine planks that were two inches thick. She was always cluttered with oyster tongs, rope, crab traps, patent dips, old lunch bags (with biscuits—he wouldn't eat loaf bread). She had a small cabin that always smelled of mildew with old clothes, sou'wester, rusty wrenches lying everywhere. Her bow was always cov ered with rope never coiled, never neat. Her bow was lower than her stern when afloat because of the weight of her engine forward. She was slow & solid with, in later years, a Lathrop 64 horse power. During the 30ies and 40ies he used Model "A" engines but they wouldn't last over a couple of years. I was surprised to see how high & proud her bow was when she was on the railway. She was a good sailor in bad weather, wet & able. (Once Vernon Page & myself went with him because the weather was so bad—blowing a gale southwest. We got so wet in her cabin that we had to put on oil clothes & get on the stern).
>
> She had no name but everyone called her the "Peter Liss." She was built with the bottom lines of the old sail boats (Skipjack, Bugeye). So she never performed too well. With an engine. No matter how much power you used she would not plane only suck-down at the stern and carry a tremendous wave from bow & stern.
>
> He put a 40 gal. gas tank on the port side (the side he worked his tongs on) and kept it filled so she always listed to port thus the man working the starboard side had to raise his tongs higher & always looked like he was getting beat (not catching as many oysters as the other man). (Competition was always keen between the men in the same boat & between boats as to size of catch. If you wanted to say a man was a better oysterman you say he could turn the boat over on him—catch so many more oysters that the boat would list to your side.) He was an excellent oysterman worked longer than anyone else but left the dock later. He was never an early-bird. His epitaph

should have been "he was a hard working man made many a dollar gave an honest tub."

The *Peter Liss* coughed, pitched, and pooped out on the western edge of Egg Island Bar. This time she seemed gone for good. We drifted over white sand marked by patches of dark weed, moving silently, not disturbing fish and crabs beneath us. I had spent weekends here treading clams as Billy had showed me: feeling them under my bare feet, diving for them, gathering them in the bucket that trailed behind me on a rope. While Billy had both hands working at the scorched engine, I watched for the black lid of clouds and the manic storms that often came up too fast for a workboat to beat it to a safe cove, but it was early morning and I knew storms came in the afternoon. The water was, as watermen say, "slick kam" and the sky a wide blue. Billy got her going again just as a blowfly bloodied my neck.

He pushed the stick forward and we bobbed back toward shore. Most workboats have a waist-high stick fixed to the washboard and connected by rope to the rudder. A steering wheel would be easier but they use sticks. Some say it leaves your arms free to lift pots, nets, or tongs. Others say it's just the way it always has been. These workboats, like the watermen they ferry, resist change the way they resist order. They aren't tidy, spare, or shipshape. They belong to no navy. Their only heritage is steady, single-minded work. Their "cabin" will hold no more than two small, crouching men as if they figure God's weather is all a man needs. I've heard them called the Lord's ugliest vessel. But not by watermen and not before watermen. They are repeatedly painted but rarely sanded, scraped, or prepared. They have thick skins and look a little like a painter's truck. Perhaps it's no wonder that garden clubs and the like complain they litter the creeks and coves. Maybe they do turn off tourists who have somehow wandered away from the phony streets of Williamsburg or the Revolutionary redoubts at Yorktown—that my brother-in-law bulldozed up for a nice piece of change. But you won't hear watermen complain, and they have to navigate around the dead boats. Sometimes outsiders come to do feature stories on the watermen and their boats. The watermen grin a lot.

I had come to Bull Island as an outsider. Now I was aboard the *Peter Liss* and moving into a faint breeze tinged with the smell of pine and deep water. I was thinking how I had got where I was. I hadn't yet thought about what I was. Somehow I was now an insider, or else I would be having no part in burying a man's boat.

Maybe any beginning is arbitrary when you start having a sense that the events of your life are and have been inevitable. This morning had started two weeks earlier when I stood on the boat dock at Langley Air Force Yacht Club. I had been invited aboard a forty-foot Hatteras for a day of trolling in the Chesapeake Bay. I was carrying gear on board when a small boat roared up to the next dock some thirty or so feet away. It was what watermen call a bateau. A man was shouting for help as he let the bateau die against the pier. People gathered quickly and I went for more gear. Later I saw a master sergeant bent over the body of a man on the dock. He seemed to kiss the body, then pounded its chest. At one point he leaned over the water to spit out somebody's vomit. A few feet away, back to this scene, a man dangled his legs from the dock. He rolled his waders down to mid-calf. Then he rolled them up. Then back down.

A Hatteras yacht moves like a Cadillac. I sipped my banana daiquiri as we glided into open water. I never imagined that man on the dock was Peter Liss, or that Peter Liss could die. I would have said, anyway, that Peter Liss didn't sail on Saturdays, not at age sixty-eight. But it was him, and he had sailed. For one thing he and Miss Homer needed something to eat. For another George was home and maybe he meant to come on the water at last. But the most of it was that a waterman can't stand not working on a bright day, can't stand the roof overhead. This is why he won't have a union—though he knows very well the buyers are killing him—because he can't stand the idea of someone saying he can't work. Liss had sucked himself up and sailed. George said they were pulling crab pots and his Daddy leaned over the hot motor to check weed in the wheel (propeller). Then he laid down on the motor and didn't flinch. Doctor Cecil Evans, kin to almost everybody in Bull Island, said "his heart plain give out."

It seems to me now that I saw every instant of that day unfold, as if I, not George, had gone with Liss. But I was miles out in the bay, into daiquiris. I did not see much more of subsequent events than of Liss's death but I have them in my head as if I had invented them. There was a wake, three days of it, with Peter Liss dressed in somebody's suit. He lay in the bed where he had got himself eight children. There was an abundance of good food, none take-out, brought by wrinkled women who spoke briefly with Miss Homer, sat in the living room a spell, and left quietly in sun that hurt their eyes. There was, as Liss would have said, "a right smart of drinking" by men who did not remember not knowing him. Watermen mostly, they wore what looked like somebody's suit. They lied a lot about what a fine man Liss had been. On the third night, behind that house jacked up on blocks against floods, its three rooms jammed, there came a clutch of black men to stand mute until Miss Homer passed them a pie out the screen door. Except for some white hair and a little shining, they were part of the black night.

"What the hell them niggers doing round here?" somebody said. The room slammed silent and Somebody left. The lying backed into the old days. Liss had sailed with Blacks. The watermen kept their boats on the James River then, nearly fourteen miles south. They walked over on Sunday night, worked all week on the boat, then walked back on Friday night. There weren't men enough willing to do that, so they'd taken Blacks on. A full third share given. The names of black men, old or dead, darted through the air. But only Miss Homer spoke through the screen to those who had come to pay respects to a man that had been part of their history, as they were part of his.

Bull Island is as racist a place as I have ever known. It is home to no Blacks. There are some families who are, technically, black, but they grow lighter-skinned and bluer-eyed every generation. The Blacks were gerrymandered when the town formed, put in their place—which was just outside the town line. The year Peter Liss died, 1969, the town had maybe 5000 people. It has more than doubled because of all the white souls from Hampton, Newport News, and Warwick who say they dream of living on the water. Few Blacks seem to have this dream. No Bull Islander was ever a greater bigot than Peter Lisle Carmines. That is what Billy has always said, at any rate. Yet here were the faces of black men on that white ground, what the Wanderer might have called "Old comrades." How did they know Liss had died? Why did they care? Why had these bigots not stopped that nigger-hating Somebody from taking a hasty, tactful leave? Why, when these Blacks began a low, moaning spiritual, were so many dabbing at their eyes? How is it possible to know the *idears* at the soul of such a place?

Peter Liss went into the ground pretty much the way everyone he had ever known had gone. Hymns. Prayers. The summer sun steamed through stained glass. Rows of ladies' hats bobbed; bald heads gleamed. Then they went home. They probably told more lies about the old days, about the fine men they all were. Little said, I suppose, about the Blacks. Life went on as it must for watermen, a life of habit and work that they can't get enough of and don't understand. Most didn't ask what it all meant. Most didn't think about or hope for a change. There wouldn't be any, except for the *Peter Liss*.

I don't know where Liss left the scrawled, illegible note that was his will, but Billy had it, as he had the duty to bury his father's boat in the place and the manner Liss prescribed. It sounded simple enough: take her one last time around the point, over the bar, and at the appointed hump of marsh run her aground. The hole he'd knock in her bottom would leave her to the slow repossession of water and weather and time. He knew the place. As a boy sailing out with his father, he'd seen the boats mount up there. They had been sailed by men who could not remember not knowing Liss, four or five of them stove up on each other, mostly underwater, broken casually, looking for all the world like children who'd raced to a point and bumped heads. This was what manhood, a life, had come to. A body had gone into the ground but this was where Peter Liss would spend eternity, with the marsh, the water, and friends. He had ordered it.

I would be a long time knowing these were more than dead boats. Some men, I knew, kept their father's boat or sold it. Or traded it for a fiberglass fishing skiff. Billy never said why the *Peter Liss* had to be buried. But he stalled. He meant to do it when the wake was over, meant to. He waited a long two weeks. He drank hard. Liss had been a prodigious drinker. George drank. He called and harangued Billy. Billy harangued his wife, me, anybody near him.

The telephone woke me before dawn that Saturday. Billy had been up all night, drinking though he could not get drunk. He had gone to bed but woke terrified he was having a heart attack. He sat through the hours in his small knotty-pine den, stared at the framed photographs of the *Peter Liss* and the others like her, and he knew. It wouldn't speak but it was there, punching him in the chest even through the mildewed Bible he clutched against it. He drank hard to shake himself free of his father's ghost but he knew. I was less literary then and did not think, when he told me this, of Hamlet's father on the battlement. I think about it now. When Billy could stand it no more, he called me to meet him at the dock by dawn. He didn't ask if I wanted to. I didn't say.

George ignored me but he didn't like me being there. I wasn't even a lost cousin. But Billy was the oldest son and he had decided. If George meant to bitch he'd done it when Billy called him. I knew Billy had called him first. Somehow I knew that. I still couldn't help feeling I didn't belong any more than the bateau roped to and bobbing at our stern. I don't think I even knew why the bateau was there.

By now the sun beat in my head like a gong. I had not worn my waterman's cap, the baseball cap that farmers wear—except instead of a tractor's name it has a leaping swordfish above the brim. Billy and George wore them. When workboats pass these caps are dipped ever so slightly in salute, unless there's been an insult in the preceding hundred years.

I knew the cove but not its name. It was shaped like a Mateus wine bottle and we were in its neck. Parachutes of jellyfish like small angels hung in the water. Along the shore were newly built docks to starboard, empty marsh to port. At the docks were sleek, expensive speedboats. Beyond pine trees there would be brick ranchers, barbecue pits, and garden clubbers. All white. I also knew this land had once been hunted by Powhatan's subtribes.

Ahead of the bow, three-quarters of a mile off, the tin roof of Bennett's Crab Wholesalers flashed high above the stilts it stood on. All over the cove stobs, sapling trees pruned of limbs, rose from the green water; workboats tied to them faced us. The tide was coming in. A hundred yards more and Billy tried to idle the *Peter Liss*. She died. Now I could see where we had been heading, where the *Peter Liss* had been heading for forty-six years. Suddenly, there was no breeze. The crabhouse stank. Heat and humidity greased us. Gnats, mosquitoes, blowflies swarmed at us. I slapped. Billy knelt placidly at the engine. George smoked. Oddly, there were no voices drifting from the ranchers, no boats moving out yet.

The place where we would put her was marsh grass about waist-high. A foot or so at the edge would be black mud festered by the holes of fiddler crabs. As a boy I had dreamed these holes were doors to a magic city underground. I could see the remains of a few boats canted in the sun. A wheelhouse with glass windows still unbroken, no vandalism here. This had been a dredge boat. The outlines of several washboards. Workboats. They seemed to me whole, not broken, just resting in the shallow water. Maybe that's what is in my mind now. They seemed to be grateful for the sun. They seemed to be waiting, full of themselves.

Once again Billy eased her forward, already turning her into position. He told George he meant to run her over Jumps. He didn't say "the Jumps," for he made no distinction between the man named Jumps and the boat the man had left. Nor did that man and his boat belong to some dateless history. They were a being forever, there, waiting. I don't know what it means to be an American, a Southerner. I'm a Bull Islander. If I wasn't anything before that moment, I became a Bull Islander. No pledge of allegiance, no flag or card to be carried, merely the obligation to a sleepy, forgotten place. The obligation to be a man among men, maybe.

Billy and I had climbed into the bateau. He got her running, told me where to take her, then went back aboard the idling *Peter Liss*. When I tried to back this mufflerless bitch I saw she had no throttle. But I wasn't going to ask for help. I sweated. Impatient now, Billy called at my back that I should use the valve on the carburetor. I looked over my shoulder to see George sitting in my place on the cull-board. He had an ax resting on his shoulder. I drifted with the tide away from them.

A workboat's ugliness may be exceeded only by its steady dependability. In this it is like a good mule. Jury-rigged, ad hoc, its sparkplugs apt to be rusted to its cylinders, these boats work—though God knows why. She had died on us all morning, but now the *Peter Liss* gave Billy her best, hard rpms.

He backed her lightly, like a car stuck in snow, then shoved the throttle. She did not leap or surge. She simply dug through the water. Almost, I think now, almost she did plane. I am certain she tried and, almost, I see a gap of light between her severe bow and the water. Not quickly but with heavyweight dignity, she rode up over Jumps. I think I heard those belabored, weak planks groan in recognition. Then the little cove rocked everywhere with a spreading wake. Even the workboats tied to stobs swayed gracefully like nodding tufts of white hair. It was over, I thought.

Billy came aft and unplugged the Peter Liss's seacock. George went forward and made three feeble swipes with his ax, the flash of sunlight on the blade becoming, as it does in James Dickey's poem "At Darien Bridge," seagulls in flight.

"Goddammit, George, don't do that," Billy screamed. Fifty yards away, he was clear over the racket of the outboard under my arm. He grabbed the ax from George and threw it in the water. I watched them jaw at each other. Then Billy turned and waved me to take them off the back-filling *Peter Liss*.

I reached my right arm back for the throttle valve, holding the metal brace on the front of the motor with my left. This was what *Peter Liss* had steered with. The valve wouldn't budge. Mosquitoes were all over me.

"Push it goddammit," Billy shouted.

I pushed hard, ashamed, failing my part. The valve stayed stuck. Then it didn't. Instantly the motor was wide open, the bateau lifted like a bike doing wheelies. Ahead of me, when I looked, was nothing but greasy bateau bottom. I was about to mount the *Peter Liss*.

"Turn the motherfucker. Turn the motherfucker," George screamed. I'd heard this anger in his voice once when he'd come to borrow Billy's Coast Guard .45 after hearing some assholes were oystering the underwater beds that Peter Liss had rented from the state of Virginia for ninety-nine years. There was no fear in that voice, only outrage.

I hauled on the cross-brace and felt the bateau heave sickeningly. It dug around. I felt like I was riding a banana. Between trying to force the valve back and screaming out my problem, I kept leaning out too far to see what stob, boat, bank, or pier I was going to die on. I hauled, compensated, overcompensated, and hauled again. I knew I was spinning in an oblique circle when I started to bounce and skid over my own wake. Periodically I lifted free of the water, as if I had sailed somehow out of time.

I don't know how I got that valve unstuck. All at once, it was awesomely still and I was putting forward. My wakes were lapping audibly, like a mocking applause. Blood pounded from my ears to my tennis shoes.

"You stupid college educated son of a bitch," somebody said. I'm sure I heard that. Billy, who was turned toward the marsh, swears he did not speak. George faced me. He had said nothing. Peter Liss, who had often enough said this to Billy, was dead. Maybe it does not matter who said it. But why did I feel so worthless, so ashamed? What illusion had done this to me? How can I apologize and for what?

When Billy and George had settled in the bateau I crammed myself so far into the narrow vee of the bow that I pinched bruises on my thighs. I faced forward while Billy took us rapidly back where we had begun. I knew his eyes under his cap were black and hard as a seahawk's. In less than half an hour we sat shoulder to shoulder in George's battered 1956 Chevy pickup truck. We faced Back River and for a long time did not speak. Drained, hungry, we watched a line of fat Hatterases ghost out of Langley's yacht basin. Beyond them Lyndon Johnson's tower cast a long shadow like a dead hand toward Bull Island. The fifth of Early Times that George pulled out was hot, but we drank it. I didn't rub the bottle's mouth on my sleeve and neither did they. All I could think of was it felt right to be in that place in that time, connected with these two to something so huge I could feel it but not think it. With the second bottle, Billy's, George spoke.

"Got to go back. Gone have to knock a hole in her."

"Know it," Billy said. "Got to take her wheel off first, else somebody will."

"Motherfuckers," George said.

But they did not knock a hole in her, as Peter Liss would have done, when a week later they did go back. They took off her pitiful little brass and left her. Billy thought, so he said, she was in safe enough. That fall a nor-easter floated her free and the *Peter Liss* does not rest where she was buried. No one knows where or in how many places she may be. If she had broken up in that cove the low tides would have revealed her. Maybe she found a way into the deep water of the Bay. Maybe she's nestled against Egg Island Bar somewhere. It's even possible she might have made it into the Back River channel. All that is certain is that she doesn't lie where Peter Liss wanted her. And that is because of a failure of love, because Billy loved his father and his father's boat too much, and because he was human enough that he paid too little attention to the history of his place. It's a subject he broods upon and is unwilling to discuss. It's why he wakes abruptly, convinced he is having heart attacks. But this is only part of how that day ended.

I remember that, at least to my way of thinking, there was an ample willingness in that truck to rehearse, inflate, and lie about the details of my part. We drank the second bottle slowly, beginning to laugh. George, I think, brought up the matter of any man's having *some* common sense, enough to work an outboard I believe is how he put it. Billy agreed, though he did point out that "she were a bad-rusted piece" for the reason that she had at least twice gone to the bottom, once when George tied her too close to the dock before a high tide and once when Peter Liss, drinking some, had forgotten to bolt her onto the transom. Most of what we said after this has grown as murky as the water over Egg Island Bar, water that watermen will tell you now leaves oil on your body. But all of it remains with me like a grand illusion. In that illusion, I am convinced, are a few idears of crucial importance. I may have expressed an awareness of them but probably I have not made a clear communication of them. I mean to try one more time, for it is by idears that men must live if they have any hope of living with purpose. I have not heard watermen speak of obligations to bury boats or anything else so tribal as that, certainly nothing was said about the abiding spirits of the dead to which we must be responsible. Billy would say that you only bury a boat when she is dangerously rotten. Watermen squirm in the presence of idears.

We buried that boat ceremoniously because we were witnessing what it means to be a man. We did it to be watermen, because we couldn't resign from what we already were, good or bad, because we were acted *upon* by ideas that made us know a man has obligations in and to the world. He has to *do* and to *know* what he does. Burying a boat, a man witnesses his history, the intersection of forces that make him what he is. Like a writer, he puts the boat where he can keep it in sight, a little alive, testifying to the character he must keep alive in order to keep himself alive. As long as men pass on that water they will pass the shape of their character, what they have made and been. What they must keep faith with. I do not mean they are required, even by the dead, to meditate or worship. A waterman would not discuss what, if anything, this meant. But he knows, he feels, in that passing that some things durably *are*, just are, and these seem to say to him you are "one of us." In the spiraling dark of time you shall feel you are connected to the greatness of the world for a moment, and even forever.

Sometimes I think the luckiest thing that ever happened to me was to get slowly drunk, exhilarated, full of joy and lies at what must sure to God be the end of the world. I may have agreed we had buried a boat only because a numb-nutted old man wanted his way and because his boat wasn't worth any trouble to keep it. OK. It doesn't matter what lies we tell ourselves so long as they help us know we are indivisibly part of something, are a self and a part. For many of us, when the text or the critic or the professor whines that we are the hollow men, merely entries, we are obliged to whisper *Bullshit.* We are still ourselves, Somebody or not; we are the dead who live because idears live us, and in us, like genes. Sometimes we feel very good because we have been faithful. We have given our honest tubs and earned some kind of right to say fuck fate. This sustains us as we sustain the dead and their place. My life as a writer, which seems to me to begin in the ceremony I have described, consists in my obligation to become aware and to communicate the place where I know life is, just is.

I was drunk again the night before I left Bull Island to go to graduate school. I had already begun to publish poems in magazines, poems that were vaguely focused because I didn't know what they were about. They were about ideas and illusions I didn't recognize or even know I had. With my wife and Billy and his wife, I sat up most of the night. I don't remember what our ugly black quarreling chewed over except that I was leaving and Billy didn't want me to go. I swayed in the door the way the *Peter Liss* had as it settled over the Jumps. Billy screamed at the night beyond me, "You son of a bitch don't you know people are the same everywhere? Why the fuck do you want to go?" Then, almost tenderly, he said "Will you ever come back?"

My words keep saying yes. And no. They are my obligation, my crossroads, my faith. I send Billy a copy of everything I write. I do not know if he reads my words but he knows what they are about. They are stove up on his bookshelves, piled together like friends, where he passes in and out every day. I hope they gladden his heart as the writing of them has gladdened mine.

Passion, Possibility, and Poetry

■

Poetry is passion and possibility. Naked, it is more passion; intricately clothed, it is more possibility. At its finest, it is both. We speak of how poetry is all language, the beautiful contrivance, but I am not one who cares much for form without content, or even content serving form. The poem whose language is indivisible from its content—and how few of those excellencies there are—is the balance we must honor, for it is the dynamic body of passion which both celebrates and is possibility. This dualism, like anything that matters, is complex and scarcely permits the easy resolution of flat statement. James Wright tells us that all he can do is speak in a flat voice but Wright's voice is not on the whole a flat one. Wright is a singer whose primary characteristic is complexity, especially of rhythm, and a sense of the multiplicity of thing and meaning which he trusts to reveal itself in the plainest of words. If the world and our lives were simple, if flat and honest statement were easily possible, there would be no need for many poets and less need for our feeble attempts to discriminate toward excellence.

The fact is that poems of passion and credible possibility are ideals we do not often achieve. That we fail our poems does not, however, mean we should abandon either the task or those monuments of our poetic heritage which show us what is always possible. Those poems are our first and primary teachers of what art is, not sociotherapies. When we set up to evaluate poems we are then the teachers and it is our function, or

Note: This essay, as originally published, included an extensive critique of three poems by students, poems chosen by the editor of *Poets Teaching*. I have thought it appropriate to reprint the essay with that critique and the poems excised since the essay itself was constructed as a pedagogical and aesthetic statement meant to explain the basis of my criticism.

ought to be, to insist on standards of excellence and to do what we can to suggest how such standards have been and may be attained.

Like many of us, I grew up throwing one sort of ball or another. I did it for pleasure, without thought of excellence. It is impossible to do anything without learning to do it with *some* increase in efficiency, accuracy, and understanding. But it is also possible to learn wrongly, to impede growth and skill, which is what coaches hope to prevent. And, I think, teachers of writing. It is equally possible that one's inherent abilities, in spite of the American vision of equal opportunity and common-man-ism, are so limited as to preclude the highest achievements. There is no shame in this, though some would have it so. Time and experience taught me that my ball-throwing abilities were limited. I wasn't going to pitch for the New York Yankees or even the Norfolk Tars. At fifteen, I did not have to be told this. So I dedicated myself to football and basketball. I soon learned that I hadn't the speed, the size, or the reflexes to continue beyond high school competition. Nevertheless, I loved these sports and watched, as player and as spectator, so closely that I gained a good knowledge of athletic mechanics. Dynamics, if you will. By a fortuitous turn, I became for a time a high school coach, and a good one. If I couldn't personally measure up to the standards of excellent athletes, I could and did make them available to players with greater ability. Many of America's finest professional coaches have been only mediocre athletes. Perhaps it is because they became excellent students and developed the ability to transfer what they knew. I know what makes extraordinary basketball, what it looks like, why it happens, and how it may be encouraged. I take almost as much pleasure at ex-coach Al McGuire's broadcasts of college basketball as at the games themselves, for McGuire sees and announces what is going to happen and how before it does happen. Gaining such a knowledge takes a long time and is, in many ways, earned.

Poetry takes a long time and must also be earned. Before I go too far, I will say that I recognize the dangers of comparing basketball and poetry. I'm aware that all games have, ordinarily, a clear, ordained intention, which is for one team to score more than another and to win. Games are competition in ways that poetry is not. But only the reader entirely disinclined to consider similarities will insist that the two activities have nothing in common. Such readers, I am certain, will have pressing matters to attend to beyond the space of this little essay. My point is merely to suggest some principles that were important to me in playing, learning, and coaching are also integral to my teaching of poetry writing.

I begin with the consideration that everyone has inherent limits and has a right to discover those limits with and without me. It would be criminal to say to a student, "You haven't the ability to write anything." When I was an undergraduate at the University of Virginia, a professor did tell me that. But it isn't criminal to help a student discover, through one's own experience and knowledge as well as through the student's explorations, what his limits and possibilities might be. To recognize a student who is either unable to write even competently or is woefully ill-prepared and to slick that over with untempered praise seems to me equally criminal. Which is to say, I have little patience with anything less than the judicious and gentle pursuit of excellence. I have no time for poetry as therapy and only contempt for touchy-feely teaching. Let me add here that I am speaking only of the teaching of poetry in colleges and universities, for I believe that if such institutions do not devote themselves to the pursuit of excellence, then whatever else goes on in our society will not much matter. Standards of excellence, then, are not going to be met by all students. I was not an excellent athlete. We are all *not* excellent at something. I try to give my students patience, attention, intensity, honesty, and the lessons of my own experience. I try to help them avoid the mistakes I have made and seen, to recognize the benchmarks of excellence. I encourage them to believe in possibility and to love knowledge, for I believe that knowledge is the necessary love. Teaching for me is largely a matter of developing an attitude toward experience and the language which both expresses and creates experience. I cannot teach anyone to have passion, that which the true poet is never without, as passion is a product of some mysterious conjunction of genes and desire that is the poet's given.

If I begin with an awareness of limits, that is not to say I stand watch for weaknesses to triumph in student work. Indeed, I do stand a constant watch over the poems of my students and it is always a readiness to clap my hands with delight and ask, "How in the world did you do that?" All of us know that it happens, the true poem, and though we may carp a little to keep our pride intact, what is more wonderful than the surprise of that moment when we discover the poem that could not have been predicted and cannot be explained? This is the moment when passion and possibility are so fused that I stand in the presence of a poem humanly beautiful and nearly original. It didn't occur because of me, but in spite of me and, with luck, somehow beyond me. But such poems do not occur in voids. They come because of preparation, knowledge, hard work, and the lonely commitment of the writer to push to his limits. In the presence of such an achievement, there is little use to cant of structure, vision, and so on, all those matters submerged in the poet's process. The thing, happily and enigmatically, exists. It testifies that its process of becoming also exists.

The process of teaching writing, and of writing, as I know it, is my subject here. With all of us, this process is more intuitive than rational. If it were not so, if we had a formula, what results we could expect from every student! All I can do is to try to say how I conduct each student as far as he or she can go toward that moment of delightful hand-clapping, and to say it with the knowledge that my own informing attitudes may be revealed, if unspoken.

Doesn't it seem a bit unnatural to begin a workshop of college students by immediately throwing their poems into a public scrutiny and asking that public for a response? The ordinary routine is this: instructor meets a dozen or so unknown, and mutually unacquainted, faces and to them issues a command that they shall each present a suitably duplicated poem for the next class, these to be discussed at length. As instructors our justifications are various and even predictable: they did register for the course; they are people and they have emotions; they appear to want to write poems and to know something about poems; poetry-writing is a study of literature; the best way to learn is plunge right in; assignments could be made but these blunt the enthusiasm. So it goes. We instructors all too often ignore important considerations for such an activity. If the students have emotions and a desire to express themselves, they may have little or no idea of what constitutes excellence in poetry. To say that they know nothing, true or not, is no excuse for a failure to remember that we are the knowledge-bearers. The fact is that most students have read very little, have at best a rudimentary understanding of poetry, and have only in the rarest instances a vocabulary which permits the articulation and exchange of helpful criticism.

Those who have taught or taken workshops will recognize what I have described. I have taught in this way. The second class arrives and when asked to make a response the student says, tentatively, the poem is, well, it's well-done. What does the student mean? According to what standard? Another student says that she likes the poem. Her voice is filled with kindness, like a loan. If we ask whether this is the same response one might have to a salad, the student is apt to qualify the response by saying there is a line, a phrase, an image which is in some nebulous way attractive. For some teachers of writing I have known, the rule of thumb is let us like and dislike and leave time enough for a beer after class. I think a more properly prepared instructor, a more thoughtful instructor, one who really means to take his students seriously *as writers,* must plan his workshop so that it builds toward the same principle that defines an excellent poem: diversity embraced by unity.

A good workshop might begin with a couple of sessions spent examining poems not written by class members but by previous students, the instructor, or "published" poets. I am not personally skittish about criticizing the poems of known writers, but students often are. In order to avoid the weight of those names, poems from good little magazines might be offered without the author's name. I ask my students to make marginal notes on these poems, to be prepared to discuss the good and bad features as they see them. Initially, I make no attempt to guide their discussion. I listen and direct the traffic. I learn what and how the students think because, not having to confront their as-yet-unknown peers, they are not cowed. They know the poems in question are neutral. They respond. Importantly, this process introduces them to each other. They begin to test each other not on the level of ego but in the act of criticism, in the application of intelligent and justified observation. This first step builds trust in the group, and I think no workshop goes very far in helping its members without trust. I don't mean, of course, back-patting and hand-holding. I mean the recognition that each person is capable of useful and provocative criticism that he can modify with impunity and respect. Even uninformed students have valuable things to say and it is important that members of the class see that participation is essential; that the act of commentary is directed at the object and not the author. Clearly it is critical that the poems I choose and employ in this manner be selected to represent identifiable degrees of quality. If I haven't the experience to know a good poem from a bad poem, according to standards that at some point I am going to have to articulate, I am being paid by my university for the wrong reasons.

Some of the students, quite naturally, will praise the bad poems and attack the good ones. Some will know intuitively which are bad and which are good but will have difficulty saying why. Some will be openly puzzled. When the class has scoured each poem and the discussion has begun to decline, I take over. I have been making notes from their comments, and I begin to address the salient points, both the obvious and the implicit. I take care not to undermine anyone's enthusiasm or seriousness and I go to whatever length necessary to demonstrate my respect for his or her act of the mind. Neither am I loath to point out what I believe to be the rightness or wrongness of that act. That everyone's response is equally right, however divergent and pluralistic, is a heresy I will not accept. I will encourage disagreement, and even heat, but only where the student can bring to bear an argument, an evidence, a standard as sufficiently convincing as my own. Among the splendid benefits of such a class is the making of friends, the encouraging of citizenship, the progress each makes toward a full humanity—but we are not precisely here for such benefits. We are here to learn what excellent poetry is, what it might be, by what various and fundamental ways people have made that poetry. This process begins, in a classroom, with the generation of a modest commonality: with establishing some critical zones in which to work, a language, a mutuality of respect and integrity, a sense of standards, a sense that the product of our labors is always going to lie before a reader, inert and vulnerable and in need of the best efforts we can muster toward helping it live and bloom.

Clearly, all that I have said and will say is a code of partial expressions, all intentions as often as not honored in the breech. But a vague sense of direction is better than either a rigid direction or no direction. Totalitarian instruction is not more desirable than touchy-feely. I once worked as an assistant coach under a man who had absolutely no sense of play, of improvisation, hence of possibility. I was given the scrubs to coach against his intensely disciplined first team. His boys were furious blockers so long as my defenders remained where he had shown them to be in blackboard diagrams. Yet they could make no progress against my inferior defenders who played creatively, darting unpredictably, adhering to unannounced rhythms and counterrhythms. My head coach was enraged, dogmatic, and Pavlovian. At one particular practice we scrimmaged until it was so dark players facing each other a foot apart could see only outlines. Finally I instructed my defenders to fall to the ground, to let the first team score, so that we could all go home. Such discipline is not only funny, it may be injurious. But discipline, even if it must be breeched by any artist worthy of the term, is yet necessary and fundamental.

When I enter my class's discussion of those first, anonymous poems, I am introducing my code and my discipline. I tell them that the rules, the standards which inform my responses and theirs will be, for us, a framework that each, in his own way, will transcend at the moment he or she begins to do important work, at the moment those inherent limits are pushed. I also tell them that the framework will create in each what Auden once called the censor in the self. It is a kind of fog detector and we have, individually, enough fog to need whatever help we can get. I tell them that the best and truest help will always come from inside, from the censor.

But the discipline needs initial tending, so I create a code. It is really a three-part formula, and I am aware of all the nasty implications of that word. Haven't we all noticed in our composition apprenticeships how

Directors of Compositions marshal their formulas? First, I ask, what is the poem about? What is its subject, its object of focus, its plot (if it has one)? There is no poem which, in its literal dimension, is not about something. I want that laid out in paraphrase as clearly as we can do it. Generally, students will respond with interpretation. The poem about the used-car salesman is actually about cosmic injustice. I disallow this kind of comment initially. I want the salesman, his cars, his place of business, his emotions, the weather, the conflict, the point of view—whatever the elements are—to be specifically and without judgment or interpretation identified for all present.

Second, how well does the language present these elements? In part two, knowing the landscape and objects, we must consider how well or badly they seem to coexist. This means, of course, we have to consider what the writer intended to do, as best we can discover that. We must try to place ourselves in the writer's passion, to understand what complexities he approached, to see what design underlay this committed action. The writer is not allowed to tell us, only the poem on the page. The instruction is, I hope, clear: meaning, expression, coherence, clear sense, possibility, passion, beauty are all in the language employed and shaped or they do not exist. But how could we talk of these ineluctable qualities so necessary to poetry if we have not previously determined the elements out of which they must rise and in which they can only be found? Part one of this formula was nonjudgmental. Part two must move toward judgment but must also attempt to restrain emotional effusion while encouraging hardheaded attention.

Part three, however, consists in deliberately subjective evaluation and properly causes apprehension among those colleagues to whom I have mentioned it. The students are initially suspicious of this step but generally come to see its value, sometimes becoming so passionate in its pursuit that they need a gentle curbing. Part three asks whether what the poet has attempted was worth doing. I believe there is nothing in the world which is not available to poetry, but I also believe that poetry may be demeaned by triviality, by deliberately adolescent acts, by a refusal to be ambitious for art. If a poem is something done solely for an assignment, done for self-aggrandizing fame, something done for a purpose other than the obsessive joy of its doing, it is very likely to be a stillbirth. If the poet has clearly demanded less of his or her abilities than might have been asked, the poem often becomes a sham and a personal deception. This poet is at fault and should be told so. Part three of my formula involves judging the poet's maturity of intellect, quality of perception, and ambition to catch the world in durable words.

Poets and teachers of poetry commonly refer to the act of poetic composition as playing. The play of the mind is fundamental in writing but it is a special sort of play, one which should always be challenging for the highest stakes. It is an absolute necessity that we teach our students that we write and read poetry for pleasure, for delight, yet this must be balanced with the constant reminder that this play is that superior intellectual play whose end is to know, to apprehend, to test, to challenge—not to win. In this regard, the poem is significantly a moral act. I do not mean a moralistic canard, a pious statement, a simplistic and sentimental lip-pursing; I mean the poem is an act of celebrating human health. Even the darkest visions are nevertheless such celebrations. Who is darker than James Wright, as moral a poet as exists among us? We should not expect to condemn or embrace our students' poems according to the identifiable moral value. It is enough to bring our students to understand that all true poems, even the lightest verse, participate in the continuous and incremental recognition that we are one body in this world, one life in need of witness, celebration, understanding, and beauty.

Can we deny that there are poems, and even books, which are mean-spirited, evil, life-defeating? Anyone who has taught writing has seen student poems reveal, quite unknown to the student, prejudices and convictions which are intolerably ugly. If we content ourselves with innocuous comments about the language of such poems and do not identify the rottenness which rises through the language, then we are merely impotent technicians. Those relativists who would argue that the moral value and seriousness of a poem is a bogus issue are often those who claim students have nothing to say. And say it badly. I have been constantly gladdened by seeing students respond keenly to the life and the issues in a poem, and not as abstractions but as tangible realities. It is up to the keepers of poetry to insist on the poem of discovery and the poem of revealed possibility. If life is not beautiful—and for many it is scarcely that—the most faithfully accurate and heartrending poem may be. Auden's elegy for Yeats says poetry makes nothing happen, but the poem which says this makes Auden's words a lie. That poem makes something happen to anyone who reads it, unless the reader has wooden ears.

In my teaching, particularly at novice levels, I try to establish three standards. These are clarity, beauty, and value. Obviously the best poets haven't a need for such a code, but those poets haven't a need for a writing class. I am not, of course, denying that there are other values and other approaches for the sophisticated students who take advanced workshops. Too, I want to add there are various and quite different approaches to teaching at the beginning levels and their successes are documentably evident. I do not rigorously adhere to my own pedagogy since each class, like each student, requires adjustments to its particular personality and needs. In general, however, I have found my approach capable of creating confidence in students who often despair of saying anything that matters and it has often enough provided a good base for the intelligent and critical exchange of responses which is the heart of the educational act.

This essay was written in answer to an invitation to critique, with two other poet-teachers, three student poems. It is, however, not so much a critique as a statement of pedagogy. Therefore, one last comment seems in order. Implicit in all considerations about the pedagogy of creative writing is a continuing quarrel between writers and teachers. Are these two always, sometimes, or never the same person? Several years ago a questionnaire from the Associated Writing Programs asked: "Do you consider yourself a writer who teaches or a teacher who writes?" The question implies a necessary and inevitable division. I confidently answered I was both. Now I am less certain. Increasingly I suspect that the ardent teacher gives his own censor and his own energies so fully to his students that he has little left for his own work. Or he protects himself, restricts what he gives, and develops anxieties about what compromises he effects. The writer and the teacher vehemently advance certain aesthetic positions when they meet, often opposed positions. I once heard a famous novelist harangue an audience to the effect that a writer writes and a teacher teaches. Some of us are so passionate about this division that we might, I suppose, insist on separate but equal toilet facilities. The fact is that we ought not be surprised at such passionate partisans. They exist in one body, in our individual bodies. The writer in us wants, like a jealous lover, all of our attention. The teacher in us wants no less. The student makes a third, equal claim. Most of us simply don't know how to divide our service to obligation, responsibility, and function. As teachers and as writers we sometimes don't know what to say to our students, and the confusion, the anxiety, backs us into corners within ourselves. We fall into and out of strident pedagogical and aesthetic positions. Though it may be heresy, I believe this unresolved fragmenting of energy and affection is sometimes a good and desirable situation: it means we are concerned about what we are doing, concerned for our students. Of course, some of us can never serve two, much less three, masters, and these ought to make the hard choice not to serve what destroys them. In any case, we must all make choices, for that is what it means to live maturely.

I have chosen to teach creative writing with a realization that what I do will not show full, visible results in the short range. With many students, my instruction may lead to nothing. This is equally true in biology, psychology, calculus, and basketball. I have not believed, and have been disturbed by, the contention that instruction in creative writing accomplishes nothing. At best it enhances knowledge and provides a vital community for writers who must always live among the Philistines. At worst, creative writing breeds good, close readers. There is a widely held opinion that creative writing instruction does little more than produce safe, academic clones whose future is a self-perpetuating system in which true art disappears and is replaced by something like a committee product. This argument began, not surprisingly, with the system's have-nots but it has become the scholar's argument. Of course the scholars, who invited writers into the academy, have always been suspicious of uncanonized writers and often enough have merely condescended to them. They are fond of announcing that neither Faulkner nor Hemingway needed workshops, that neither Eliot nor Stevens was a teacher. Their memories are as short as their pedagogies are fixed, as short as our own memories. They forget that the teaching of contemporary literature is a historically recent innovation, however well entrenched now. Of their examples we might say a great deal with respect to changes in society, cafe "workshops," commercial climates—indeed we would need a large and enormously informed sociological study of influences on writers' lives. Would it tell us anything valuable or definitive? Perhaps we need only to say those writers offered as exemplars made a free choice, one which cannot be proven to result in art and one which is, therefore, not to be taken as a reliable guide. There are equally unreliable examples of writers who have taught in universities, unreliable because this choice also does not guarantee art. Such examples might include Theodore Roethke, Saul Bellow, Elizabeth Bishop, Robert Lowell, John Gardner, Robert Creeley, and Denise Levertov.

If the scholar suspects and dismisses the writer, it is also disturbing to find the writer, particularly the writer who teaches creative writing, who contends that the teachers of literature are the enemy and that their teaching of workshops is merely something done to keep food on the table while they write. Of teachers of literature, we might say they have kept alive writing itself. No society could kill off all its writers; writers are too hardy, like wind-driven spores, for that. But what society has so encouraged writing and writers as our own? And this is quintessentially the gift of teachers of literature. They have taught us to love and respect what many would not otherwise have known. As Milton says, they also serve. Not a few of them have served immeasurably well. If they are the writer's enemies, who are his friends?

The creative writing instructor who believes that he need expect nothing from his neophyte students is, whatever else he may be, not our friend. He is the one who approves or disapproves indiscriminately whatever the students give him. Refusing to teach *some* standards, he refuses to teach. "What's the use?" he says. He fails to demand ambition in students, the ambition for art and excellence. This reflects either his disinterest in teaching or his own ignorance. Within the past six months I heard a young poet, tenured in the University of California system, preface a reading of his poems with ridicule for professors of literature. He said that he was glad to stand among people who, like himself, must distrust ideas unconditionally. We cannot hold anyone specifically responsible for a contemporary collusion of stupidity, democracy, and poetry, but ignorance should not be tolerated. Ideas are part of life; they are part of poetry. When I think of that young poet sitting among his writing students, I imagine them being cheated of a rightful heritage. The kind of teacher, his kind, who refuses to encourage their ideas *in* poems and *in* class implicitly professes a constricted experience. He condescends to his students because he does not take them seriously. He does not, as the true creative writing teacher must, teach art or teach artfully. If humility before the intellectual and creative endeavor of mankind is of value anywhere, it is mostly so in the teacher—and not less for one teaching creative writing.

The instruction of creative writing, perhaps more than literary instruction, does teach art—the process, not the product. It is and can be a respectable, important segment of a young writer's education. It ought not be the primary part of that education. We must understand and be tolerant of the limits of our instruction, as of the limits of our students. And we must not overrate ourselves, because what we do is so little available to objective quantification. Neither should we belittle our own knowledge, experience, and commitment to excellence in writing. We must try to be what we would have our students emulate and surpass. In every art, in every craft the world has ever known, there have been masters. Those masters and their works have provided models for students. These masters have been willing, as teachers, to say a loud *no* to inadequate accomplishment. They have been singular in their demand that students comprehend the heritage of particular and general art. We are obliged to do no less. This afternoon I watched a televised report about a man considered to be the finest kite-maker in America. Many would consider that an irrelevant pursuit at best. Yet this man was so devoted to his passion that he had apprenticed himself for three years to Europe's finest kite-maker. He said that he *hoped* his apprenticeship would prepare him to accomplish something unforeseen in his future. Unlike that man, many of our students and our colleagues appear to believe that successful completion of a specified number of hours in creative writing will certify them as masters of poetry, the Queen of the Arts. Many of our writing programs graduate these masters in only two years! Perhaps those of us who teach creative writing need to remind ourselves that life is short and art is long. Just so, we need to remember, and to make clear to our students, that creative writing courses can only form an appropriate part of a necessarily larger study. That larger study is man himself, what he has been, what he has known, what he has recorded, and what he has so far only apprehended.

We will be able to take ourselves seriously, and be taken seriously, only when we recognize the need for integration of creative writing with literature and other disciplines. We cannot insist on isolation and simultaneously reduce the suspicion of what we are and what we do. We cannot be everything to everybody. If we set up as masters, we must be willing to say no to work that is inadequate, unpromising, clearly lacking excellence. We must demonstrate allegiance to standards which will liberate the imaginations we would nurture, remembering always that the true master of an art exercises mastery and responsibility in equal measure: he masters in order to achieve and accepts the responsibility for keeping the art he has undertaken, not for the keeping of the lives of his students. His function, and his students' in turn, is to tell the truth and the beauty of his kind. Insofar as we are masters and teachers of poetry writing, we are not meant to be the social workers of verse, but witnesses to civilization's highest values. If we manage to sustain a continuing excellence in our work and in our students, we will perform a most valuable social service indeed. We will, in demanding the best of ourselves and our students, be doing what writing has always done—teaching the inarticulate to comprehend, express, and shape human experience. That is not only a very human act, but is exactly the divine function meant by the name *poet.*

Notes on Responsibility and the Teaching of Creative Writing

■

In the late fall of 1966 I was one of a thousand high school football coaches to attend a clinic on coaching held in the ballroom of a major Washington hotel. After a long day of seminars in tackling, weight programs, experimental offenses, and a long night of boozy anecdotes, we gathered on the second morning for yet another revelation, this one advertised as "Secrets of Winning: Life and Football." In my hard steel chair, I had pen and paper ready to diagram and annotate but my mind was on the lightly falling snow outside. Looking back at the presumption of the man who named that seminar I am chastened to remember that the best secrets usually remain secrets, profound and enigmatic and demanding our attention. Robert Frost's little poem "The Secret" describes aptly what most teaching and criticism amounts to: "We dance around in a ring and suppose. / The secret sits in the middle and knows." What I have to say here is in the form, mostly, of notes—because that is a kind of dancing around which exists in contradistinction to the presentation of fact or formula.

The seminars at this clinic represented three kinds of teaching by men of proven success in the win/loss columns. The first was a dazzling performance with film, sound, and multiple personnel, big budget extravaganzas whose flash and sophistication left most of us stunned. The second sort was a quieter two- and three-man demonstration of, say, quarterbacking techniques. This involved a blackboard, a display of Xs, Os, and arrows which would impress an experimental mathematician. But the third version was and is still for me the memorable one. While I dreamed of snow, a slightly seedy, slightly bowlegged, mostly stumpy and potbellied man, of an age past forty but otherwise not to be distinguished, shuffled to the center of the stage. No one introduced him. He gave his name and an incredible won-lost record, then said he had no idea what he ought to say—all in a raw West Virginia drawl. Then he picked his nose.

After a long silence, he announced that he would just answer questions as best he could. Looking back I believe he might have answered, entirely without eloquence other than the granite bluntness of conviction, all the great and impossible questions men ask about, say, the nature of time, God, reality, and death. Unfortunately, we had no questions; we had hangovers. Moreover, how should a hayseed nose-picker be taken seriously by teams of men neatly decked out in matching shoes, slacks, caps, windbreakers, and jargon? At length, he broke the silence, barked some sort of command, perhaps an "Awright," and spread apart his arms like Moses at the Red Sea, so that unbelievably we rose and folded our chairs and peeled away from the center aisle until it became, as if by magic, a playing field. He barked again and twenty-two scruffily uniformed boys of mostly unimpressive physique appeared. He called a number and the boys went into a half-speed scrimmage before our eyes.

For a long time this seemed to me not only excessive but also absurd. Now I see that coach had taken us into the actual presence of a dream, his necessary dream. Like the artist, the writer, he had placed before us and meant to fix in our minds an image of man. For him this image was not available in graphs, statistics, playbacks, diagrams, devices of measurement, or theory—for those lead only to a hypothetical man, not a man in action. And who among us will claim to be a hypothetical man or would not shun the company of one? So entirely real was the image the coach had created that soon he had got down among his players, was oblivious to his audience, and walked in the heat and heart of the action until the scrimmage ran full tilt. And how could he have resisted that being swallowed into his vision as fully as Jonah had been swallowed by the whale of his evil? He had become responsible to the living shape of his dream, and it alone, not the amazed crowd of critics we now were, claimed his entire attention.

After lunch, we gathered for the guest speaker's remarks. Coach Duffy Daughtery, of Michigan State University, resplendent in three-piece suit, said *his* secret was simplicity and illustrated this by telling us how he trained behemoth defensive tackles. They were, he said, paired off on the first day of practice and required to spend an hour daily slapping each other. One slapped one's comrade on his outside and inside shoulder, as he faced you, and he would shout "Dive" or "Sweep." In a game, when a tackle faces an opponent, that opponent's physical pressure will tell the tackle that the ball is going in the direction from which he receives the pressure. He will shout "Sweep" if the ball is going to his outside shoulder and "Dive" if it is going to his inside shoulder. He is, thus, responsible for his team's countermoves. This training had worked so well, Daughtery said, that one night in a movie his wife had leaned to greet a player in a dark theater and her touch brought forth a ringing "Sweep!" When his joke faded, Daughtery, astonishingly, brought the old high school coach to the podium and asked him to discuss the "simple" secret of *his* success. The old fellow scratched and shuffled a little, then said, "They run fast." Daughtery waited. We waited. Daughtery, at length, asked the coach how he got them to run fast. More scratching and shuffling. Heavily then, with that voice which courteously rebukes its hearer for not knowing the obvious, he said, "Ah makes them boys run home after practice. It's dark then, see. They can't see how big the mountain is and they most all live on top, 'bout eight miles up. Them is tough but they still boys and they fear the dark much as you and me." He paused. "Everybody knows it ain't no opponent tougher than a eight-mile run up a fearful dark mountain. It gets them to see what they can do."

Robert Penn Warren, the finest living American poet, has written, "Man lives by images. They / Lean at us from the world's wall, and Time's." Joseph Conrad once wrote that his task was to make us *see* before all else. What that coach did for his boys, he did for us: he created an image which communicated simply and powerfully, through the immediate senses, what he knew and what he valued. He did not lecture us about honoring civilized virtues such as pride, courage, teamwork, discipline, sacrifice, responsibility, and even love. He showed them to us. He did what Mae West once advised when she said, "Use what's lying around the house." His task, the task of the writer and the teacher of writing, was to help people see what they were and what they might be, not as the hypothetical average, but as individuals in the living dramatic context.

It is going to require a heroic leap of faith to move from that coach to the business of creative writing, but no greater leap of faith than that of any teacher who believes, as I do, that the end of teaching is to reveal, test, and reaffirm the values by which men have found it possible not merely to survive but to live with dignity. The first question we must face is: what is creative writing? In time we are going to discover, as we always suspected, that there are more questions than answers, and not a little contradictory opinion. Creative writing is no more and no less than all writing. By convention, however, "creative" means the writing of fiction, poetry, plays, and sometimes hybrids; it is distinguished from nonfiction prose, journalism, and scholarship. But, of course, all writing that has interest, value, passion, durability, and vision is necessarily creative. For the sake of proceeding let us define instruction in creative writing as the performance of practical criticism, by an instructor and members of a class, upon original poems and stories submitted by members of the class. All who participate in this instruction are, therefore, literary critics. Allen Tate once wrote, "literary criticism, like the Kingdom of God on earth, is perpetually necessary and, in the very nature of its middle position between imagination and philosophy, is perpetually impossible." We might well ask why. Tate's answer is a further question: "Is literary criticism possible without a criterion of absolute truth?"

Most teachers of creative writing, when they are writers themselves, take the position that writing cannot be taught, though it can be aided. But few go so far as Allen Tate toward identifying the problem that arises in any consideration of teaching creative writing. If we live in an age which admits to no absolute truth (and we do), hence no consensus of literary standards, how is criticism possible? And upon what grounds does one make a critical comment? For the teacher of creative writing, even as he or she is an apprentice writer, has set up as a literary critic. In fact, in the greater number of cases he has set up with little thought of pedagogy, intention, results, or awareness of limitations. Writing programs do not require study in the history of our language, let alone the history of criticism. Student responses, as critic, are necessarily formed by the model of their instructor and passed on when they become the instructors. Ordinarily these students have little knowledge of the origin, nature, or real utility of the aesthetic ideas which they fuzzily articulate as gospel. To what and to whom is the teacher of creative writing then responsible? The variables and complexities involved in such an answer are so overwhelming that I can hope for only modest sketches of this business. Yet, perhaps, something of a portrait of the affair, as it is currently carried on in the United States, will suggest we might do well to consider our responsibility and to bear in mind Emerson's injunction that "There is then creative reading as well as creative writing."

The Associated Writing Programs Catalogue lists 251 colleges with instruction in creative writing that ranges from a scattering of courses to the Ph.D. in English with a concentration in writing. No information exists to reveal how many other schools provide some regular writing instruction but conventional wisdom says such instruction is increasing everywhere. One has further to imagine, based on a history of expanded financial support through state and federal agencies, that this instruction is becoming a staple of public school curriculums (President Reagan seems determined to reverse this trend). For example, the Poets-in-the-Schools program exists in virtually every state and sends poets into the classroom at even the lowest elementary levels. For some time *The*

American Poetry Review featured articles on the techniques employed by visiting poets who meant to teach the children how to do art. It was rumored that these pieces were published because they generated grant revenue for the magazine. Numerous states have collected, published, and touted poems culled from these PITS programs. Courses which imitate the pedagogical methods of these visitors have evolved in public schools all over the country. Clearly there are many questions to be asked, if there are few answers, about the nature, scope, relative quality, and per-tax-dollar value of such courses. About all that one can legitimately say of what is often called the creative writing industry is that it has exploded and mushroomed downward from the top to the bottom of the education industry.

Nevertheless, few commentators have seen fit to examine carefully what has happened or why. There are some obvious explanations, of course. People do seem to want to write. Some want to write better and some want a built-in audience. Where there is a demand there will be a supply. People want to avoid being condemned to the inarticulate average. The more cynical among us might, however, agree with Andy Warhol that everyone will sooner or later be famous for fifteen minutes and it is mostly fame these people want. Some, as always, are misled by money. They imagine that a writing course offers a secret which can be learned and employed for instant riches. Still others tell us that in English departments there has been a steady decline of students for reasons which may have to do with employment markets or woeful teaching or both and more, but an equally steady demand for creative writing courses. This demand leads to expanded graduate programs for teaching writers, jobs, more classes and students, and onward. I have taught at one large state university where the chairman vigorously beefed up the writing program by hiring name writers in the singular hope that students attracted to the graduate writing classes could be influenced to become regular doctoral students, a breed he had seen to decline in both quality and quantity. Such an expansion is supported by many literature faculties, albeit with strong suspicion, because they realize that writing students can be required to fill their otherwise poorly subscribed classes in literature specialties. It is also said that this expansion is a phenomenon attributable, at least in part, to the boom and temper of the sixties and seventies; that is to say, it is part of the educational move away from mastery of a body of literature and some ability to be critically articulate about that body, and toward a sort of therapy of souls with a common interest. This is sometimes called touchy-feely teaching. It is characterized by an emphasis on democratic participation and a minimalization of negative response. Alberta Turner's collection of essays by creative writing teachers, *Poets Teaching,* suggests we are engaged in everything from finding a way to keep the monsters stilled to saving souls. How all this is done, and with what success, even according to what standards, remains mostly unexamined. If literature teachers regard creative writing with suspicion, one can hardly blame them; they have long been suspect in a world of Yankee pragmatism. Increasingly one finds critics in the journals and little magazines speaking disgustedly of a self-perpetuating system which, it is contended, has succeeded in installing a literature both mediocre and vastly overrated. Unfortunately, much of what is written is not only biased but also surprisingly uninformed.

In the March 1, 1981, issue of the *New York Times Book Review,* Daniel Menaker implies that hordes of sad American would-be writers are ill served and duped by creative writing instruction—apparently because false hopes are raised—and he writes, "There is general agreement among professional writers and editors that with some exception—prominent among them the M.F.A. courses at the University of Iowa, Johns Hopkins, Columbia, and Stanford—these curricula are of extremely dubious value, except perhaps to the institutions themselves." One notes first that Mr. Menaker has duped himself: neither Johns Hopkins nor Stanford offers an M.F.A degree. Perhaps the point Mr. Menaker makes is valid, though neither his "general agreement" nor his unidentified subscribers can be tested for factuality, but it is odd that he fails to note that nearly twenty-five other M.F.A. programs are staffed by graduates of and modeled on the University of Iowa's program. This means there is, essentially, one curriculum. Logically the curriculum cannot itself then be strong here and weak there, only its staffing, implementation, resources, etc.

Charles Molesworth has argued in his recent study of contemporary poetry, *The Fierce Embrace,* that there is no genuine audience for art; there are only masses of poets going in uncharitable and diverse ways, having no common mission or understanding of what poetry is supposed to be or do. A more temperate and trustworthy but not less polemical study of these matters is Christopher Clausen's recent book, *The Place of Poetry.* That there is, in these generally conservative times, a new and reactionary critical anxiety about the untidiness of the literary world no one can deny. In a recent issue of America's most prominent literary magazine, *Poetry,* Karl Shapiro in "Creative Glut" argues that "Reading itself is discouraged, perhaps in legacy of the destruction of libraries in the Sixties and of the Yahoo cry for Relevance. Not only is the student ignorant of craft and craftmanship: he is ignorant of literature itself. He has no models. There is no common pool of information, no point of reference, no common vocabulary, no cultural bank-account." Professor Shapiro's peculiar choice of computer and commercial metaphors aside, the conservatism of aging poets aside, his essay remains an oddly popularist and demagogic view of writing and teaching in the last thirty years. Professor Shapiro, like editor Menaker and professors Molesworth and Clausen, relies as often on polemical opinion and innuendo as on factual information. We may find no answers when we ask questions about creative writing instruction, but it is irresponsible to ask no questions and irresponsible to publish comment so weirdly uninformed as to actually discourage unprejudiced investigation.

Surely we would all agree that the purpose of creative writing instruction ought to be the engendering of progressive improvement in compositions. Such teaching, in practice, ranges widely. William Faulkner gave his first novel to Sherwood Anderson to read. On a bench in New Orleans Anderson said he would get the novel published if he didn't have to talk about it, which is a critical evaluation. I heard once of a writer who began his class by plopping a hog's leg on the table and commanding the students to write a poem or story about it. I am unable to imagine *his* criticism. Our teaching includes all sorts of gimmickry, assignments, and methods of response. It would be interesting to chronicle the more bizarre of these but I will resist turning what I have to say into a *Popular Poetics*. The point is that we range from technicians to theorists along the common road of belief that something valuable can be taught about the process and product of writing without divorcing it from our lives. Is it worthwhile to learn about writing? The ages have thought so. Chinese emperors, we remember, used to have to demonstrate technical facility in poetry to assume power. We teach by conference, by reading, by acting like writers, by literally infinite clues, obvious and subtle alike, as to what a writer is and what he does. Yet it might be said that creative writing instruction falls into two parts: we teach the history of writing, craft, and literary models, and we teach what it means to be a writer.

The most common model for this teaching is the workshop. Its historical pedigree is overlooked frequently but nevertheless exists from the pre-Socratic philosophers to the Scribler Club of Swift, Pope, Gay, etc., to Ransom, Warren, Tate, and other Fugitives, to the Harlem Renaissance, to the Beats, to Black Mountain, and unto university programs in creative writing. In the current form the workshop operates by requiring students to write and duplicate a poem or story which is submitted to members of the class for criticism. Theoretically, each student will receive an equal share of the class's attention and this is (or is not) supplemented by conferences with the instructor. It is generally assumed that each student will learn something that will improve his writing. Obviously such learning will depend on many unknowns. What is the instructor teaching? How deep and broad is his experience, knowledge, and ability to transfer what he knows? What do the students know? Are they able to express anything helpful? What does improvement mean? Is any such learning or teaching measurable? Does a workshop necessarily urge individuals toward a committee aesthetic? What personal and group dynamics are involved? What, if any, values of a moral, emotional, social, or literary nature can or should be taught? Each question leads to a nest of yet more troublesome questions and beyond all this is the greater question of what kind of teaching, from blanket endorsement to close discrimination, is appropriate for each level of students from elementary to doctoral. So far as I am aware, these questions are asked and answered, if at all, solely in the minds of conscientious instructors. Perhaps it is after all the same in home economics and physical education. In any case creative writing instruction stands accused of irresponsible proliferation, undemonstrable value, corruption of art, financial boondoggling, pettifoggery, ignorance, cultural malfeasance—such sins and wickednesses as would take a new Bible to enumerate. That is to say, everything we expect of the United States Congress.

Can we not, then, even discuss what might be called the responsibility of the teacher of creative writing? I think we can and we must, if it is only within the most tenuous of frameworks. Creative writing instruction, like dreams and death, is not going to go away. If we have already institutionalized it, perhaps what we need is not less but more attention to what it is, what it can do, and how it ought to be regarded by all concerned. To this end I am going to propose a limited set of further questions and brief answers, both to be taken as points of departure rather than finite arrivals. And I begin by suggesting what I take to be the value of art and whatever form of education serves to enhance that value. In Isaiah one hears this curse: "Make the heart of this people fat, and make their ears heavy, and shut their eyes." Who will not agree that this is a living death we must struggle at all costs to escape, as well as precisely a description of what we are in our worst moments? Against this curse it is man's nature to set the revelation of words, the rebellion of truth expressed that it might be lived. I will say the value of writing in simple language, that of A. E. Housman, poet and Latin master, who wrote that "good literature continually read for pleasure must, let us hope, do some good to the reader: must quicken his perception though dull, and sharpen his discrimination though blunt, and mellow the rawness of his personal opinions." Our responsibility as teachers and writers is to remember Isaiah and Housman, to ask:

1. *Can creative writing be taught?*
Writing can be and always has been taught. One may teach both the forms and formulas of literature. One cannot teach how to write masterpieces of great art. Art history, art appreciation, and studio instruction teach a great many valuable things about painting. There has never been a course which could teach even the most talented apprentice to be a Michelangelo. But was Michelangelo self-taught in a void? In writing what is taught is respect for time, history, discipline, struggle, expectation, and accomplishment.

2. *What good is creative writing?*
William James once wrote that the value of a college education was that it enabled one to tell a good man from a bad man. Is this true more of music, astrophysics, carpentry, or religion than of writing? In the state of Utah the school board has now required all high school students to complete a course in morals. In writing one enters into the dynamic and dramatic engagement of life as it rises to representation in art. The good teacher of creative writing is in the position of testing the value and validity of that representation, hence of moral, ethical, social, and cultural values. Writers before and after Emerson have spoken of the writer as both revolutionary and priest, teacher and soldier of vision. As Allen Tate said, the critic stands between imagination and philosophy. He is like an antenna, except that he must be willing and able to know what to transmit and what to receive. If the teacher of creative writing does not know what a good man is then he will not know what art is. Jean-Paul Sartre has written that "Health consists in the absence of disease." He is half right. The good of creative writing is the good of art itself: it creates receptive, perceptive, discriminating critics of what is true and false in the world, and it may result in great images of individual and communal health.

3. *What tangible values has creative writing instruction?*
Many values of such instruction are apparent to those who have taught writing and to those who have taken such instruction, perhaps less apparent to those who have no experience with it. These may be summed up in the words of Henry James on Nathaniel Hawthorne: "The solitary worker loses the profit of example and discussion; he is apt to make awkward experiments; he is in the nature more or less of an empiric." That is, we benefit from the knowledge, community, and common interest of others, though not infinitely of course. More practically, we do not and should not expect to make all students into Miltons. The biology major does not often become a Darwin. But we help students to realize that language is a living, vital reality: it is what we possess to experience

and shape everything we can know. Art is what we have to prevent the deadly and dehumanizing languages of technocracy by which we are transformed into the hypothetical average of inputs, outputs, interfaces, digits, texts, and body counts. Creative writing is one of the few formal opportunities in education for self-discovery and self-creation. It leads a student less to right answers than to right questions. It creates more intelligent, informed, and responsible readers by immersing them in the actual process of imaginative exploration and accomplishment. Creative writing engenders, or ought to engender, an appetite for excellence in the dramatic images of man. In any age dominated not only by the shallow and delusionary images perpetrated by television, and movies, and pulp books, but also by the anarchists and polemicists of fringe culture, good instruction demonstrates the historical successes and failure of ideas, actions, beliefs, dissent, taste, tolerance, beauty, and knowledge.

4. *Who should teach creative writing?*
In one sense, everyone engaged in teaching ought to teach imaginative inquiry. The difference between the teacher of creative writing and the orthodox teacher of literature is that in literature one begins with an established text and context. There is always critical help for the discussion of the text, whether it be historical, polemic, generic, or peripheral. The creative writing teacher must be all this at once, for he is expected to receive, evaluate, and constructively discuss what has theoretically never existed until the moment it is presented to him. He must provide not a lecture but a response which is the terrain of discovery.

There is, among teachers of creative writing, an argument as to which degree sufficiently prepares a teacher for employment. The argument is irrelevant, for no degree guarantees preparation or success. The job market has for some years been shrinking, while graduate writing programs have been expanding. There are now approximately thirty M.F.A. programs in operation, graduating perhaps 150 people annually. Another 50, perhaps, annually take Ph.D.s. But only some 50, I would guess, actually find teaching positions. Over a hypothetical five-year period this means 750 people do not get teaching positions. Yet, is it not a mistake to think of any collegiate specialization as vocational training? The fact is that a teacher of writing ought to be hired because he or she demonstrates excellence in writing and in teaching.

That is, as employers we must look for the teacher of writing who is capable of simultaneous humility and conviction. We shall ask of this person the wisdom of but not an enslavement to the tradition of literature, a vision of literary excellence which is synthetic but not prescriptive, and a character sufficiently visible to both lead and follow the students.

Theodore Roethke, one of America's finest poets, may serve as the prototype for us. His students have constituted an impressive collection of accomplished poets and teachers, including James Wright, Richard Hugo, Carolyn Kizer, and Tess Gallagher. They record Roethke as a demanding, sometimes tyrannical, sometimes doting, always impassioned teacher whose end was to leave the world's body of poetry not only better served but also extended through his students.

We ought to teach our students to write what they will not be ashamed of having done in ten or twenty years. We must teach them that to be a writer is to examine, dramatize, describe, understand, and enter wholly into the world as words. We must, therefore, be intersections of values, priorities, conventions, philosophies, and possibilities. It is old-fashioned to speak of being a model for students but in no other way does a teacher of writing so totally serve the future of his student and his art. Our teaching proceeds in a very great measure in snatches of conversations in halls, offices, and classroom aftermaths. We teach by what we write, what we think, our enthusiasms, prejudices, faiths, and willingness to let the world speak through us.

5. *How can we measure the quality of creative writing instruction?* Immediately, we must trust the judgment of students who take our classes, realizing their perspective and their knowledge is limited. It is, I think, possible to determine if our instruction is putting them into contact with their world or, conversely, to see if we are merely replicating ourselves. We must seek to measure ourselves. My football coach sees his results in clear wins and losses, every Saturday. With us it must be otherwise. In time we will have the measurement that is the writing itself. We shall see some of our students become the writers whom we value and trust for what they reveal in images of man that we could not have expected but which, please God, we may have helped them toward. For the most part, however, we shall not know the harvest of what we have sown. Unless, of course, it is mightily and visibly bad. But surely we shall see that in the short run.

Creative writing is no panacea for individual or social ills. If it were we should have long ago discovered how to prevent Vietnam and the collapse of Chrysler. Because of the horror of the Holocaust, George Steiner said, "After Auschwitz, no more poetry." And it is hard to sustain a fervent belief in art as humanly affective when we know that Nazis read Goethe, heard Mozart, and cultivated refined tastes by night after a hard day of eliminating Jews. Yet did not art always tell us about that darkness in the human spirit, and what worse would we have been without those images of ourselves in Homer, Chaucer, Dante, Shakespeare, Dickens, the Brothers Grimm, Kafka? I have mentioned critics who complain of the spread of writing instruction and argue it dilutes the quality of our writing. Have they got their facts in perspective? One of their complaints is the size, the cost of a writing program. It is worth remembering that one Air Force bomber costs more than the entire budget for the National Endowment for the Arts; that no school in this country provides the salaries, support, or attention to creative writing that it does for computers, music, engineering, biology, or ROTC; that in every state university we have the athletic budget for laundry alone exceeds the budget for creative writing. The point is that we are a tiny, tiny operation but we are entrusted with envisioning, recording, and even sustaining the best that has been and will be thought and felt about human nature. When we seek to measure what we are doing, and we must do that, let us do so in appropriate contexts.

6. *Should the artist, the creative writer, be in a university, college, or school?*
If not there, where should he be? This certainly depends on what we expect universities to do and what we expect artists to be. The common argument is that universities mold academic writers who are not in touch with American values, whose writing is anemic and isolated. But who else so pursues truth and challenges it? Where? Boston University's President Silber defiantly said not long ago that no university is a democracy. If it is not, what is it? If the artist can find our intellectual country, he will find it nowhere else. It is up to us to insure students the opportunity to dream freely, but not capriciously. The artist and the teacher, in spite of a wide American streak of shame about it, are intellectuals. Their charge is precisely to be literary and traditional while they are democratic and revolutionary. Freedom, Janis Joplin's followers used to echo, "is when you have nothing left to lose." We may agree, but that is also a definition of anarchy and of death. The university and the school exist as the witness to and the embodiment of complexity in every aspect of human experience. To the artist playing demagogue and brat in the streets we must always counterpose the living memory of history. Henry Ford said history is bunk. That attitude results in war, poverty, industrial rapacity, and ecological destruction.

7. *What are the abuses of creative writing instruction?*
What but the curse of Isaiah, that we make the heart of the people fat, and their ears heavy, and their eyes blind? That is, we fail our responsibility to art, to students, and to ourselves. We allow ourselves to be indulgent, ignorant, uninformed, and lazy. We become complacent, cyni-

cal, privileged, and uninterested. We surrender to apathy and inactivity. We lose faith in possibility. We forget, for reasons of comfort, that life is short and art is long. We forget that you get to grandmother's house only through the hard cold and the dark woods. We forget that many will not get there at all. And what of the mediocrity we are said to perpetuate? What of the network of friendships and connections that is said to become a virtual cartel with control of jobs, prizes, and publications? What of the fact that we are training, as critic Molesworth says, "more people [to] write poetry than [to] read it"? One despairs of such questions not only because they have *some* truth but also because they are irrelevant questions finally. Are not these writers also readers? Will they learn something better on assembly lines? Universities have, as Molesworth's questions clearly imply, created new opportunities for encouragement of writing, of hope for countless readers and writers, of publication for books which cash value might have killed off. How can this be thought without value or wrong? W. B. Yeats once said, "There are too many of us." He meant mediocre writers. He is our century's greatest poet and we do ill not to attend to his least remark. Yet, having heard him, what action should we take? Shall we clamor to cut off publications? Sadly, the majority of those echoing Yeats's whimsy are writers who have not shown they merit our attention, often critics who imagine they are poets and novelists of superior but unrecognized abilities.

Those who have asserted the corruptive influence, the basic worthlessness, and the collective irrelevance of teachers of creative writing have yet on their shoulders the burden of *specific* argument and detailed evidence. Our instruction is not without weakness and abuse, but we require our critics to leave aside demagogic bluster and literary McCarthyism. We require them to articulate what is valuable and what is not, where it is to be found and where not, how it may be accomplished and how not, while we are all reminded that, as Melville said, "He who has never failed somewhere, that man cannot be great. Failure is the true test for greatness." That is very like Allen Tate's contention that as critics our task is impossible. Yet if we are doomed to failure, Tate does not tell us to shrink from failure.

I said early on that these notes would raise many more questions than answers, being a sort of portrait of writing and the teaching of writing. I have, I believe, been faithful to that prediction. And I am acutely aware of how much I have left both unasked and unanswered, even unhinted. Nor do I mean at this point to bring about a crescendo of conclusions, but instead to abandon the subject. That is, after all, what the poet Paul Valéry said we do with poems. It is what we do with students and they with us. What is left then? Well, the images of man in the writing, the images by which we find it possible to dream of ordinary human dignity. These we must continually seek for and covet and laud for what they fix in our consciousness as possibility. We must regard them as the secret and necessary dreams of being which we may enter into with our simple hearts and complex passions, entering so entirely that we recognize no division between what we are showing and what we are being. That is why I remember that old football coach, the tones of his voice among the sounds of boys banging their bodies together on the bright red carpet of a posh hotel, and the snow falling outside as if to seal us all into something like an eternal, dynamic, and luminous moment. What I did not see then, but see now, is the teacher's and the writer's principle of responsibility, that we can, we may, get it right. We can be what we dream.

Beagling

■

My neighbor has a handsome adolescent beagle which, as anyone knows, is a universe of energy and assertion. Sunrise and sunset, he yips, yelps, and yodels. I have stood by the tall wooden fence that cages him and watched, impressed by the signaling range of his voice. Sometimes he is lyrical and brief, sometimes he is cumulative as a fugue. Occasionally he sits abjectly and cocks his head as charmingly as RCA's dog. He can't see beyond the fence but often appears perfectly receptive of all that is distantly, unknowably, continuingly there. When he has latched onto something which affects him, he sounds off.

To speak of a poet as a dog is reductive and comic. A beagle is not even one of God's hugely admirable creatures, scarcely wolf or dane. But a beagle is an actor and an action, fulfilled only in collaboration with the man who sets him loose and controls, loosely, what he does. The poet is both beagle and beagler. The poem is a passage from ignorance, or stasis, through particular thickets, meazes, mudholes, road-ruts, cabin debris, and—increasingly of late—suburban landscapes, to mystery. I do not say from innocence to experience, from arrogance to humility, from restlessness to contentment, from ignorance to wisdom, though the true poem is surely characterized by these patterns. The true poem is not deliberately functional but experiential. It must have its ghostly spoor, as the beagle has its rabbit, and it must proceed in successful circles but its greatest pleasure is not in arrival and cessation but in its contested, testing, revealing movement.

Beagles, like all hunting animals, are images of witness and faith and, especially, obligation. Dog hunters say it is a matter of genetics, of blood. Dogs are obliged to hunt because the world is there, because the summons is in their blood. Like poets, a beagle cannot choose *not* to hunt. Unlike poets, a beagle cannot choose *what* to hunt or what will be the shape of his voiced response. The other half of a hunting beagle is his owner. Some of these hunt for meat but others, the true hunters in my mind, hunt only for the mysterious pleasure derived from the sounding of their dog's circling announcements of the world's shape. These usually hunt at night and their hunting consists of sitting at a campfire, as at a desk, alone or with others where they listen intensely. Between the looping, singing voices of dogs, these hunters shape and reshape both the quality and content of what their dogs say. This is ordinarily done in a constant awareness and even reverential (sometimes debunking) evocation of history's dogs, hunts, and sounds. One has only to see the otherworldly glory in these faces to know such men have come into a direct engagement of all that is real and durable in their lives, though the hunt is partial and temporary.

Why do dogs hunt? Why do men sit in the night to hear dogs hunt? What is the nature of such hunting? The answers are never simple or complete. It suffices to say dogs hunt because of a blood-gift. Men hunt them because it gives them pleasure. Such hunting is circular, ritualistic, and ordered by manners. The poet does not choose to become a poet, I think, so much as he becomes one by default or destiny. He could choose otherwise but does not because writing poems pleases him and fulfills the demands of his nature. The poem is always circular, ritualistic, and informed by manners. Its particular form is the result of self-negotiations between what feels *right* and the continual assertions of all those voices which have been lifted before him and of which he cannot declare ignorance. For the poet, each poem must be a reentry into the night-barking mystery, each entry having its local and inevitable logic of circumstance, personality, formal character, and meaning. Yet if the poem does not or cannot establish cohabitation with the past as with the unanswerable mysteries, it is—as hunters say—a dog that won't hunt.

I imagine my neighbors listening, as I do, to the young beagle next door. Their speculation is almost audible to me: pain? immaturity? loneliness? fear of intruders? Is it hunger for food, his mother, a young bitch? Why don't they take him in, make him feel better for Christ's sake? No questions affect the dog's noise; no answers account for it. There are no resolving answers to explain why a god's delight comes to the hunter listening confidently through the mysterious darkness nor why a similar delight comes to the poet. We do try to account for why we write what we write and how we write because that is our nature and one of our obligations. We feel obliged to know and to say, to bear witness in image and narrative and rapture and dirge, to make a discrimination of values and defects and causes and effects, just as one beagler speaking with passion to another. And like them, we slip reflections of the world into our remembering and conjecturing: the absence of the heroic dead, the meanness and infertility of our kind, the loss of good fields, the war against change and for change. While we speak critically, the right dogs keep hunting for us and with us, and we are glad to be alive then. We are glad to praise life, even in our annoyance and speculation.

I am suspicious of making prideful statements of accountability or prognostication. What may be said of poems seems to me often partial, wrong, and inconsistent; or it is self-defensive, posturing, inflationary; or it is illogical, sentimental, hysterical. I mistrust the poet who would legislate my emotions, induce ameliorative behavior, or stump for a patriotism of aesthetics. I mistrust those who would huddle us forward as if to a doggy obedience school and distrust those who would value us according to our pedigree charts or our field trial certificates. Even in poets the critical effort is proprietary and oppressive. The true poem will have none of this. It has all it can do to answer the opposing calls of the poet and the world.

Milton thought of the poet as God's translator. Others have regarded him as physician, legislator, policeman, psychologist, etc.—all distinct and distinguished functions, social functions. Conrad describes him as a kind of therapist of the senses, Eliot as a catalyst, and Adrienne Rich as a self-appointed Equal Opportunity Officer. Auden reflects the world's opinion: the poet makes nothing happen. All of these figures are true. And false. They reveal only that the poet values what he signifies and suggest the particular subjects to which he is most susceptible. I might have chosen the figure of the poet as spy (John Hollander and others have done so) since in the jittery instability of contemporary existence the spy has moral authority, privileged perspective, formal control, and all the world to roam in. Even television's archetypal gumshoe, Columbo, constantly journeys from ignorance to revelation. But, no. For me there is something appealing in the homely, divided figure of the beagle and his hunter that rings true. One is useless without the other. I write because it is a blood-gift I can't ignore. I write about what I know and have known and would know better: evocative places, significant human actions, ethical and moral and consequential mysteries, the indifferent and holy urge to live, which is freedom. I write to go beyond fences I did not erect but must acknowledge.

Of all a man might say about his poems, the least reliable observations concern form, or sound. All poetry exists on the spectrum from image-pictograph to abstract rhetoric. There is too little heartbeat in the image and there is no body in the rhetoric. Neither organic nor mechanical metaphors unequivocally explain what balance we choose—and the poet does choose—for the individual poem. I find my poems occupy various positions on that spectrum and I regard that as healthy. But the poems I take the greatest pleasure in are those whose principal organizing feature is neither a dominant picture nor a faithful metric, but is a circling, a slowly circling forward motion that is the movement of planets. Or the mind. Or of beagles on a night hunt. It is a motion whose cadences are strong, repetitive, idiosyncratic; whose pleasure is to seek, to apprehend, to announce; whose source is in the blood-beat of my ear; whose end is in its beginning. It is a kind of beagling that swings away and back to the self that waits before the looming fence of the night, the self who must find within the lovely orchestra and chorus his own rising, falling, entirely alive voice. To find the poem one must lose the poem, letting it go and drawing it back, letting it become as Frost says "a wild tune"—though not so wild that it escape intelligible, necessary, and revealing witness. The poem, then, that sings as it hunts, simultaneously and significantly. Not the poem that merely sounds off.

Heroes of the Spirit: An Interview with Dave Smith

■

PETER BALAKIAN: In much of your work, especially in *The Fisherman's Whore* and *Cumberland Station,* there are seamy places—outcast environments—alleyways, flophouses, abandoned seacoasts, and these landscapes are peopled by downtrodden characters. Why do you go to these places and people in your poems?

DAVE SMITH: Well, I have thought about this as I have written poems during the past few years. In fact, there's a poem in my book *Homage to Edgar Allan Poe* which talks about those places. In "Nightcrawlers" I am thinking about those people to see if they were what I thought they were. In writing about those people I am trying now to imagine what the truth was in what had been previously attractive to me. I wrote about the fishermen of the Atlantic coast and the kinds of lives they represented and the circumstances they found themselves in because they seemed to me in some respects exemplars of virtues I admired; for example, they seemed to me men of stoic courage, of passion, of a certain dignity, and of a certain integrity which I value. And it might be, I think, that they were heroes to me, I mean in the sense that Joseph Campbell means with the heroic figure; this could be a very different kind of hero from a king or prince in literature but not entirely different from the kinds of heroes one finds in Anglo-Saxon poems such as "The Wanderer."

I suspect it is partly true that I gravitated toward those kinds of people because I grew up around them, although I had been educated out of living among them except in purely emotional ways. I began to write about them partly because they were people I knew and partly because they remained intensely mysterious and partly because I very much admired the way they lived, so that early on in my poems there is a romantic description and embodiment of those lives. At the time, I'm not sure I realized what I was doing in seeing these people as heroic figures. I mention "Nightcrawlers" because its speaker goes back to the fish docks to greet another fisherman coming in, to see if the fisherman is what he had been described as, a hero. I have come to see also that my admiration of such people, and fascination with their places, partially reflects my suspicion of the intellectual life—as a partial life. American writers are schizophrenic about being verbal laborers and physical laborers. We hate and covet both sorts of existence; hence we romanticize and distort whichever of those lives we currently feel estranged from. In art we want to repossess the truth we feel we have not lived. But what is the truth we see in other people?

During the last few elections the people in the rural places I have written about voted almost entirely for archconservative candidates, out of stubbornness and out of fear. They are Ur-conservative, bigoted, racist, narrow-minded, even sometimes ugly and uncivilized. That's both repulsive and attractive to me. They are still people. They are also virtuous and decent. I mean I have a great interest in a man, for example, who doesn't have a bank account and what money he gets he has to spend at a grocery store where his credit is extended from week to week, month to month, because he and his family, his ancestors, are part of the life of that place. He is, apparently, a known, simple commodity. Yet he is also a man, and complex. His is not a life of leisure. It is a life of hard, brutal work. But it is not entirely different from any life in which a man has to live pretty close to what he believes in. I have tried in my recent poems to know how and where I exaggerated so that I made these people less and more than they really are. It would be sufficient for any poet to know the actual truth, a whole truth, and I am trying to do that. That is why I have written a number of newer poems about racial relations.

PB: Now, in your going back you're once more checking yourself on your romantic and mythic tendencies. It's all right for the poet to make it mythic; are you being too hard on yourself?

DS: The poem that lies is no good to us. You must continue to ask yourself where you are lying in the good sense that you are lying toward the truth and where your lying is self-deception. Or ignorance. I am interested in those people who have—I don't want to say who have been defeated by the world—literally suffered lives which many of us couldn't endure and yet they managed to do it with dignity intact and with spirit unbroken; I admire that in them. At the same time I want to see them as people and not as caricatures.

PB: Do you consider yourself a Southern writer?

DS: Your question raises many answers and many conflicting impulses in me. Robert Penn Warren, whom I regard as not just a great Southern writer but as the best living American poet, was asked in an interview if he considered himself a Southern poet. Warren said he didn't know how to think of himself as anything else—that was his heritage. That's one answer. Harry Crews, a fine Southern novelist, has also written that no writer wants to be labeled anything that will limit what he might be. One has to hope that whatever he's writing has the ability to be a felt reality for literate readers anywhere. To be a Southern writer is merely an accident of birth, though it does reflect certain cultural and aesthetic traditions—either in practice or rejection.

It is fair to say that I feel myself to belong to a region of this country and its heritage in a way that I don't feel myself to belong to other regions. I deliberately determined to make my book *Goshawk, Antelope* set in the West, a part of the country entirely foreign to me, even though I'd been living there, because I wanted it to be imagined rather than precisely informed by local experience. I have since written poems which return to a Southern place. But it was important for me to write *Goshawk* to test the limits of what I could do. I think what it really means to be a Southern writer is not so much a matter of geographical orientation but of the immediate and felt reality of history in a place. I think when one grows up as I did and most Southerners do—in the immediate presence of living history—you realize intensely that life of the past around you. It's vivid, it's actual; one lives in very old houses, very old places, where events happened you have read about in school and hear about through one's family lore. The books purport to be objective. The families are fiercely subjective. You grow up in that intersection, as I grew up near Jamestown, Yorktown, Williamsburg, and Civil War battlefields. Anglo-Saxon history in the West is very different and really begins in the mid-nineteenth century. People growing up in Utah have little sense of the reality of the Civil War, of slavery, of the military occupation of tidewater Virginia, which has been continuous since 1861 and consists now of more than fourteen major military bases.

I was talking recently with Red Warren and I found myself marvelling—stunned even—to be talking with a man who, as he has written in numerous poems, once sat under a tree and heard his grandfather's memories of cavalry experience with Jeb Stuart. This makes history a living fact. The Civil War is something that Warren knows not as a book fact but a human fact—in a way that your father or brother or girlfriend might say, "Do you know what happened to me yesterday?" Warren has a great line in which he calls the past "the great rebuker," echoing George Santayana, who says we are doomed to repeat the past. I think Southerners know keenly the living history around them. That you are what your parents and your grandparents and neighbors and friends *were*—that what they did and had to do made you what you are. That sense feeds into an individual and a communal identity; one knows what one is by what has been and what is around him.

Place becomes very important. When I was a child I used to go to my grandmother's house two blocks from Hampton Roads, a great body of water, and I would look out and know that the *Monitor* and the *Merrimac,* the first ironclad ships, had battled just off that shore. And know that not only was this the Civil War but that it was the beginning of modern naval warfare. That sense of history is appalling.

In this respect, I am a Southern writer and couldn't be anything else. It's also, to be more specific with your question, said that Southerners are natural storytellers. Is this like saying black folk have rhythm? I have known many there who couldn't be tortured into telling a story. The hero of my novel *Onliness* is such a person. Yet there is something about a Southern writer which inclines him toward stories and the employment of myths, and we seem to fall into urging the necessity of myths, we of the defeated country, as it's often put, which is interesting and helpful but in the end I don't know that this really distinguishes a Southerner from anyone else. Could it be proven?

PB: Would you say some of the narrative impulses in your poems are connected to your being a Southerner? Did you grow up around storytellers?

DS: Yes and no. That's part of why I'm suspicious of what an interest in storytelling reveals. My parents were not in the ordinary sense literate. My father was a mustang naval engineer and my grandfather, having been a B & O Railroad foreman, was forced by the Depression to become a mustang aeronautical engineer. Any books in our houses tended to be stress tables and design manuals. I suspect the men in my family have not read a total of three novels. This would not prevent them from telling stories but they were laconic, private men. For about eight years as a young boy, I would get up before dawn and go into the woods with my grandfather to hunt squirrels. He'd choose a fallen log and we'd sit there from dawn till noon, utterly silent except for the occasional bang of our shotguns. He taught me a great deal, but he did not tell stories. On the other hand, my mother and grandmother made certain I knew the stories of our family which *suggested* we were of genteel and authorized stock.

My sister keeps genealogical books. I have been made aware of ancestors who fought in the Union *and* the Confederate armies, of lands and fortunes held and lost, of family beauties, heroic acts, and the like. Just as the women of our family wished me to remember.

Yet my family, a prototypical American family, seems to have been always on the move. We began in Lynchburg, Virginia, tobacco people I am told. We moved to West Virginia, to coal mining, and my grandparents grew up in Cumberland, Maryland, as railroad people. When the Depression came my grandfather took us to Baltimore and then to tidewater Virginia.

Much of my inheritance has been literary, coming through literature. The first book I read at the University of Virginia, where I walked past Poe's old dorm room and where Faulkner was then writer-in-residence, was Robert Penn Warren's *All the King's Men*. It was a monumental influence on me, its way of being and its rhythms. I read a great many Southern books there. I discovered William Styron there, who wrote about my hometown.

I will mention an irony here. If you talk to Southerners from Mississippi, Alabama, Louisiana, you see that many of them still regard Virginia as a marginal Southern state, if Southern at all. I have in fact been called a Yankee in some Southern states; that is when I presume to note the dominant sites of battle during the War. Yet people who are not Southern often think of the South as monolithic and of the people as all the same. Southerners are as much in flight from each other, and their places, as from anything else.

PB: Would you call yourself a tidewater Southerner?

DS: To some extent. Tidewater is a maverick community. One Southern literature critic, Louis Rubin, once wrote in the *Mississippi Quarterly* that, oddly, there had been no Southern writer of any consequence from this area except William Styron. I took that as a personal challenge. I said, well, I'm going to be the second one. Maybe I will be yet.

PB: What are the most serious limitations of contemporary American verse?

DS: Anyone who writes has opinions, and ought to have them. If we don't read with intelligence and discrimination, if we are guilty of reading without examination, then we will only delude ourselves. My opinion here is no more authorized than anyone's; it's just an opinion. I will substitute *poetry* for your word *verse*. I think there is a great deal of exciting poetry being written. I'm not at all convinced that there was ever a more propitious or exciting poetry. I say that with a full awareness of what has happened with, and since, High Modernism, the Fugitives, and so on.

Nevertheless, I also think our poets demand too little of their poems. It seems to me many don't press themselves to be better than they are; one often hears, for example, that it is so hard to publish, meaning we don't recognize the good stuff. It ought to be hard to publish. I think, quite to the contrary, it is too easy to publish. A lot of mediocre books get published because people seem to lack a kind of humility which would allow them to discriminate between the good and bad, the better and best.

Jim Wright used to say that he was nothing more than a third-rate lyricist. When you pressed him on this he would say, "My God, compare me to Horace. I can't lift a finger to Horace. Or compare me to Swinburne, or the worst you can imagine." That kind of humility is rare. It venerates excellence. Many now regard excellence as elitism; we are democratic levelers. We operate aesthetic standards as a function of self-importance generated, perhaps, by the kind of times we live in and by the hunger of magazines to have copy and the hunger of book publishers to meet quotas for Blacks, women, American Indians, etc. Our innocent arrogance and our innocent populism seem to bury the excellent poetry with the mediocre and the bad. How many editors are accomplished poets, or even informed? Can we find three critics or professors who will agree about what is excellent? I do not mean what is socially, politically acceptable. Our will to do good devalues the past but only the past, that heritage, will help us to know what is excellent and what is passing. On that Eliot and Williams clearly agreed.

PB: We're a bunch of amnesiacs as a culture; Wright is a very literate man and knows the history of Western literature, and this enables him to have historical perspective on himself.

DS: We Americans live in a curious situation. We poets are able to say, as a given, that there's no money in poetry. Therefore we need not be measured by the American stick of value, which is the dollar. This helps to make art independent of our people. I can say I don't care how much a book earns or sells, I'm simply writing for myself or posterity. The end result of this might be that I don't care about readers, what they think or hear or feel—or don't. If they can't understand me, too bad. Perhaps we have allowed ourselves a protective indulgence in writing that may be harmful to us. Perhaps sales ought to be *one* of the tests of value. Henry James, Conrad, Virginia Woolf, Faulkner, Frost, Joyce, and Eliot were not uninfluenced by the need to sell books, though they are the great artists and changers. The necessary connection with a reasonable reader had *some* effect on what they wrote, on how they wrote. We must be aware, as much as we can, of what we are doing and why, of the choices we make. Perhaps it is not entirely true, as we appear to have assumed, that excellence is congruent with obscurity, gamesmanship, and solipsism. It is fair to think that poetry ought to be clear, accessible, at least as a general goal; it ought to be some kind of expression with communal significance and an individual, felt reality. I often want to say to poets I am reading, "Why should your particular angst interest me?" The answer of course must be in the particular marriage of language and thing, not simply the thing itself. Too often we are asked to accept words lineated as poems when there is no art, no poetry. We want the poem which has the necessary, inevitable pressure of the world and the right words.

PB: Are you referring to a pre-Romantic idea of the poet having a relationship with an assumed public place? Have poets taken the idea of Philistine public to such an extreme that they feel it no longer necessary to speak publicly? Is this the decadent end of Romanticism?

DS: I don't know if we've gone that far. I do know that we have allowed ourselves an extreme privacy, an extreme indulgence in our experimentations with form and language. What else is *Finnegans Wake?* To that extent, we risk writing ourselves out of an ordinary human connection.

Modern and contemporary poetry is, in spite of anything Eliot and others have said, Romantic in impulse and in the formal action of that impulse. I do not suggest any return to republican verse, to Pope or the like. I'm saying that something that disturbs me in our poetry, and that I might regard as a weakness, is the refusal or the inability of talented poets to try to speak clearly of what concerns us all.

There is also a popular poetry that seems not to take seriously what it means to struggle to live, which I find jejeune and silly. There is a chattery poetry and a poetry which drones in charming ways. These fill our magazines. Critics say these are the worst of times, that we have no great poets. I am not so sure. Perhaps this was always a complaint; perhaps we too readily forget that John Esten Cooke was thought greater than Walt Whitman. In Richmond, anyway. Robert Penn Warren is a great poet. We have many splendid poets, if we are intimidated by the word "great." These include Galway Kinnell, Louis Simpson, Mona Van Duyn, Sterling Brown, Don Justice, Anthony Hecht, Gary Snyder. Many others. James Dickey has been a national asset. Jim Wright and Richard Hugo also. Philip Levine is a favorite of mine. There are W. S. Merwin, Mark Strand, and even Robert Bly, for those inclined. You make your own list. I very much admire the poems of Norman Dubie, Carole Oles, William Heyen, Fred Chappell, Stephen Dunn, Michael Harper, and on and on.

PB: Is there such a thing as the moral imagination?

DS: That's difficult. Especially since the word *moral* is being thrown around with a new political edge to it. If I say that all literature should be moral, there will be people who imagine I am a card-carrying member of the Jerry Falwell contingent, that herd insanity.

PB: But I mean it in the Arnoldian sense—talking about moral in the sense that Whitman or Arnold would talk.

DS: I think this is a real issue, an issue about which I wish I could believe young poets thought more than they appear to. A basic Romantic question: Does the poem, or the poet, change the world? Is a human being bettered by exposure to poetry? Auden, even, was ambivalent. The Romantic conviction was a resounding yes. For another response, there is George Steiner saying, "After Auschwitz, no more poetry." He means we now know that Nazis could burn up Jews by day and enjoy poetry, or Mozart and Beethoven, by night; art did not prevent butchery and gross human brutality. My feeling about this is complex. We must grant Steiner the right of his argument. On the other hand we do feel that what we say is crucial, important, that words matter, that poetry is the most significant of human expression. Surely this is the value of the Bible. Yet we may be only justifying what we have to do. It could be argued that we don't know what worse would have happened if there had been no poetry to temper our brutality through history, if we had had no civilized people thinking about themselves, about what happens, no one dramatizing our darknesses.

PB: That's one way of looking at it.

DS: But beyond all that is one's own conviction about what people are. On the whole people are a pretty damn sorry lot. They are quite capable of evil. Evil does exist, in spite of Dr. Spock, and it is unlikely that poetry is going to drive it out of us. I don't ever think than I am going to save the starving children of Indochina with a poem. That is a great mistake for a poet to make. Bly seems to imagine that his moral indignation and righteousness will translate into an alteration of human behavior. Has it? His is the attitude of Lutheran zealots, preachers. I cannot accept it. Yet perhaps art may restrict our worst abuses. It is certainly in the human to try to soften the evil he contains, to try to find ways to live as best he can. One of these ways is to witness the beauty and grandeur that life sustains, maybe without purpose. Michelangelo did not prevent Il Duce, but the richness of my life is increased by Michelangelo's testimony. Art does seem to have the ultimate effect of reminding us of what we are and might be. It doesn't necessarily change us.

Too many poets, hearing Rilke say "you must change your life," become simplistic evangelists for whom poetry is the gospel according to me. The Black Mountain poets and the Deconstructionist critics have all but founded a church for which poetry is liturgy, sermon, Talmudic code, and new commandments. Do we need a new Ecclesiastes? If I tell people to change their lives, then change to what? And how? Nevertheless, poetry has a function and it's a moral function, if by moral we mean art witnesses the health of the human spirit.

PB: Are you saying that your poetry must be connected to a lived-in world, and in this sense I take that to have something to do with moral. Has much of our poetry become solipsistic and broken those bonds?

DS: That seems true. I don't know if I'd put it exactly that way. I want to avoid clichés, but great art affirms dignity, beauty, the hope that's possible in life. The human being is, after all, in spite of his compulsive behavior as beast, a great creature. I'm never as excited about dogs as about people. Robert Bly has a long-standing position about solitude and its relationship to art. It is a nearly otherworldly, ethereal position. He really does believe that to be a good-hearted spirit in the world you have to sit under trees a lot—in poems. This ignores much human crisis in cities, suburbs, rooms. If I can go back to those people I admire, the fishermen, they don't have the luxury to sit under trees all day. They have to feed children and work hard hours. They don't have the opportunity to pursue an enlightened life. We may say that anyone can choose to do so, but cultural, social, and economic pressures make such a choice generally impractical, if not impossible. The poet has the opportunity to educate us about choices, alternatives, perceptions through the dramatic and lyrical engagement of values put at peril and tested. He must, however, engage life as it is and has been lived; otherwise he is merely preaching, usually to the converted. He must seek truth with humility, that is his morality. He must recognize that art can indicate a right relationship to all that exists. Art does have a consoling effect, but beyond that it helps you to *know*, simply to be aware and to see through. In this sense also, art is moral.

PB: In the sense that you are talking about humility, I think of Roethke's sense of the sacred: his insistence that there is something larger than the human self before which we come and efface ourselves. Now that's not a popular notion with many poets today. Would you say that you have a religious disposition in this way?

DS: Oh yes. Most have such a disposition, realized or latent. In reading the critical and aesthetic statements of our senior poets—I'm thinking of Ted Hughes, Elizabeth Bishop, Warren, others—I've found an interesting image that recurs from poet to poet, something that is often described as a current of electricity in all things. Warren says in *Fugitives Return* that a poet tries to lay a finger or a hand onto this current of reality. His image is an electric wire—but it's the touch, the religious image of the hand-laying, on the thing alive with current which is interesting. By implication, we have all lost touch; we've got disconnected. Hughes said in an interview that he wanted to contact "the elemental power circuit of the universe." If one imagines all matter as participating in a constant stream of energy, then the next step is energy as something sacramental, as possessing a certain kind of holiness which, when one contacts it, one possesses and is possessed by. Without that contact, one is not energized; one lacks an authorizing power. It is as if the lights have gone out; we are disembodied.

Now I am not talking about orthodox belief or even mystical vision. I'm talking about the sense that there is something greater, not necessarily anything anthropomorphic, than we are and which powers us until we are divorced from it. It would be quite possible to argue that all poets, in their ways, seek to reconnect with this power source. In that sense, we are all religious. In some way we are all sacramentalists, all looking for sacraments to authorize the intuited life, the felt reality.

PB: Does this religious impulse have to do with facing death?

DS: John Gardner has said that in any fiction, any poem, the main character is death. This is an interesting observation. Richard Eberhart recently wrote that "poetry is a spell against death." One way to look at poetry, what it does, is to see it combats that main character, even when the combatants are not identified. The reconnection and movement with sacramental energy is our battling that enemy, death.

Poetry's religious dimension can be identified as celebrating in the face of all evidence to the contrary the wonderful thing that it is to be alive. Part of what poetry does is to help me want to get up another day. That's where the impulse to poetry begins. The poet, as Faulkner said, gives courage. We need that.

PB: Do you have a need to define what you are talking about—this larger grand electric current—in any way that uses some traditional religious terms?

DS: I start with the assumption that there is something greater than I am. It isn't necessary for me to be too specific about what that might be. But one writes one's poems as speculations about how the world operates. Probably we live in an age which, more than any other, is characterized by uncertainty. We just don't *know* so much of what we once thought, believed, felt. The irony of that is that science tells us how much more we know about everything.

We can't account for the world we know and the world we have but we want to say it is there and we love it and we're trying to understand it. In some ways it is as simple as that. More specifically, I sometimes do and sometimes do not employ traditional religious terms and concepts. When I do it, I do so for the sake of referential communication with a human audience for whom Christian myth remains emotionally affective. This use is that of a language, a furniture, not an assertion of Belief.

PB: This is what you mean by sacramental?

DS: Well, much of what I have said tries to define my meaning. Poems for me still have on some level the very real dimension of prayer. That's why they have the power of consolation, even if it's no longer public consolation.

PB: Some of the things you are saying make me think of Whitman. Has he been crucial to your work?

DS: Yes. I read Whitman in school, as all of us have, and I thought he was often a windbag, an oaf, a posturer. I thought he wasn't in control of himself. I read him again periodically. What I thought remains true. But that is only a small part of Whitman. I wouldn't hesitate to tell you that I think Whitman is the greatest American poet yet. I've just finished reading Justin Kaplan's new biography of Whitman.

PB: It's a tender book.

DS: It is a tender book. Kaplan didn't do the one thing I had hoped he would. I may try to write my own book about this. Whitman was one kind of poet before the Civil War, something of an American jingoist and junior chamber of commerce huckster-poet. After the battle of Fredericksburg, he was a changed man. His change paralleled the change of the American nation. It was as if this country, in spite of the Revolution and other wars, was still an innocent; but the Civil War bloodied the country in the way that a young hunter is bloodied after the killing of his deer. Whitman was big enough as a spirit, as a visionary, to become the voice of that change and maturity—not just the voice of democratic/populist ambition but also the voice of life's sadness. When Whitman says the real war will never get into the books, he's talking about the war to be alive. I don't know anybody who has more of that in the books than Whitman.

PB: Most critics who have written about Whitman have failed to see this. It's as if to admit Whitman changed is to betray America.

DS: I don't know. Whitman's important to me, not in a structural way, but as if he were our father, the American Shakespeare, with all the funny ironies that brings up. Whatever it means to be American now is already there in Whitman. When he says, "I was the man, I suffered, I was there," he's right; he was and he did and he was.

PB: What other poets and poems have influenced your work?

DS: The poet who wrote "The Seafarer" and "The Wanderer"; the *Beowulf* poet. Those poems have seemed to me—not merely because of the tough and lonely language, the odd and visceral music of the poems—to be at the heart of what I wanted to write. I can't think of a poem that's more contemporary than "The Wanderer"; here's a poem about a man who goes out and lives on the water, shakily, and who is left in exile—away from old friends, comrades, and home, his life has come to grief and what he misses most are place, companionship, love, and the kind of understanding that's provided by those who value you. This poem is a thousand years old. It tells us art has a continuing vitality, true art.

I have a sustained interest in Chaucer. G. M. Hopkins is an enormously important poet to me. I'm not talking about his sprung rhythms but simply Hopkins's stuttering passion for what it meant to be alive. His letters show us that while he did not publish he had a clear idea of who he wrote for and why. Hardy is an influence. Auden, I think, in spite of himself loved Hardy. I feel that. Perhaps this is a place to say that I think the essential strength and beauty of American poetry derives from our Anglo-Saxon cadences, stresses, vowel combinations, and rhythms, less so from Romance language influences. Both strains are our heritage and resource. And our poetries are invigorated by diverse ethnic and linguistic immigrations; nevertheless the base of our language is Germanic, or Teutonic, and nothing will alter that. Excepting American Indian poetries, the heart of our cultural speech is English.

Eliot comes to mind here. I think the matter of Eliot's influence by the Symbolists may be somewhat overstressed. It is there, of course, but the attention given to that influence inclines us to neglect the influence on him of his home ground, St. Louis and the Mississippi River. I think Eliot is finally pretty muddled, especially in "The Waste Land," but I respond strongly to him. I would also argue that in *Four Quartets,* if not elsewhere, we're listening to a great midwestern poet. I don't know if that can be defended, but I feel it emotionally. It's the phrasing and music, the yearning for a wall of piety where all is sky and dark wind. Well, I feel it. And I think Eliot will stand in the Anglo-Saxon line, being more heartland American than even he would perhaps admit.

I don't really know how to answer you about the poets who influenced me. I would guess all the poems I have read, remembered, forgot—these are influences. I didn't come of a culture that valued poetry, as I've said. In college I hid from poetry so as not to be thought "freaky." I was not one of those people who wanted to be recognized as different; I wanted to be normal, like everybody else. But I can say that I discovered and imitated, in turn, Frost, Robinson, Eliot, and Yeats. Then I moved backward historically as my interest deepened. Coleridge's "Mariner," Gray's "Elegy," and Milton's "Lycidas" are lodged in my memory. Keats, Shelley, and Byron seemed fine to me, but "soft." I have never had a great interest in Blake, and don't now; he has felt programmatic to me. I read Arnold, Swinburne, Tennyson, Browning, but not with great passion, with a certain technical interest. Without explaining it, I think I am temperamentally attuned with pre-Norman Conquest literature.

PB: Your interest in a body of poets who use/exploit the powers of the Anglo-Saxon language, the heavy stressed, alliterative lines with dense, often heaving, pressured powers—often this is congruent with the world you go to in your poems. The landscapes demand such language.

DS: This ties into your first question about the outcasts of this seacoast place. I think it can be argued that in that tradition you described there is a continued exploration of what it means to be heroic in the world—heroic in spirit and in one's attitudes toward the world. In the life of a man there is something valuable, admirable, sustaining in crisis. What is it and how do we get to it? How does a man live? That's what *Beowulf* is about. This is what "The Waste Land" is about. The heroic story begins with a man but a man begins in a place; he is a place, a carrier of it. All places are dangerous and difficult, because life is so, and none more so than the ocean. Life is a journey, the great ones tell us. To know life, then, we chronicle the journey, from where to where, experiencing what, valuing what, leaving what for our descendants?

PB: This gets us back to the moral question—poetry that shirks the question of how we should live cuts its legs off.

DS: Obviously we cannot make laws by which poetry will be written. We can hardly tell poets to take the high moral road, or else. Yet I think we are obliged to recognize poems which are silly, weak, trivial, perhaps immoral. A poem which demeans or trivializes human struggle is immoral, for example. It seems to me unlikely that one is going to write a great poem about a knife and fork. Perhaps. Such poems exist but they do not sit well beside Ben Jonson, *Paterson,* or Emily Dickinson.

PB: Yet we have poets who are doing this all the time.

DS: The world is not a fair place. Much in it is ephemeral, perhaps necessarily. We should beware of our desire lest we become Laputans or, worse still, Puritans. I will say only that there are certain kinds of poems I do not enjoy and among these are those by American surrealists. One of my students called this brand "the helicopter on the fire hydrant school of poetry." That's a perfectly apt description of the arbitrariness. His response, and mine, was why should he care about a helicopter on a fire hydrant; that's a wrong ambition.

The word *ambition* now means something pejorative, an abuse of power. Nixon would be a sufficient cause for this, though there are other reasons. But we can't live without power, without exercising power. If we haven't the power of conviction, we're spineless; if we haven't the power to act in right ways, we're in social trouble. There is certainly much ambition in literary circles that is careeristic, the desire for money, fame, glory, and power as a manipulative force.

But ambition for the poem, for art, is something finally different. We want power in poetry. I think poets ought to want to compete with "Lycidas" and to try to write a better poem. When I hear tender souls cluck about there being no competition between the "real" poets I wonder what world they are living in. Of course we compete. When we read and admire a true poet's work, we begin to test ourselves against it. We learn our weaknesses and hone our strengths. We seek to empower our best creative abilities. This is ambition for art. Perhaps too many younger poets are forced to compete too little; perhaps they are not ambitious enough.

PB: You're talking about permanence, then?

DS: Faulkner said he wanted to write on the wall of time, Kilroy was here. I would agree with him. Joyce wrote *Ulysses* for the ages of men.

There is, perhaps, a tangential issue here. Critics seem fond of saying that our poets write too much. I wonder. I would ask them, what is the alternative? If one wants to write, needs to write, how is it possible to write too much? It is possible to publish too much, I suppose. It is possible to write badly. Yet if one writes less, will he write better? Publishing and writing are divorceable acts. It's impossible for me to imagine a poet in his room saying to himself, Look here I'm writing too much. I'll stop for a year or so. This seems ludicrous. I don't think you could be a great poet like Whitman unless you'd written as much as Whitman. And as badly. Bulk comes to be important. Our timid talents do not like this idea. But you must span a great stretch of time and experience and create a large, full-dimensioned shape before you can be called great. I have some real enthusiasm for Elizabeth Bishop and Mark Strand. Can we call either of them great? She published fewer than ninety poems in a lifetime. I have not, I think, said this very well, but I mean that our poets seem too willing to accept too little when conferring laurels. Let us be as ambitious for the poem as Marvell and Dr. Williams and Hart Crane and Robert Lowell.

PB: Many of your poems deal with American adolescent experiences—rites of passage that are really at the heart of American experience. Sex, athletics, confrontations with nature. This is difficult ground to tread; you tread it well. It's easy to lapse into sentimentality, cliché, with this experience. Dickey and Wright are great poets who have done this so well. What must a poet do to pull this subject matter off?

DS: I am tempted to say he must be lucky and then to remark, as Jack Nicklaus did when told how lucky he was to sink a long putt, it is funny how constant practice makes a man lucky. Well, all these experiences you mention are part of what I am calling the heroic tradition. By that I mean witnessing that one is part of a long line of writers who write about what it means to be heroic in life.

I mean it in the sense that Joseph Campbell identifies the archetype of the hero in society, or in the sense that Emerson talks about the poet as priest. Or prophet. I think that the poet writing in the heroic tradition is obliged to reaffirm and to witness and perhaps to validate the rituals by which we pass through stages of initiation. The poet tries to seek out what's important and to show this in dramatic ways, dramatic in its immediate felt reality, to show life in motion. This life is both what we have experienced and what we are able to imagine. Those rites of passage you describe are not uniquely American. They are the heart of Joyce's *Portrait of the Artist;* they are Melville's as well as Conrad's. They are our moments of individual crisis, intersections of idea and act. Where else would we look for knowledge tested, known, proven?

The old man who teaches the young man to hunt, track, skin, etc., is only a Virgilian guide. Literature doesn't make him; it adopts him. This man passes on the seed of *pietas*—it means something like respect, awe, humility, obligation, the knowing how to do a thing, knowing the grace that surrounds the doing of the thing, understanding the grace, dignity, and humanity in our every act.

I think my poems may be about one thing, in the largest sense, and that is obligation; it flows directly out of this notion of *pietas*. The obligation that has been failed or the obligation that one's lived up to; obligations imposed by oneself according to the acts one has committed or has not committed, the obligations one feels to the dead and to the living, to tradition, to history, to country, to place. I think my poems are rituals of obligation.

Bill Heyen wrote me once that it was odd how all the best poets are ex-jocks. If you allow his term to include people who recognize and delight in a grace of the body, then you want to say yes. Frost, baseball; Maxine Kumin, swimming; Jarrell, tennis; Ransom, baseball; Whitman, baseball; Keats, swimming. It goes on. And speaking of Ransom, he has a wonderful line: what a poet must have in the right order is the head, the heart, and the foot. That's a physical description of a rhythmic and intellectual activity, of poetry. You can't say it better. It is hard to believe anybody could argue that the grace of the body is not absolutely necessary to the grace of a poem. We're out here trying to learn to be heroes in our bodies in order to be, truly, heroes of the spirit.

It is fair to say that any advocacy of superheroes can lead to abuses. This is obvious from Hitler to American college basketball to television's Incredible Hulk. Nevertheless, you don't want to throw out baby with the bath water. If it's valuable to sing about the greatness of what it means to be a man in the world, then we ought to do it. If you can't say something matters more than something else then you are saying, in effect, that nothing matters.

PB: It's a way of articulating values.

DS: Certainly. I think we have to be willing to articulate values, and the way we articulate and dramatize those values is in our awareness of history, of time, of the past, of all that resides in memory. Without this awareness, ruthlessly examined and tested, how can we hope for a dream of freedom, let alone validly express that dream of the future we must have?

PB: In *Goshawk, Antelope* you left your central place, the seacoast. *Goshawk* has a different quality than the earlier books. How has moving inland affected your imagination?

DS: Somehow the western American landscape suggested spiritual deprivation to me, but also the ruggedness and strength of human passion, of will. I set those poems vaguely in Wyoming because I imagined that Wyoming corresponded to emotional crises I wanted to write about. I had wanted to write about domestic life, pain, love, betrayal, the ordinary sadnesses not revealed in obvious or dramatic ways, but felt as hard and continuous. I thought Wyoming was empty, severe, yet nevertheless *there* as was the heart I had in mind. For me it was a move to the country's interior, and the soul's. I wouldn't go see Wyoming until I had finished the book. Later I realized it was a more remote book, harder to read than I had expected. It is important to me as an invented, imagined vision, less biographical than other books I had written.

PB: Do the increasingly metaphysical preoccupations in the book come out of the fact that you couldn't know the land the way you knew the Virginia land, so it became more appropriate to move into the metaphysical and meditative, philosophic, mythic?

DS: I don't know. I know that some readers have found the book less accessible than my earlier books, but that doesn't bother me. Well, yes, it does bother me. I willingly risked obscurity in an attempt to write a poetry less dependent on narrative and increasingly given to a softer, flattened speech which seemed appropriate to the emotional landscapes I had chosen to write about. To the degree this was a mistake and a failure of clarity, I regret my lack of skill. I did feel compelled to approach a more intensely cerebral poetry; I am reluctant to call it metaphysical or philosophical, though aware I wanted to find a way of writing about ideas as I had not previously done. I hoped, through the employment of a slightly different language and an orchestration of certain image patterns, to explore the nature of love, fidelity, despair, death, and the human will to survive life's defeats with some dignity. There are also certain mythic contours to *Goshawk, Antelope* as well: the book is a progressive, though not entirely obvious, movement west and I was aware of the American urge westward in fact as well as in spirit. The long poem at the book's heart, "Settlement," may be the most obscure in the book but it is also the enactment, I think, of all that is in the book. To answer your question, it is entirely possible that both the changes represented by this book and its failures are results of my being not a native of that western landscape but an interloper. It is possible, too, that my imagination wasn't strong enough; the events in this book, generally, are not autobiographical. I made them up.

PB: Your language has changed in this book—from the insistent heavy stressed lines of *Cumberland Station* and *The Fisherman's Whore* to a more serene, contemplative language.

DS: I think this is somewhat true. Perhaps it only means that I was becoming a different personality while writing the poems. I did not make a decision to change the language. I did not know such a book would exist until it was before me, hidden among the many poems which did not cohere into this book. There are also poems in *Goshawk* which do not show the change you mention, "The Roundhouse Voices," for example. Still, at some point I realized that I was developing a less declamatory language, a more lyrical and more imagistic texture, and I believe I gathered poems—and excluded poems—according to this characteristic. This language is, perhaps, given to more patient, more subtle rhythms, rhythms I thought would be more appropriate to the increasingly private, less public events of these poems.

I believe the book which follows *Goshawk,* the one called *Dream Flights,* will show another slight shift in the language. No one, I think, can entirely abandon his particular language since it rises from his body's physical rhythms, but in this collection I have tried to write poems that would be more open, more accessible, that would breathe better—as I have described it to myself. I have tried to resist the cramped, gnarling clusters of stresses which have always appealed to me. My hope is to allow readers to come into the imaginative experience more quickly and more directly without being hampered by any conventional poetic idioms. I hope to be faithful to Joseph Conrad's desire to make the reader *see* all that may be seen. None of us is going to be freed entirely of the poetic conventions of our time. These are helpful. They are also distressingly comfortable. That is one reason I submit to writing metered and rhymed poems from time to time. One wants to bend, stretch, and break the given possibilities of poetry, its conventions, but there is only so much that may be done before sheer eccentricity is reached, and that is what we dignify falsely as "experimentation."

PB: Has anything else influenced your quieter, more spare language in *Goshawk?*

DS: There are no specific influences I can cite. I can say that I had felt a danger of becoming too loud, too melodramatic, a need to see what other tones, ranges of voice, my poems might manage. I would like to be a poet of range, not a one-note poet, however successful at that one note. I may have been influenced by the simple desire not to bore myself with self-repetition. Beyond all this, I suppose that language evolved to reflect the spareness of the Western landscape, and the emotional landscape, I had chosen. It's pretty hard to be an exuberant Anglo-Saxon in the Western desert, because what you see is an indifference of rocks, sage, sand, and sky. It isn't a turbulent, greenly consoling, passionate landscape. It is often glorious, sometimes sublime, but it is almost always a landscape of emptiness, space, slower rhythms, one in which individual loneliness is pronounced—and individual passion to survive is heroic there, too. To some extent one seeks a poetry to reflect the presiding emotional temperament of a place. I don't, however, believe there is one language for the desert, one for the mountains, another for the ocean. This would be absurd. But with my change of landscape in the poems I found a slight change in language. It did happen.

I might add that in *Dream Flights* I have returned to my seacoast landscape and the poems have become somewhat as they were in that stressed, earlier language. Still, there are changes. The poems are less assertively heroic, more speculative about human relationships and failures. I have written about racial problems, high school life in the late 1950s, the need to show our children their complete heritage, as well as returning to subjects that have continually interested me. These poems seem to take a shorter line as well as to be less conspicuously Anglo-Saxon in texture. They seem that way to me, in any case. I do not know what this may mean for the future. I do not plan ahead; I write one poem at a time.

Nevertheless, I have now completed another collection which Harper and Row will publish in 1983, called *In the House of the Judge,* and these poems differ from previous work, I think, by an increased preoccupation with questions of ethics, of what ordinary human responsibility might mean. They are both lyrical and narrative in structure but there is a greater willingness in them to be brooding and joyful at the same time. There are numerous poems about the life of that seacoast but also poems about ghosts, writers, animals, etc. The book is, I think, a kind of extension of the dream-memory journeys I started in *Cumberland Station.* I hope that the language, however, is increasingly direct. I might put it this way: if in *Goshawk, Antelope* I was dreaming in the desert, then in *Dream Flights* I was dreaming in airplanes and on various temporary but domestic locations. In the new poems I am dreaming about and inside of houses. I am trying to enter the secretive life of families. I am no longer locked into that spare but elegant desert.

PB: Being landlocked was a compelling metaphor for the flight then. Is that right?

DS: In hindsight, yes. It is a metaphor both for flights to something and flights from something, which I think is a good image for poems. It may be that poetry is especially a going forward in space, time, and imagination, but it is also a constant return to what and where we have been. This movement, then, is a survey, a measurement, a series of measures by which we seek to know and delimit all that is. If the world did not change some, we could get it fixed. If it changed predictably, we could adjust and get it fixed. Or if we did not change. . . . Yet every point of reference seems constantly, if subtly, fluid; we are both predictable and aberrant. I have the fundamental conviction that the matters of the human heart, which define us, do not change. A man and woman in love, as Hardy's little poem "Breaking of Nations" shows, are the same creatures in the same fix in the year 10, the year 1000, or the year 1982. If there is anything constant for us, it is that human story of love, hate, fear, pride, jealousy, obligation, failure, and so on. We do, however, have need to tell the tales in Ecclesiastes in our own tongues, how the sun riseth and falleth for us. Those who remain heroes of the spirit among us provide the points of reference, the marks for measurement of what we are yet, what we may be. They allow us the poem which is above all the song of our being alive. That is surely what Whitman means by "The Song of Myself."

Index